Taming My Elephant

Tshiwa Trudie Amulungu

UNAM
PRESS
UNIVERSITY OF NAMIBIA

University of Namibia Press
www.unam.edu.na/unam-press
unampress@unam.na
Private Bag 13301
Windhoek
Namibia

First published:	2016
Cover drawing:	Pena Brock
Family trees:	Wilfried Brock
Maps:	Martin Hipondoka and Andreas Amukwaya, UNAM Department of Geography, History & Environmental Studies
Copy-editing:	Mutaleni Nadimi, Lushdreamer Creative Services
Design and layout:	Vivien Barnes, Handmade Communications
Printed by:	Times Offset (Malaysia)

ISBN 978 99916 42 18 5

Distribution
In Namibia by Namibia Book Market: www.namibiabooks.com
Internationally by the African Books Collective:
www.africanbookscollective.com

Contents

A word about the title of the book

Metaphorically, in Oshiwambo, my mother tongue, the elephant is likened to the most challenging situation that can face humanity. The Aawambo believe that if an elephant shows up, everything else, irrespective of its nature and urgency, is put aside. Dealing with and getting rid of the elephant becomes priority number one. For this reason, when elder people plan an activity for the following morning, their concluding sentence is always as follows *'Ongula osho tatu ningi ngele uusiku inawu vala ondjamba'* or 'We will do as agreed if the night does not give birth to an elephant.' If the night happens to have given birth to an elephant, all planned activities are put on hold and the villagers immediately join forces to get rid of the elephant. In my case, since I was alone and the elephant showed up so many times, I had no choice but to tame it.

Prologue

'I now turn to my new daughter-in-law. From a humble place in Owambo, she went to Zambia, then to France and back to Namibia with a French Master's.'

These were the exact words of my father-in-law as part of his speech at my wedding when I married his son in December 1990. My father-in-law has captured the exact scope of the landmarks of the route I, and so many others, had to travel to arrive where we are today. It has been an unusual route, full of challenges but also full of pleasant surprises.

Why did I decide to write this book? Well, I started feeling awkward being with people who did not know that much about me. I know that this sentiment may be hard to believe, but, for me, the awkwardness only intensified when it came to those I lived with.

I first thought of sharing my story with my family. Although so dear to me, they do not know half of me, maybe even less than that. They are, however, convinced that they know me well. Yet, there is so much about me that they cannot know. Individuals' lives are often most elusive to those closest to them. Not by choice, but that's just how things are. I had to travel a long route to adjust to my life as it is today, but they don't know much about this effort. I initially smiled when my children asked me questions to which they expected nothing less than answers that corresponded to their frame of reference. In the end, I too assumed that the tooth-fairy, Easter eggs, Christmas trees and other such customs were the natural way of doing things. Habit simply and gradually set in.

It only, unexpectedly, clicked one day when a car guard unintentionally, but boldly, drew my attention to this obvious fact.

This attentive young man must have observed us, my husband, my children and me, over a period of time as we arrived regularly at the gym. Interestingly, it all started with him offering to look after our car. There being nothing unusual about that, we always welcomed the offer. One day, it so happened that I went to the gym alone. Our usual car attendant confidently approached me and asked me, this time in Oshiwambo, whether he could look after the car. *Sure*, I responded and was about to rush off. But he politely wanted to know if he could quickly ask me something. *Sure*, I answered and slowed down. Clearly, he was satisfied that he could confirm his long held suspicion about my mother tongue. His question to me though was: *Who are the people with whom you always come to the gym?* When I explained that these were indeed my husband and children, his next question was: *Do you mean you live with them?* As soon as I had responded in the affirmative, he fired the next question: *How do you communicate with each other?* When I told him that we did so in English, he wanted to know whether this was what I was doing on a daily basis. Again I responded in the affirmative. Although he appeared not to have further questions, his look expressed nothing less than genuine sympathy.

From this brief exchange with the car guard I realised how much my present family life perplexed an ordinary Namibian who shared my background and experience. I later on also established that a good number of my peers initially wondered whether my marriage to a white man was not stressful for me. I still remember how one of my close friends confronted me with an unambiguous question: *How do you deal with a white husband?* I of course was also surprised by the shift of my own mind set between the first time I had set eyes on my husband in 1988 in Lusaka, Zambia, and the time all these perplexities came to the fore 24 years later when I began writing this book.

My first concern was to provide my children with some account of my background in order for them to get some understanding of the society I was from and the path I had travelled before settling into the posh Windhoek suburb of Ludwigsdorf. Before putting anything on paper, I reflected a bit on what to include in my story. This obviously made me think deep into my past in order to sort out the relevant information. I went as far back as some forty years, to the earliest days of my life. I was amazed about the whole lot I had gone through. I clearly recall my natural upbringing, my native village and school life at the Catholic mission stations in Okatana and Anamulenge and my very first step into the unknown, a liberation movement that would become my guardian for twelve years. This liberation movement for the independence of Namibia would secure home for me in Angola, Zambia and France with temporary shelter in Tanzania, Kenya and Senegal.

When I look into the eyes of my four daughters, I see their absolute conviction that I have always lived in Ludwigsdorf. Little do they know that I had moved here just shortly before the last two were born.

When my children excitedly ask me what gifts they are getting for Christmas, how could they possibly know that Christmas was the only day of the year that I got to drink tea? For them, tea has always been in the house and it is drunk by choice. Sugar is a household item that we keep in the same place year in and year out. As a child, I devised plan after plan on how to steal sugar. My poor mother had to find hiding places to protect the sugar from us, yet we always managed to find it. And, of course, once we discovered it, we showed no mercy and ate as much as we could. Although punishment was guaranteed, it never deterred us.

My recollections brought back fond memories of this typical village girl who, like any village girl, had to learn every household activity, ranging from all that it takes to produce meals for an entire family without any measurement, to looking after siblings in the absence of both parents. A mere look at the amount of water in the pot or a quick dip of a finger in a hot liquid was enough for me to know whether I would have enough porridge for everyone, or whether the mixture was ready for fermentation for the next day's drink. And, in like manner, a stern look at a younger sibling was sufficient for him or her to understand that, in the absence of the parents, I was in charge.

With this typical traditional upbringing and every day filled with nothing but work, I faced challenges on arrival at the first Catholic mission station for school. Here, I had to adjust to a new order, especially the regulated way of doing things. The adjustment was not that hard as there was the dominant element of workload, just like at home. The only difference was that one had to be very attentive to the time according to the watch and no longer according to the position of the sun, and to the exact sequence in which things had to be done.

After having comfortably settled into and perfectly adjusted to the structured life of the mission station, I was to find myself, from one day to the next, in a completely different set up across the Namibian border. The explanation is simple: within the blink of an eye, we, a large group of school learners, crossed the border into Angola and joined the liberation struggle of Namibia under the care of the South West African People's Organisation (SWAPO).

Initially, it all sounded unbelievable. Very quickly we were to discover Namibians who had left the country earlier, some as early as 20 years before us. We learned of their true identity, which was far from being what the South African apartheid government portrayed them as back home. These brave countrymen and women had set up a network of camps, centres and settlements across the neighbouring countries to receive and care for Namibian freedom fighters. As unbelievable as it may sound, they had secured trust and solidarity across the world. After three months in the camps in Angola, we were simply put on an aeroplane to go for further studies. The sky was the limit! I picked up the courage to study at the United Nations Institute for Namibia (UNIN) in Lusaka, Zambia, and went on for university studies in France, studying in French.

Since there were hundreds and thousands of us, a sense of purpose and discipline was a requirement. In a very short time, we connected and fully embraced the liberation struggle of our country and made it our real daily business. It did not matter what was assigned to us, we simply picked up the order and went for it. From serving in the People's Liberation Army of Namibia (PLAN), to studying in very distant countries and in languages we were not familiar with, to serving in camps and settlements or in SWAPO offices across the world, we served wherever required. Our mindset was solely geared towards securing the independence of our country. And we were fully aware that we had a lengthy, arduous path ahead of us.

One, however, is not shielded from challenges in precarious situations such as the ones we found ourselves in. It was during these 12 years away from home that I was to receive the sad news of the sudden death of my mother, leaving behind my eight younger siblings. I was further to get myself into a very short marriage which left me shattered for a number of years. But as the saying goes: challenges can be turned into opportunities. My motherless siblings and my baby daughter added to my sense of purpose and further sharpened my determination to move on and work harder. Soon afterwards I met a remarkable young man whom I was to marry some two years later. His skin colour became a challenge for me for some time, but it gradually became a non-issue. We both, however, had to find a creative but convincing way of introducing each other to our respective families. And this had to happen upon our return to Namibia, in the wake of the excitement and anxiety of our national independence. Can you imagine the magnitude of such a partnership in a country like Namibia those years when skin colour was a real issue and mixed marriages were as good as non-existent? As the late Mosé Tjitendero the first Speaker of the National Assembly of the Republic of Namibia put it in his speech at our wedding in December 1990, our marriage was a bold statement.

This is the story I wish to share with those who care to read it. Today, I find the story unthinkable. What is amazing is that I did not really plan any of the many things that happened to me. Neither did I realise at those particular moments how extraordinary these happenings were. This is particularly true for my 12 years in exile. In reality, things just happened. As many like to say: one only needs to be at the right place at the right time. And this is all I did. In the final analysis, one cannot take credit for any of these happenings. In a way, these events reflect a collective achievement. Those of us who went for studies could only do so because others were waging the liberation war and some others went around the world campaigning for solidarity, including scholarships. In the end, each of us had to bring our little pieces to the liberation struggle puzzle, although, evidently some brought bigger pieces than others.

Just as there is that visible leap between my childhood life to my children's lives, so was there a huge leap between the lives of my grandparents and that of my own parents, and of course between my parents' lives and my own. Each of the four generations has had completely different life experiences. It is far from being a simple evolution.

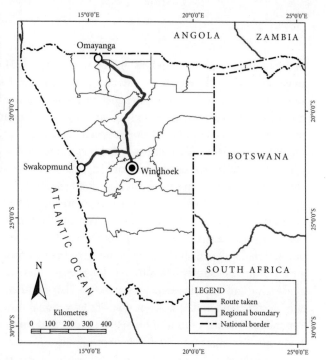

Map of Namibia showing my childhood home in the north; Windhoek, where Wilfried and I settled with our family and Swakopmund, where we visit Wilfried's parents.

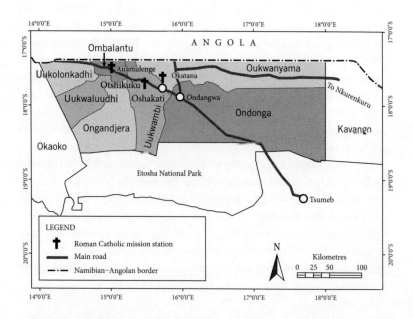

Map of the seven districts of the former Ovamboland and three Roman Catholic missions.

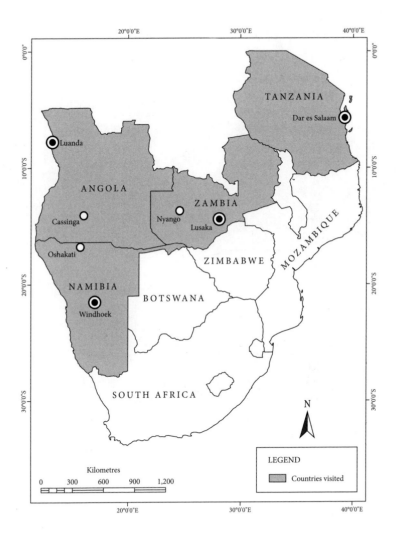

Map showing the countries in southern Africa that I visited during my time in exile.

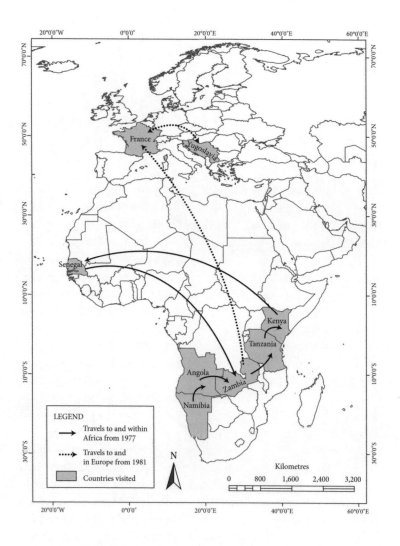

Map of countries I visited within Africa and Europe.

A word about Namibia

Namibians will certainly not need these tips but our colleagues from abroad may find them useful. This is the background and events that influenced and shaped my life and may offer some explanation as to why I reacted the way I did to certain occurrences in my life.

The country Namibia: Namibia lies in southern Africa and because of its location, it was first known by its colonial name South West Africa. Namibia was a German colony between 1884 and 1918 when Germany lost all its colonies at the end of the First World War. Like all other former German colonies, Namibia became a mandate under the League of Nations and was placed under South Africa who imposed its laws in Namibia, including the apartheid system. Namibians fought against foreign domination and a war for liberation against apartheid South Africa between 1966 and 1989. In 1989, the United Nations supervised elections, and on 21 March 1990, Namibia became an independent country.

The people of Namibia: Namibian people have a vast cultural diversity. Although the apartheid system strived for decades to divide Namibians along racial, tribal and cultural lines, the people of Namibia identify themselves as Namibians first. Due to the apartheid laws, deep division in particular between Whites, Coloureds and Blacks was unavoidable and the country is still struggling to erase the ugly scars of apartheid.

Northern Namibia: This part of Namibia was completely rural until the time I stepped out of it into the outside world. This is the part of the country where the Aawambo or Oshiwambo-speaking Namibians live, and derive their livelihood from land cultivation and cattle. They live in homesteads, traditional homes constructed from wooden poles with thatched grass roofs. Each homestead is surrounded by a crop field and a grazing area. During the pre-colonial era, the Aawambo lived under traditional kingdoms ruled by *Ohamba* or *Omukwaniirwa* depending on the location and dialect. There were about eight traditional kingdoms and each of them was divided into districts that were further subdivided into smaller areas. As such, each *Ohamba* or *Omukwaniirwa* was supported by senior headmen, headmen and village headmen to govern the kingdom.

The Aawambo attach importance to clanship. In other words, each Oshiwambo-speaking person belongs to a clan with a specific name and everyone in the same clan is supposed to be a relative. It is a very useful social structure phenomenon because clan members are supposed to support each other irrespective of whether they know each other or not. When arriving in a new area, stating the name of one's clan was sufficient to secure temporary shelter and other means of support to settle in the new place. With the constructs of modern society, a clan is no longer as useful as it used to be.

The Aawambo lived this traditional life until the arrival of the missionaries. The first group of missionaries was from Finland and the second group was from Germany. The Finnish missionaries were Lutheran and the German missionaries were Roman Catholic. It was not a question of choice; people were baptised by the missionaries who settled and established themselves in their area. The missionaries demanded that people change their traditional lives as they considered the local traditions as pagan practices. This change was later reinforced by the South African government and people's lives changed for good. The social structure was in particular disturbed by the introduction of the contract labour system under which all men were required to work in mines, factories and farms in the urban areas for meagre salaries. Labour contracts could last as long as eighteen months.

1

My ancestors

As there is no way I could have complete information on my ancestors beyond my grandparents, a general picture can be painted from stories told by various relatives and family friends. As usual, there are always variations in what many people make out of the same story. What really matters in this case is the general idea of the situation.

My great-great-grandparents originated from the various parts of the former Owamboland area situated in northern Namibia. The available information indicates that both my paternal and maternal great-grandparents originate from a place called Uukwaandudhi in the Uukwambi district. Initially, my maternal part of the family originated from somewhere in the Ongandjera district. My maternal great-great-grandmother arrived and settled in Uukwaandudhi with her only daughter following some social disturbances in the district of her birth. There is no talk at all of a great-great-grandfather.

Around the turn of the 20th century, some of my forebears immigrated towards Uukwanyama, Ondonga as well as Kavango. During that time, children would normally move with their mothers, and not so much with their fathers. Similarly, sisters or nieces would move with or to their brothers or uncles, brothers of their mothers, or to their maternal grandmothers. This is due to a strong inclination of the matrilineal kinship among the Aawambo.

The paternal side of my family can be traced to a woman by the name of Naambo Atshipara. The name Naambo would run through the family. Two of the daughters of Naambo would be my great-great-grandmothers. These are Nambudhi, the maternal great-grandmother of my father and Vute, the paternal great-grandmother of my mother. Naambo had five daughters: Noa Amurondo, Tuuthigirwa Amurondo, Nambudhi Nekuta, Vute Uumati and Niipanda Uumati. Three of the daughters, Noa, Nambudhi and Vute, had offspring.

Noa had two daughters: Naambo Ekuwa and Katarina Iinkono. Nambudhi had two sons and two daughters: Iipumbu Amukuma, Ndetshuuva Amukuma, Naalokoshe Iimbili and Ihepa Iimbili. Vute had a daughter and a son: Mpingana Angombe and Akongo Iipinge.

One of Nambudhi's daughters, Ndetshuuva had a daughter and a son: Naambo Nekundi and Kandenge Uusiku. Naambo Nekundi had three sons and a daughter: Hifivali Taukondjele, Amunime Erastus Amulungu (my father), Namutsheko Aili Amulungu and Nuunyango Lukas Anghome.

Vute's daughter Mpingana and her husband Kathere had three sons and four daughters: Akapara, Angombe, Iitura, Noa, Nangombe Martha, Karunga and Kuushuru. The third child, Iitura, would be my mother's father.

♋

The family stayed in Uukwaandudhi for a long time until a young fellow by the name of Tshikongo put things into motion. At the end of a lengthy and eventful move, Tshikongo finally settled in Kavango. He was the youngest son of a cousin of Naambo Atshipara, also known as Naambo, but her full name was Naambo Tshivoro. Naambo Tshivoro, with her husband Nanyeni, had six children, five sons and a daughter: Kambidhi, Nangoro, Tshikesho, Tsheehama, Nangura and Tshikongo.

The move was triggered by a pregnancy. Young Tshikongo made a girl pregnant. And in those days, this was an intolerable error in the Uukwambi district. When it happened, and it unfortunately did happen, there were only two options for the poor girl. The safest, but most challenging option was to make a hundred per cent sure, but really one hundred percent without fail, to be outside of the Uukwambi district before anyone got wind of the pregnancy. The second option, which was not an option at all, but a hard reality, was to face death. It sounds harsh today, but that is how things were done. From the stories I have heard, there was no consequence for male culprits. The fair part of the story is that all girls in the area were well informed about the practice. And this explains why, along the Uukwanyama villages, the next district bordering the Uukwambi district, there is a considerable number of inhabitants who speak with a remarkable inclination towards the Otshikwambi accent. Of course, there are those who came to settle there by choice, but there are also those who are there because their great-grandmothers had to move there.

It is not clear why the people in Uukwambi were so intolerant towards girls who fell pregnant before *olufuko*, the traditional marital ceremony. Whatever the reason, it warranted death. And there was one cruel method: to build a grass structure around the girl and set her alight. There was no sympathy whatsoever, including from the closest person, one's own mother. Cultural practice came first.

Tshikongo seemed to have been a gentleman. He thought of dealing with his trespass in a responsible manner. To save the future mother of his child, they both fled to the Uukwanyama district. Arriving in Uukwanyama, the natural thing to do was to search for a prominent individual from the same clan: *ekwambashu*. Clans were and remain solid bases of kinship and social relationships among the Aawambo. Tshikongo did not need to search long before he introduced himself to *elenga enene*, the senior headman, in the area named Kondjamba. Kondjamba was more than happy to get an addition to his extended family. He soon introduced young Tshikongo to Ohamba Mandume, the king. An impressive and daring young man himself, it did not take Tshikongo long before he was appointed *elenga* (a headman). He knew how to behave himself around *Uuhamba*, the palace, and he made full use of the opportunity to prove himself and to earn himself the liking of Ohamba Mandume. This was unfortunately going to be to the detriment of the subjects of the area.

All started well for Tshikongo. In no time, Ohamba Mandume was very impressed with the newcomer headman and placed a large area under Tshikongo's jurisdiction. Tshikongo however, although already powerful, felt uneasy in this foreign area. As is customary, he thought of surrounding himself with his own kin. He would feel safer and would have a sense of belonging. Nothing was wrong with this, and he soon sent for his second-degree cousin Nambudhi. The young Nambudhi joined Tshikongo in the newly acquired territory. She took the wishes of her cousin seriously and had four offspring. Tshikongo had reason to feel very comfortable. His relative Kondjamba occupied a senior position that automatically made him one of the close collaborators of Ohamba Mandume. Tshikongo himself was also part of the leadership of the district and at the same time, he occupied a senior position in the district army. And to his delight, his cousin had produced kin that consolidated his clan in the new land. Things could not be better.

The *eehamba,* kings of Uukwanyama were obviously also very pleased with the performance of Tshikongo, especially with his warfare abilities. His performance and charm saw him serving three consecutive *eehamba.*

But, as the saying goes, successful people end up outgrowing their shoes. Or they simply end up running out of constructive ideas. Tshikongo ended up doing both. Ohamba Mandume liked and relied on him and this conducive environment which provided nothing else but privileges convinced Tshikongo beyond doubt that he could get away with anything. He lost no time before he tested the waters. To harness his popularity and glory, he had to get certain individuals he considered as threats out of the way. In those days, threats in the Aawambo society were always wealthy or well to do people. Since eliminating someone those days could only be executed on the order of the *ohamba,* Tshikongo had to get Ohamba Mandume to issue the required orders. But there needed to be a reason for a subject to be eliminated so Tshikongo geared himself to invent those reasons. The base of the invention would obviously be the tarnishing of the names of his targeted prey. There was no doubt that Tshikongo was at the same time taking Ohamba Mandume for granted. He would nevertheless give it a try. Those were common practices among people in power. You eliminated your threats before you became a threat to them.

A wealthy man became Tshikongo's first casualty. He made up an unbelievable story, yet he told it. He claimed to have seen the chickens of this wealthy man lined up on their way to a water point, with the leading rooster carrying *eholo,* a milking can, around his neck. Ohamba Mandume found the story outrageous and ordered the killing of the man. How dare this man possess supernatural chicken in his jurisdiction, which carried *eholo* around, and, on top of that, found their way to the water point in such an orderly manner! This was a deliberate show of wealth and of course of supernatural power which was tantamount to first degree provocation, threat and disrespect of the *ohamba*.

Next in line to fall prey to Tshikongo's cunning operation was a man who possessed a lot of cattle. Tshikongo told Ohamba Mandume that as he one day passed the house of this man he heard a thundering sound of milk flowing during the milking of the cows. Again, Ohamba Mandume did not hesitate and ordered for the elimination of the man. The flow of the milk during the milking of the Ohamba Mandume's own cattle did not come close to the sound of thunder. Tshikongo was of course quick to round up all the cattle of his victim and shared them with the *ohamba*. Did the sharing really match the order of the *ohamba*? Only Tshikongo could tell as he left his part at home when he took the share of Ohamba Mandume to Uuhamba. It did not take long though for Ohamba Mandume to wonder why the sudden disappearance of the thundering sound when the very same cows were being milked in his own kraal. Tshikongo did not take note of the eyebrows of Ohamba Mandume and was already busy devising the trespass of the next victim.

Cattle were not the only sign of wealth among the Aawambo. *Omahangu* (pearl millet) gave a similar status and Tshikongo decided to shift his trap to the subjects who derived their wealth from this popular crop among the community. One day, Tshikongo stopped at the home of one of them, bringing along *omahangu* in an unusual container, *oshikayiwa*, a head tie normally worn by women. It was rather a peculiar sight. *Oshikayiwa* is an item which is solely associated with women and not at all with men, let alone headmen. Secondly, *omahangu* was a commodity which was not moved around easily. When the need arose, women normally carried *omahangu* in baskets on their heads or, in case of a heavy load, it was placed in a strong bag and carried by men over their shoulders. Carrying a few grains of *omahangu* in *oshikayiwa* in one's hand was unheard of. But that is what Tshikongo did and surprised his host.

Although surprised to see the headman carrying *oshikayiwa* in his hands, the host was above all flattered by the visit. It did not happen very often that one had a headman stop by for a visit. Tshikongo told his host that he was on his way to Uuhamba and wanted to leave his *omahangu* for a while with him. As he was aware, Tshikongo explained to the host, Uuhamba was not only a huge place, but also a very busy place. Being offered a meal there, although common practice, was not a given. Should he not be offered a meal he would stop by again on his way back home, to eat his *omahola* (boiled *omahangu*). *Omahola* in the Oshiwambo culture is not a proper meal, but something comparable to a snack. And important people in society did not go around having snacks.

Getting such a request from a headman was an honour in itself and the man, who was flattered, gladly took *oshikayiwa*. He would also, and gladly so, have *omahola* prepared if Tshikongo deemed it necessary on his way back. Such requests for little services from those in the leadership could only mean recognition and could only work in one's favour. So, it was important to make full use of the opportunity whenever it arose.

After taking leave from the welcoming and enthusiastic host, Tshikongo went straight to Ohamba Mandume to inform him that he had gone around some homes and had managed to secure him a quantity of *omahangu* in the neighbourhood. All Ohamba Mandume needed to do, Tshikongo explained, was to send enough servants to collect *omahangu* from a certain homestead where it had been gathered. Ohamba Mandume was very thrilled with such a thoughtful headman and asked Tshikongo to give the necessary instructions to the servants. The servants of course, when they arrived at the indicated homestead, explained that they were there to collect Tshikongo's *omahangu*. For the homestead owner, the message was crystal clear. Tshikongo was there not long ago, and it was true that he had left an *oshikayiwa* with some *omahangu*. That Tshikongo did not return himself to pick up his *omahangu* and chose instead to send the servants from Uuhamba to do so on his behalf, was none of the homestead owner's business. Those in power had many responsibilities or could as well do as they pleased. Now, what was required from him was a simple gesture and that was to hand over *omahangu* as the owner had sent for them. Why there were so many servants for so little *omahangu*? Well, that was Tshikongo's business. It could also be that they had stopped there on their way to or from somewhere else.

Ohamba Mandume felt so belittled upon receiving the small package. He had more than enough *omashisha* (*omahangu* containers) full to capacity and this subject dared to make fun of him by sending him a handful of grains of *omahangu*, and in *oshikayiwa* for that matter. This was nothing else but a sign of disrespect and for that, the man had to die. Before Ohamba Mandume could get a full explanation from Tshikongo about the whereabouts of the tons of *omahangu* he had secured for him, Tshikongo was already busy with a wonderful idea of trapping Ohamba Mandume into eating geckos. Yes, after dealing with subjects, Tshikongo was about to deal with the *ohamba* himself. As unlikely as it may sound, Tshikongo pushed his luck. Geckos are a source of power and protection, he explained to the *ohamba*. Although sceptical, Ohamba Mandume allowed himself to go for the game. He would draw Tshikongo in. If geckos were a source of power and protection, Tshikongo himself would surely benefit from them as well. Ohamba Mandume made sure that Tshikongo was at his side when the geckos were ready. As soon as they were brought in he offered Tshikongo to take the first bite, just to taste whether they were well done! Tshikongo did not expect the offer. But as smart as he was, he quickly found an explanation why he could not taste the dish. He would have happily tasted but this time, an error was made. Female geckos had been cooked together with the male ones. '*Ihaa pi mumwe nomakadi!*' They should have been cooked separately! Well and good, Ohamba Mandume decided not to take any action as yet.

Tshikongo seemed not to have read Ohamba Mandume's facial expression correctly. Sure, Ohamba Mandume did not appreciate Tshikongo's malicious 'assistance' in strengthening his power and protection, but he did not take action either. For Tshikongo, the non-action meant only one thing: he was a powerful man and could get away with anything. But he had at least learned one thing: he would leave Ohamba Mandume alone for the time being. It would be safer to return to the subjects.

What would he do next? He would continue with the elimination of the subjects and this time he didn't see the need to go through Ohamba Mandume. He would just do it himself straight away. To start off, he decided to eliminate a subject for the simple reason that he possessed too many cattle. Accumulating so much wealth was not healthy for the area. As soon as he had the man out of the way, Ohamba Mandume confronted him. Tshikongo first denied his action and when he realised that Ohamba seriously wanted an explanation, he ended up admitting to the murder. He received a stern warning. With that, Tshikongo found out very fast that his idea of killing people was not on. He also got wind that he was about to start losing the liking of Ohamba Mandume. He had to find a quick tactic to sustain the *ohamba*'s attention, which he obviously needed if he was to continue consolidating his own power base. He knew too that he had by now made enough enemies who would use every opportunity to influence Ohamba Mandume to take action against him.

Tshikongo seemed to have run out of ideas, but he badly needed constant interaction with the *ohamba*. Headmen moved around on horses provided by the *ohamba*. One day Tshikongo went to Ohamba Mandume to launch a strange complaint about his horse. Something unusual had happened. His horse that had served him magnificently over the years had suddenly become so slow that it was recently overtaken by a chameleon! As much as it might have been a joke, Ohamba Mandume did not find this funny. He ordered Tshikongo to be flogged. It was high time. Yet, Ohamba Mandume still gave Tshikongo another horse to replace the slow one.

In those days, when aggrieved by an *ohamba* in whatever form, it was unheard of that subjects showed ill feelings towards him. After having suffered punishment, the subject was expected to make a gesture to demonstrate no ill-feeling towards the *ohamba*, but in a practical and generous manner. Tshikongo knew that too well and decided to appease Ohamba Mandume. He decided to go into Angola and there he raided some wealthy members of the Ovimbundu community and captured a lot of cattle. He brought a good number of them to Ohamba Mandume as a sign that the flogging had in no way changed his respect and admiration for him. Ohamba Mandume accepted the cattle, but this generous act did not stop his sudden scepticism towards this brave man.

As expected, things started going wrong for Tshikongo. A girl got pregnant. A pregnant girl seemed to be part of the reason for each of Tshikongo's unprompted moves. And to make things worse, this happened to be one of Ohamba Mandume's lovers. This time, Tshikongo was not directly responsible. One of his servants was! But all the same, Tshikongo was in charge of his servants, and he had lately become a thorn in the flesh of Ohamba Mandume. As the saying goes, when things start going wrong, they often go wrong all the way. This was going to happen to the brave Tshikongo.

By sheer coincidence, the pregnancy incident happened just at the time when the Portuguese were approaching from Angola to attack Ohamba Mandume. All of a sudden, Tshikongo became vulnerable. The subjects who had suffered tremendously at Tshikongo's hand were well aware of his sudden vulnerability. They wasted no time in taking full advantage of the situation. They made Ohamba believe that when Tshikongo went to Angola not long ago, he went to incite the Portuguese to attack Ohamba. They insisted that the capturing of the cattle was only a pretext. This news was more than Ohamba Mandume could take. It was one thing to mislead Ohamba, including having his subjects killed, but it was a different matter to try to topple Ohamba. It was not a matter of a modern coup d'état with external assistance, it was a matter of providing first hand information to the public enemy number one to destroy the entire kingdom. And that was not to be taken lightly.

An assembly was called the same evening, to which Tshikongo was naturally not privy. Ohamba Mandume informed his entourage of his decision: Tshikongo had to die. Given the seriousness of the offence, this had to happen the very following morning. But Tshikongo was amazingly lucky. And it is really a kind of luck that is not easy to come by; Tshikongo's case is what the Aawambo call 'odhikwa homakondo ihaga tokoka' or someone who has been carried in a baby carrier with solid and unbreakable straps. In the early days, Aawambo women carried their babies on their backs with baby carriers made of entire goat skins. The baby on the back was carried in the entire skin and the four leg skins were tightened around the chest of the mother. However, it could happen that straps broke although it was not usual that babies fell. Tshikongo was one of those babies who had the fortune of being carried in a secure odhikwa and would always survive life's hurdles. One of the senior people in whom Ohamba Mandume confided went straight to whisper to Tshikongo. Tshikongo had been around *eehamba* long enough to know exactly what that meant. He lost no time. Ohamba Mandume would not get a remote chance to come any closer to him, let alone catch up with him.

Early in the morning of the following day, Tshikongo was on his way out of the Uukwanyama area. He had to take his relatives along, as well as his servants, and of course his cattle. They made good progress and by evening, they were the other side of the border of the Uukwanyama area and could safely take a break for the night. Strategically, they put up *ontanda* (a camp) nearby the water point. The following day, early in the morning, they would quickly fill their gourds for the trek ahead. They made a fire and settled in for the night. Tshikongo decided to sleep a distance away from the rest of the group. One never knows who is trustworthy. As a warrior for a long time, he knew too well that total trust rarely existed.

As the rest of the group sat around the fire, they noticed other fireplaces from a distance. The fireplaces were located in the direction in which they would proceed the following morning. There was nothing to worry about. After all, they were a huge group. Maybe others had gotten further than them and could walk that bit back to draw water early the next morning. Or simply other travellers had also opted by sheer coincidence to put up *ontanda* in the same area as them. Therefore, why bother Tshikongo with distant fireplaces?

At dawn the following morning, Tshikongo's followers were surprised by their pursuers. In the panic, they abandoned the cattle and fled in different directions. Ohamba Mandume's troops rounded up the cattle and tried to make their way back home. Meanwhile, Tshikongo, as soon as he got wind of the attack, was immediately on the heels of the attackers. He successfully repossessed his cattle and made a U-turn to continue his move to Kavango.

As expected, Tshikongo's cousin, Nambudhi, was part of his exodus. So were her three children: Iipumbu, Naalokoshe and Ihepa. Nambudhi's fourth child, Ndetshuuva, had died earlier and Naalokoshe took care of Ndetshuuva's orphaned daughter Naambo. Understandably, young Naambo was also with her grandmother, uncles and aunt in this move. During the attack of that morning, Nambudhi managed to flee in the same direction as her son Iipumbu, her daughter Naalokoshe and granddaughter Naambo. Fleeing a territory those days meant being beyond the borders of that territory before the pursuers got hold of those fleeing. Obviously, fleeing persons could not take chances.

Nambudhi and her offspring did not dare to return to *ontanda* afterwards. They continued the run until they arrived in the next district, Ondonga. Once in Ondonga, they started to figure out where to stay. They were aware of Mengela, a senior headman from Uukwanyama who at one point had also fled and sought refuge in Ondonga. They managed to locate Mengela and he assisted them to settle in the new land. Ondonga became home for them, and Iipumbu married there. After some years in Ondonga, Nambudhi decided to return to Uukwanyama with Naalokoshe and young Naambo. They hoped that the *ohamba* had forgotten about the events surrounding their moving out. After all, they were only women and were not a threat to his position of power. Iipumbu remained in Ondonga and could only return to Uukwanyama with Mengela after the death of Ohamba Mandume.

By the time Nambudhi returned from Ondonga, Tshikongo had long settled in Kavango. As to be expected, he sent for his second-degree niece Naalokoshe who happily joined him. Nambudhi felt lonely after the departure of her daughter Naalokoshe and decided to go to a village called Omutemo to look for her niece Mpingana Angombe. Mpingana was by then married and had moved with her husband Kathere from Uukwambi to Omutemo in Uukwanyama. One of the sons of the couple, Iitura, had remained behind under the care of his mother's sister, Niipanda.

Iitura grew up and, as it was customary for all boys at that time, he started looking after the cattle of his grandfather, Nuumbembe. One may not take it that way, but human beings seem to be blessed and each of us in our own unique way. It is also evident that each blessing can easily be transformed into a talent, which can be used in one's favour. Young Iitura did not miss out at all. He happened to have acquired a unique and impressive kind of whistling. Whistling was particularly associated with the herding of cattle. Every tone had a different meaning for the cattle. Even the king Omukwaniirwa Iipumbu noted the special talent of Iitura as the young man whistled in distinct and elaborate tones while leading his grandfather's cattle, passing *ombara* (the palace) every morning and every evening. Omukwaniirwa Iipumbu decided to send for Iitura. After enquiring who this Iitura was and whose cattle he was looking after, Omukwaniirwa Iipumbu concluded that the cattle of an ordinary subject did not deserve such an extraordinary whistle. With such a comment, Iitura immediately moved to *ombara* and became a herder of the *omukwaniirwa*'s cattle. He spent a number of years looking after Omukwaniirwa Iipumbu's cattle until he was old enough to go for contract labour.

~

During the same period, a young woman by the name of Nambashu happened to also be around Omukwaniirwa Iipumbu's *ombara*. She too happened to be from the same area as Iitura. Her maternal family originated from a district of Ongandjera but there seems to be no information on her other relatives except on her grandmother Nekuru.

At one point, the life of the residents of Ongandjera got thrown into turmoil by the appearance of men on horses referred to as *omashwarari*, people who sleep in the bush. All indications pointed to the possibility that these *omashwarari* came from the Angolan side of the border. Their mission remained unclear but their presence in the area was deemed dangerous enough to send residents on the run and to put up *eentanda* (camps) in the forest. One of the possible explanations could be that these *omashwarari* were members of expeditions for capturing slaves.

In the panic and confusion, Nekuru and her baby daughter ended up in an *ontanda* with complete strangers. All she had in common with them was the cause of their fleeing. But this did not mean that these people were responsible for her and her daughter. Very quickly Nekuru noticed that men would leave the *ontanda* in the night to return to *oshilongo*, the inhabited area, to look for food for their families. Women and children remained in the safety of *ontanda*. Nekuru had no choice but to find a way of undertaking similar trips as the men back to *oshilongo* to gather food. With her baby on her back, she arrived at one of the homesteads bordering the forest. She entered and went straight for *elimba*, the hut where food is kept. In the darkness, she felt in the clay pots and found dried nuts in one of them. She took some and decided not to return to *ontanda* in the darkness but to spend the night in the deserted homestead. She went in *ondjugo*, the sleeping hut, and started feeding her hungry daughter. She removed the shells of the nuts and chewed the nuts a bit to soften them before giving them to the girl. The little girl found the feeding too slow and every time she had swallowed what was given to her, she protested in a squeaky voice to indicate to the mother to speed up the feeding process.

What Nekuru and her daughter did not suspect was that the owner of the same homestead had also returned to *oshilongo* the same evening to collect food for his family. In the silence of the night, in the deserted *oshilongo*, the man immediately took note of the presence of a living being in the house. He first thought of an animal of some kind. Could it be a dog? But why then did it choose to be in *ondjugo*? He quietly came closer to where the noise was coming from and he could finally clearly feel the human presence. The voice of the baby gave him courage to enquire in a whispering voice, 'Who is there?' Nekuru panicked and pleaded for mercy. 'Please do not kill me, my baby is hungry,' she kept repeating. The owner of the house was not concerned that she was in his house, in *ondjugo*, and helping herself to his food. He was greatly concerned that such a young woman was back in a highly dangerous terrain on her own and with a baby. He ordered her to immediately emerge from the *ondjugo*, to put her baby on the back and to follow him. He took enough food and they hurried back to *ontanda*.

Nekuru stayed with the new acquaintance and his family until it was deemed safe to return to *oshilongo*. For some unknown reason, Nekuru had made up her mind that Ongandjera was no longer the area she wanted to return to. Was the experience with the *omashwarari* too hard for her? Or was her experience alone with her baby the reason for her decision? Or was she after all initially from somewhere else and wanted to get away from Ongandjera? Whatever the reason might have been, she decided to make a new life in Uukwambi, the next *oshilongo* southwards from Ongandjera. When the others packed up to return to Ongandjera, she put her baby on her back to cross the forests and *iishana*, plains, to go to Uukwambi where there was no history of *omashwarari*.

No one could say how long she walked to get to Uukwambi, but her way was marked by *omashwarari*. Each anthill she saw during the night resembled a man on a horse to her. Was it because anthills did not exist in Ongandjera, or was it just an obsession from a traumatised experience? At the sight of each anthill, she stopped and pleaded for mercy, '*Ino dhipagandje, tatekulu!*' Please, do not kill me, my lord! None of the anthills killed her and she finally, with her baby on the back, arrived at the edge of Uukwambi.

Those years, a stranger could not just walk into another inhabited territory, another *oshilongo*. This could only happen in company of a native of that *oshilongo*. Nekuru knew this too well and stopped at the edge of Uukwambi and hoped that a native would take note of her. So, she walked along the edge of the first village until a certain Tshikongo took note of an errant young woman. Tshikongo (but a different Tshikongo!) came around to greet her and to enquire who she was and of course what she was doing there. The first identification, and certainly one's salvation, those days was one's *ezimo*, the clan. At the mention of the name of the clan, relatives close by were immediately identified. As soon as Nekuru mentioned that she was of the *omukwanekamba* clan, this Tshikongo welcomed her in his house as a close relative. Not only did he provide Nekuru with part of his homestead as a shelter, he also provided her with part of his field for her to make a living.

With such an arrangement, Nekuru settled in and became part, not only of her newly discovered family, but of the entire society as well. Shortly after her arrival in Uukwambi, she had a second daughter named Kamweneshe, a significant name meaning someone who will never see his or her father. The only explanation of giving such a name to a child was that Nekuru was pregnant when she arrived in Uukwambi. Her first daughter Kaposha, with whom she arrived in Uukwambi from Ongandjera, grew up here and when the time was right, she married. Kaposha and her husband Uutshopa, had six children, four daughters and two sons. The four girls were older, and Nambashu was the third born. When Nambashu was old enough, she joined other young girls to serve at the *ombara* of Omukwaniirwa Iipumbu.

Iitura and Nambashu minded their assigned businesses around the *ombara*. Each of them was there for a specific reason, but this seemed not at all to mean that they did not take note of each other. However, nothing seemed to have been said between the two of them. As it was customary that time, Nambashu had *omuushiki*, the equivalent of today's fiancé. Although she had received *iigonda* from him, valuable gifts, nothing was definite. Should she decide to say yes to another man, either her family or the new *omuushiki* had to return the *iigonda* of the unlucky fiancé. At the same time, one senior headman of Omukwaniirwa Iipumbu had an eye on Nambushu. Nambashu herself had no problem, that's how things were those days. Morally and traditionally, she was fine. She would see when the time of getting involved came. However, she knew very well that it would not be easy to say no to the senior headman. The culture simply did not allow that.

When the time came, Nambashu went with other young girls for *olufuko, a* traditional rite of passage. Once young girls had gone through this ceremony, they were ready to be married and to join their husbands. The period between *olufuko* and joining one's husband allowed one to stay at home for a period of time. It would appear that the length of this period was not determined. Girls who went through *olufuko* stayed home until such a time that their husbands sent for them.

Naturally, when Nambashu went through *olufuko*, she was going to get married to her *omuushiki* by the name of Kafura. Before then, Elenga Tshitaatara had joined the race. Meanwhile, Iitura was back from his labour contract and had started showing serious interest in Nambashu. Iitura, the way I know him personally, just happened to be a handsome man. I am sure Nambashu also made a similar observation. She however found herself confronted by a dilemma where she was to make a hard choice between Kafura, a son of a headman, Iitura, a handsome nobody, and the senior headman Tshitaatara. In reality, it was not a question of Nambashu's choice, it was rather a matter of the three men outracing each other. Whoever outraced the other two would get the bride.

Amazingly, Tshitaatara was not aware of his two contenders. Even if he was, this would have been a non issue for him. He had power, and obviously, he was going to get his way. Kafura was not a big fighter and was soon out of the race. Iitura remained put. He was determined to get Nambashu. He knew about his contender and the advantage was that his contender was not aware of his wicked intention. But this was a deadly game for Iitura, and he knew it. At the same time, he did not want to let go. He wanted Nambashu. Nambashu must also have shown interest in him. How on earth would he otherwise have dared to challenge authority?

Omukwaaniirwa Iipumbu had favoured Iitura for all the years he herded Omukwaaniirwa's cattle, and did not want to see him getting into such a dangerous situation. Iipumbu decided to warn Iitura. When one gets warned by Omukwaniirwa, one better take the warning seriously. Everyone knew perfectly well that the day Elenga Tshitaatara found out about Iitura's secret admiration for Nambashu would be his end. Iitura knew it too. Iitura and Nambashu therefore had no time to waste. They had to flee before Tshitaatara found out. But Tshitaatara too spared no time before he sent for his young bride. Faced with such a situation, Nambashu had to be very creative.

Just before Iitura and Nambashu could start their move, Tshitaatara sent a message to Nambashu's parents that he would send for her that very same day. This was an 'official' notification, and there was no way to pretend that the message was not received. Both Nambashu and her parents knew exactly what that meant. Was this just a coincidence or was Tshitaatara getting suspicious? At that time, it no longer mattered for Nambashu and Iitura. The worst for them was that there was no time for planning or preparation. They had to count on improvisation.

The men on the horses were already on their way to pick up the bride. Nambashu knew what she wanted and she had to act fast. Before the men on the horses caught up with her, she had just time to run from her parents' homestead to the neighbour's homestead. By sheer luck, this particular homestead happened to be Tshitaatara's *okagumbo*, a small homestead for an unmarried woman having a relation with a married man. The owner definitely had interest to assist Nambashu to run away from Tshitaatara. The two accomplices quickly devised a strategy. An innocent baby had to become a sacrifice. Nambashu had hardly entered the neighbouring homestead when soon thereafter, she walked out as a mother with a baby on her back walking towards the bushy area minding her household business. It is not unusual to see a young mother going towards the bush for whatever reason. Probably she was going to collect firewood. The messengers on the horses had no time to waste with a mother. Their mission was to find a fleeing young bride. So they sped by.

Nambashu spent the rest of the day in the bush with the poor baby on her back. That evening she rushed back to return the baby to the mother, and by then Iitura was ready to leave with her. They walked through the night and by dawn they were safely outside of the Uukwambi territory. Iitura, together with his young wife, went straight to his parents in Omutemo. Their first son, Mandume, was born in Omutemo, and the young couple moved to Oshuulula village to establish their own homestead.

⌒

Once Iitura had moved to Oshuulula, relatives naturally followed. Nambudhi was the first one to move. Her grand daughter Naambo had married in the meantime, and had her first son, Hifivali. Her husband had died and Hifivali moved with his great grandmother Nambudhi to Oshuulula. His mother Naambo left Omutemo for Efulula village to her only brother, Kandenge. There she met and married her second husband Amulungu. Amulungu was brought to Efululula at a tender age as a captive from Ombalantu, another district in the former Owamboland. The boy could not even pronounce his name, and his capturer, Amunime, named him Amulungu. Back in those days, capturing a person from another *oshilongo* was a sign of bravery. Amunime felt great about his fame and he wasted no time to return for more battles in Ombalantu. Unfortunately for him, he did not survive the second fight. Amulungu grew up with Amunime's mother.

Naambo and Amulungu had two children, a son and a daughter. Amulungu named his first child, a son (my father), Amunime in memory of his capturer. Naambo was sickly and her relatives were convinced that her ill health was due to her marriage to Amulungu. They advised her to leave him. She left her second husband, leaving the two children behind with him.

Amunime grew up, and when he was old enough, he joined other young men and was recruited for the contract labour system. His first contract was in 1942 when he was among those sent to South Africa to guard installations during the Second World War. In 1944, he went for his second contract and worked on a farm. In December 1945, Amunime managed to get a contract to work at the Consolidated Diamond Mines (CDM) in Oranjemund in the south of Namibia. By then, labour contracts at CDM lasted for two full years. While in Oranjemund, his father Amulungu got sick and died on 9 April 1946. Some time passed before Amunime heard about the death of his father. The only possibility of getting news from home those days was either by mail or through new contract labour recruits. Amunime learned about the death of his father by mail.

Writing letters was a new development among the Aawambo in the 1940s. It was, in any case, not necessary before the introduction of the contract labour system by the South African apartheid government. Under normal circumstances, people did not move far from home. If they did, they moved in groups and that meant moving to find a new home. When the letter writing started, it was solely between the men under the labour contract system in the south of the country to their families back home in the north. There was no post office. Letters were carried by hand. One needed to find someone going back home after his contract, and the family back home would only write back when someone from the neighbourhood was going for a labour contract to the same place. Since there was no way for people at home to find paper and envelopes, the sender would include a blank sheet of paper and an envelope in his letter. How did people back home find pens? Clearly, another creative arrangement had to be made. The enclosed envelope came with the name of the writer, name of the compound and hostel numbers written on it. All they needed to do was to write on the provided sheet of paper, place it in the envelope already with the address and lick the envelope closed. And the letter would go whenever the next person leaving for a contract was on his way.

In the case of the death of Amunime's father, the letter was written the day before the death of the old man. In the letter, Amunime was informed of the serious condition of his father. When the old man died in the early hours of the following morning, the envelope was already licked and closed. It was out of question to open the envelope and sending an unclosed letter was simply not done. Amunime had however to be informed of the death of his father. Under the circumstances, there was only one way to do so with the very same letter. One simple sentence was written on the envelope: Your father died last night. What mattered happened. A few weeks later, Amunime received the news.

Amunime could only return home two years later and this somehow put him off from working in Oranjemund. Oranjemund is the southernmost town of Namibia on the border with South Africa. It is approximately 1,700 km from Amunime's home area. It is not that he did not like the job there, but he found the two years away too long. He described the length of his being away from home through the birth of two children of a neighbour. And these were not twins. When he left for Oranjemund, the neighbour's wife was pregnant with her first daughter, and the time Amunime returned from his two-year contract, not only did the lady have a daughter running around, but she was just about to get the second daughter. For Amunime, this could only mean that a very long time had passed. In the meantime, he had lost his father and did not have a home. His mother had remarried and moved elsewhere and, culturally, moving with mothers to their next matrimonial homes, was not something boys did easily. His sister had moved with their mother after the death of their father. Amunime would not do that. He decided to move in with his uncle Iitura, a distant cousin of his mother.

Those years, hanging around at home was not what young, able-bodied men did. Men needed to work and earn money. And working for money in those days only meant contract labour far away from home and for a determined length of time. Other options were non-existent for black people. Amunime decided to go for another contract, but not in Oranjemund. He got a contract in Bethanie to work in a school hostel. This time he received a one-year contract. That was much better. But Amunime's contracts seemed to be always eventful. Perhaps that was the case for all those men who went on labour contracts. While he was in Bethanie, Iitura moved from Omutemo to another village called Omayanga. Amunime was aware of the move but he had no clue where Omayanga was.

It was also during his contract in Bethanie that Amunime's family got the news that Amunime had died. As he walked the streets of Bethanie, mourning was taking place back home with all that went along with it including the slaughtering of cattle. Amunime was not aware of his perceived death and was only to find out once he returned home many months later. It is true that he did feel unwell for a few days during his contract. He went to the clinic where he ran into an acquaintance from the same area as his family. Out of a simple story of having seen Amunime seeking medical treatment, someone along the chain of conveying this information between Bethanie and Omayanga managed to make out that the man had died.

After his contract, Amunime set himself on the way back home. Returning home after a contract was always an occasion for both returnee and his family, as well as the neighbours and friends. It was time to receive items one had no access to, and it was also a time to demonstrate one's manhood and ability to provide. Handing out a few bars of soap, tobacco, sweets to neighbours, a blanket here and there to close uncles, and pieces of cloth to a few aunts was a big gesture. Amunime had all these items for the ritual. One thing he did not know though was that no one was expecting him this time.

After a long journey, he arrived in the vicinity of the home of his mother. It was daytime and the belief was that a person returning from a contract could not enter the house during daytime. Amunime did not at all want to stay with his mother, but he still wanted to pop in and to let his mother know that he was back. He also did not know how to find Iitura's new home. He waited for the fall of the night in the nearby bush. But he was too close to the pig stall, and when his young sister Namutsheko went to feed the pigs later that afternoon, she somehow got a glimpse of him. She knew her brother and she was certain that this was no case of hallucination. She hurried back in the house and announced to the mother that she had seen Amunime. The mother was surprised. How could this girl pretend that she saw a brother who had died months ago and after the entire family had gone through the mourning period?

At nightfall, Amunime simply walked into the house. He could not understand when his appearance caused agony to his mother instead of joy. What else could the poor mother do? The mother told him about his death. Well, he was not dead, and he was there just for the night. The following day he was on his way to Omayanga. By then, he knew he would also face the same drama there.

The reason why Iitura moved to Omayanga was to take up a headman position. Traditionally, becoming headman followed a pattern of inheritance. But this was not the case with Iitura. He became headman in an unusual manner, rather an exceptional and isolated case. The senior headman of the district under which Omayanga falls, wanted a specific favour from Iitura. Iitura's second son, Angula, had horses he had bought during one of his contracts. Horses had a certain attraction and an exceptional status. Angula had left his horses under the care of his father when he went for his next contract. When the senior headman approached Iitura on the matter, Iitura had the courage to tell the senior headman that the horses belonged to his son. But when the senior headman offered a headman position of a village in return, and although the offered village was a distance away, Iitura could not resist. He would see how to explain to his son his deal with the senior headman when the time was right. After all, moving to Omayanga would bring him closer to his place of birth, which he had had to flee for the sake of his marriage.

⤳

There was absolutely nothing unusual about Amunime moving into the household of his uncle Iitura, his mother's distant cousin. He naturally became part of the family. By the time he moved in, there were already two sets of siblings. On one hand, Iitura and Nambashu's eight children and on the other hand, Iitura's deceased sister Noa's six children, a girl and five boys. Amunime took up the place of child number 15 in the house. This was however before Iitura took in more wives. By the time Iitura moved to Omayanga, he had three wives, and more were still to come. As headman, he could afford a number of wives and of course a few more sets of children.

My parents, therefore, as distant cousins to each other, spent some years as children of the same house until my grandmother unexpectedly discovered Christianity. After their move to Omayanga, Nambashu heard about and got to know a bit more about this new phenomenon known as Christianity being advanced by the Catholic Church at Okatana Roman Catholic Mission Station, just 2 km away. The Church was certainly out to find more members and Nambashu was among those who indicated their willingness to be baptised. Soon she was going to find out that the Church would not accept her as a church member in her current matrimonial situation. Sharing a husband with other three co-wives was definitely not in line with the teachings of the Church. It did not really matter that she was the first wife and possibly the most legitimate one. Such an arrangement was simply the last thing the Church wanted to hear. If Nambashu was serious about getting baptised, the first thing she had to consider doing was to get out of this 'heathen' set up.

Nambashu did not want to miss out on the baptism and thereby on becoming a member of her new discovery. She had to find a way of convincing her husband that this newly discovered phenomenon required her to move out as a condition of her baptism. Iitura was among the last inhabitants of Omayanga to be impressed with the Church and its teachings. He did not come near the building despite living very close to it. He certainly passed the mission station and the church building often, but he only purposefully went into the mission station much later and specifically to seek medical treatment. As his age progressed and his health started to fail, he took a keen interest in finding out whether Sister Wilma, of whom he had so often heard about, could do something for him. I still remember my grandfather's conversation with my mother as he sceptically wondered whether the white woman in white clothes at the Catholic hospital could really figure out what the cause of a sore lump under his tongue was. He finally ended up believing this Sister Wilma. When she told him that the sore lump under his tongue was not at all a good thing and that it was going to cause his death, he sent for my mother again and announced to her that if the white person at the hospital said that he was going to die, then it would certainly be true. Despite his condition, Iitura took his time to get more closely acquainted with the Church. He would occasionally get admitted into the hospital and, although Sister Wilma gently told him how important it was for him in his condition to get baptised, Iitura held out until his last days.

He, however, had an understanding for his dear wife's admiration of the Church. Not only did he agree that his newly inspired Christian wife move out, but he also established *okagumbo* (a small homestead) for her with a generous portion of a field right next to his homestead. For Iitura, this was not a big deal at all as this was, after all, also culturally expected from him. Nambashu remained his wife and, as such, he was responsible for her and their younger children who moved out with her. She and the younger children were a few hundred metres away. The older children were married and gone by then, and Angula, one of the two older sons, stayed in the main homestead. Young men did not move out with their mothers; culture dictated that they remained in the main homestead with their fathers.

Nambashu's moving out paid off. Iitura was taken aback by what had to happen to those who wanted to become Christians, including his wife. From one day to the next, through a process called baptism, Nambashu, his wife of more than thirty years, received the new name Regina. He repeatedly told friends and neighbours, '*Nambashu opo eli mpo anuwa paife ohe Regina.*' Not only did he express his amazement at a sudden change of name of someone he had known by a specific name for such a long time, but he was also perplexed at the simple manner of changing one's name to a name which had no meaning at all for the Oshiwambo-speaking people.

Iitura's amazement was not unfounded. When European missionaries came to evangelise they brought a list of European names. It was out of the question to be baptised with an African name. One had to select a name from the provided list. I do not know which criteria people used to select the preferred names from these foreign names, but I suppose they went by the sound of the name. Of course, the baptised people kept their African names but those names were not allowed anywhere near the mission station.

Iitura then silently looked on as his children followed in the footsteps of their mother when all of a sudden Angula, Hinahonde, Nekuru, Mpingana, Tileni and Iyambo became Festus, Albertina, Monika, Dorothea, Teofilia and Ludwig. Their eldest brother Mandume did not go along; he sided with his father and remained Mandume, and similar to his father, he was baptised on his deathbed.

⌒

Getting married to each other was the last thing my parents thought of until it was almost happening. Growing up and living in the same house made them feel like more than just cousins. In a certain way, they were simply a bunch of siblings or as people commonly said those days, they were children of the same house. Besides that, my mother was much younger than my father and when my father returned from his first few contracts, just like all other children in the house did, my mother jumped around my father to get sweets.

Not only did my father, Amunime, start thinking of getting married a bit late but he did so in a very wrong place. They were already in Omayanga. The residents of the Omayanga village were not really pleased to see them around. They came from far away, yet their uncle, my mother's father, was the new headman of their village. And his ascension to the headman position was not that clear to the old inhabitants as there was no bloodline link. This was not an easy topic for the villagers. They let things happen and stood by as this huge family settled in and took up too much of their space. A good number of them moved out to establish a neighbouring village that is today known as Onawa ha Kilian. Kilian was among the first of the former Omayanga inhabitants who moved out to establish Onawa and he became its first headman. The name of the village is also significant as its creators demonstrated their unhappiness about the influx and domination of the newcomers but at the same time they expressed their appeasement with the establishment of the new village. The word *onawa* literally means 'it is fine' or 'we have made peace with the occurrence'.

My father took a step towards the remaining inhabitants of Omayanga and, in no time, he had a relationship with one of the local girls. He managed to keep the relationship secret for a while. Unfortunately for him, the girl got pregnant. My father did not see this as a problem as he intended to marry the girl anyway. Iitura, on the other hand, did not see it exactly that way. He was in charge of his household and whoever was part of it. He was in this precarious situation of asserting his authority as headman and under no circumstances did he want trouble with these people whom he hardly knew and who clearly did not welcome his reign. Neither was he certain that marrying a girl one was not well acquainted with was the right thing to do. Knowing a prospective spouse those days meant knowing his or her extended family, their reputation, how well off they were and so many other things. He therefore had to bring his reservations to the attention of his nephew, but in such a way that it did not get beyond the household. Who was he to prevent his nephew from marrying a girl who was, after all, pregnant with his child? This was the least they could do as newcomers to repair the damage.

It so happened, however, that the poor girl lost the pregnancy, but my father was far from being out of trouble. The girl and her people were from the village and they knew its environment. They also knew about the Okatana Catholic Mission Station and knew the priest in charge of the station. They walked up to the station and told everything to the priest Father Heimrikx, a Dutch man. The inhabitants of Omayanga really wanted to fix these newcomers who were not yet quite Christians, and certainly none of them were Catholic yet. Who were they to walk into a very Catholic village and mess around with the local inhabitants?

Meanwhile, Iitura had talked some sense into his cousin. Under no circumstances could he marry an unknown girl. Should it come to worse, there were so many of his cousins. Iitura could at least trust his daughters. That way, there would be no trouble for the family. Amunime had to leave for a quick contract. Of course to earn some money, but also to be out of the way of his girlfriend's family and secondly to give some thought to Iitura's suggestion. It was not as easy as Iitura thought.

After a full contract of 18 months, my father was back at home, with his mind made up. He was going to get married to one of his cousins. He first considered one of the older girls, but by the time he returned, that cousin had a baby. What then? He had gone to think about his uncle's suggestion and here he was and ready for the wedding. After eighteen months, this little girl Tileni had grown a bit and she looked like a woman. But she was smart and had a fiancé somewhere. How come she was allowed to do so if she was also new in the area? Well, eighteen months were long enough to settle in and know the people in the surroundings. My father would talk to her. If she said yes, the wedding would happen pretty soon. And the brave young girl happened just to have said yes. My father was quick to pay her fiancé whatever gifts he had offered to her and the news went around about the intended wedding of the cousins.

The priest in Okatana was still sitting with the complaint of the deserted local girl and was expected to take action towards this man who was about to marry his own cousin. The decision whether or not to marry the cousins was solely in the priest's hands and he was expected to do justice. There was no other option except for *olufuko*, which was becoming less popular among the communities influenced by the Church. It was therefore in the interest of my father to clear up the pending issue with the Church. When Father Heimerikx sent for him, my father lost no time. The question put to him was simple, 'Whose son are you and who are the parents of the new girl you intend to marry?' From the point of view of a Dutch mind, and to the disappointment of the disgruntled local family, there was no family relation that could prevent my parents from marrying. With such a pronouncement from the priest, my father pressed ahead with the wedding. My grandmother had no problem, but some of her family members did, especially her eldest son. My mother's eldest brother had a serious issue with the marriage of his little sister to my father. He might have manifested his unhappiness at other occasions, but he certainly did so on the day just before the wedding.

My mother stayed with her mother next door and my father lived with his uncle, my mother's father. Conveniently for everyone, the bride and bridegroom's homes were very close to each other. No need to worry about distance. Traditionally, relatives stay over in the wedding home for two days to enjoy the festivities. They arrive the evening before the wedding and leave the morning after the wedding. Naturally, my grandmother's relatives stayed with her and my grandfather's, and therefore, my father's relatives stayed at my grandfather's house. But these people knew each other so well that they moved back and forth between the two homes. So did my grandfather. After all, this was his first wife's home, which he had provided. And more importantly, the girl who was getting married was his daughter too.

As they were enjoying a drink on the eve of the wedding at my grandmother's house, my mother's eldest brother, Mandume, made use of the opportunity to tell his father how pathetic it was for him to give his young daughter away to his nephew. The argument became so heated that my grandfather stormed out of my grandmother's house vowing never to return. That was unthinkable! As a father, he had to return early the following morning to lead his daughter out of the house to go to church. In the absence of a living father, the bride could not leave home to go to church.

My grandfather, however, took exception to the challenge from his eldest son. His decision was final. Out of rage, in the middle of the night, he ordered the release of his cow he had sent over to my grandmother's house for the wedding. Traditionally, the cow should be slaughtered early in the morning for the wedding. If this Mandume was so full of himself, then there would be no cow for the wedding of his little sister!

Very early the following morning, my grandmother accompanied by her youngest brother went to plead with my grandfather, but he would not change his mind. The other two sisters and a brother of my grandmother sided with Mandume. If the old man didn't want to come, let there be no wedding. And my grandfather really did not turn up. Mandume and some relatives were not bothered, but my poor parents were. My poor mother, as young as she was, fully dressed in her bridal garments, had no father to lead her out of the house to go to church for her wedding. So she sat in the hut and waited as dictated by the tradition. The trouble was that Father Heimerikx at the Okatana Mission Station worked according to a timed schedule. Whoever was not there at a given time would not get married on that specific day. And wedding dates were well spaced as priests had other duties.

My father hung around at home and observed Iitura sitting around and giving no sign of moving to my grandmother's house to perform his fatherly duty. What a horror! My father has always been unpredictable. He went through so much trouble to get to his wedding day and all of a sudden this impasse? No way! The wedding was that day and it had to happen. Yes, there was respect for culture, but if those who were responsible for performing the cultural acts were not prepared to do so, one could improvise. And my father decided to stand in for his uncle. He walked to my grandmother's house and in that confusion, offered to lead my mother out of the house. He insisted that he was much older than her, and that he was at the same time related to her father and as such, in cultural terms, he could play the role of her father. What a statement! My mother obeyed, emerged from the hut, and walked to church. Father Heimerikx did his part, and my parents were married.

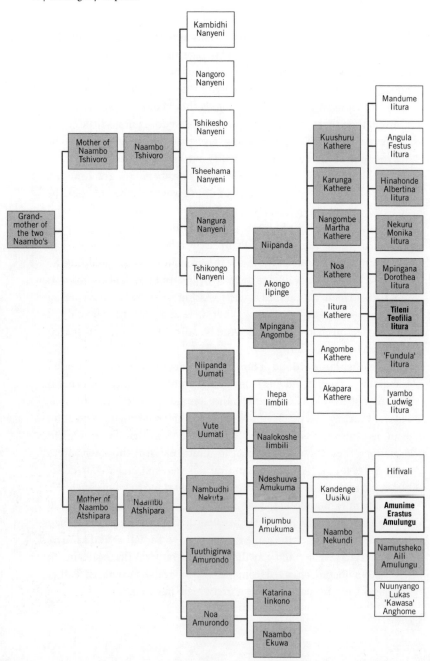

Naambo Atshipara and some of her descendants.

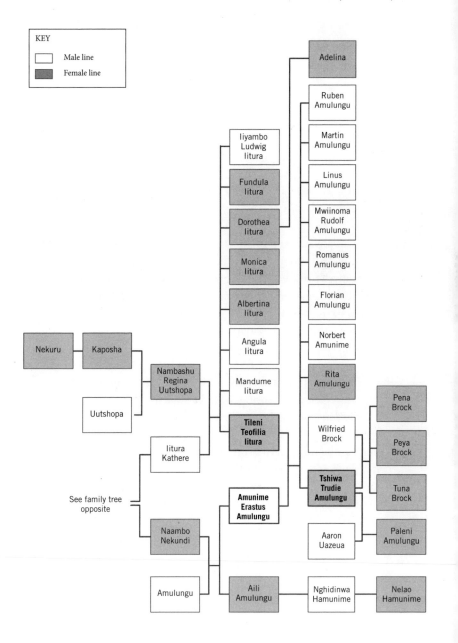

Tshiwa Trudie Amulungu: my place in the family tree.

2

My childhood

Home will always remain a place that is full of childhood memories. Every time the notion of home occurs to me, I travel back in the past and see myself running in the green *omahangu* field, or stopping at a fig tree to pick figs on my way to my grandmother's homestead. I see myself walking next to the oxen assisting my father to plough the field. Ploughing was followed by long hours of cultivation in the field and other household activities. But I also have fond memories of playing hide and seek with my father which once ended up in a real drama. I was pretty sure of having followed my father very closely as he entered a hut and to my greatest incomprehension my father was simply not in the hut! And the hut had just this one entrance and of course no window. I walked out several times, very frustrated, and every time I was outside, my father called me and the voice was unmistakably coming from inside the hut I had just left. It took me some time to figure out how my father managed to be invisible in such a small place. Evidently, children do not often think of lifting their eyes higher than their eye level.

It is this rural setting which comes to my mind when I recall my childhood. And it is not only the images of this village life, it is also the smells attached to it: the smell just before the rain, the smell of fresh milk, the smell of fresh wild spinach cooked with home-made butter, the smell of firewood in the sleeping hut. It all smelled special and different. Today, whenever I go back home, that smell is no longer there. Or at least, I can no longer smell it. Is it because I have been elsewhere? Or has my childhood village lost its origin?

I must say that I was born under special circumstances. I just happened to be born in my maternal grandfather's house. This is quite unusual, culturally at least. Well and good, there are always exceptions. As stated earlier, my parents grew up in one house as distant cousins. By the time they married, my mother lived with her mother in a homestead on the same field as my grandfather. And my father lived with his uncle, my mother's father. What really happened when my parents married, my mother moved back to her father's homestead. In my eyes as a little child, my grandparents were very close neighbours. My grandmother lived within my walking distance. For a start, this was not too bad. I practically had the team of adults who mattered in my life around me. It is obvious this was a potential arrangement of getting any child spoiled. My many siblings were still to come to constitute a real African family.

When my sister was born, I was simply taken over to my grandmother. The explanation was that this would allow my very young mother sufficient time to recover and to take care of the newborn. Of course, I could come over to visit, but for practical purposes, I was temporarily living with my grandmother. My cousin Adelina, who was seven years older than me, was permanently living with my grandmother. I am fond of her, not only because she was nice to me, but also for her creativity. She devised a system of transporting me to my mother literally on a daily basis. I was a hefty child and my cousin, out of necessity, had to find a way of carrying me on her back but without causing permanent damage to it. That time, the *omahangu* fields were made up of many little heaps of soil known as *iimpungu* on which *omahangu* was grown. Between these heaps were the zigzag gorges that people used as paths. One had no business on top of *iimpungu*. My cousin however made a creative use of them to get me to my mother. She would, after every few steps, sit down at the lower part of one of these *iimpungu* and I would simply remain on the top of it. After she had rested her back, she would kneel in the path and I would jump on her back, and the journey continued. After several rests, we would reach our destination. Later the same day, we would return, same means of transport, to my grandmother.

My first three years were really special. I had my parents and my grandparents around me. And those days babysitting was a costless affair. There were always older children around and it was part of the upbringing to look after younger siblings or other relatives' younger children. You were not asked if you wanted to do it; younger children were simply left under your care. Since this was how things were, children happily performed these tasks, and did so in an acceptable manner.

My grandfather's house was a hub of activities. Being the headman of the village, it was automatic that he had many wives. It was also not of interest to me to know exactly how many wives he had at a time, but there were quite a few of them. Obviously, he had many children too. When he moved to the Omayanga village, his children alone made up a classroom at the Okatana Roman Catholic School. Although the church did not manage to baptise my grandfather for a very long time, they did manage to do so with a significant number of his offspring as they were growing up.

In this big household, I, for obvious reasons, became somehow the centre of attention. Both my father and my mother, for different reasons, were related to the owner of the house, my grandfather. My mother was one of the daughters from his first wife. So she somehow had a different status than the other children from the second, third, fourth and fifth wives. My father, beside his status of being a nephew to my grandfather, was a dedicated contract worker and brought unusual but interesting items whenever he returned. He also had some South African pounds sterling on him. Today, such a condition will pass unnoticed, but those days, it was real privilege to have money. Besides the many people who pampered me in this full house, I was also well aware of the soft spot that my grandfather had for me, and I made use of it to the fullest. I am told that I never failed to demonstrate my grievances to him for everything that happened to my dislike. It is a pity I cannot recall much of that interesting time. A few things kept being repeated to me though.

All the stories are based on food and eating which, in the end, earned me a nickname from my grandfather which some courageous people still call me. One of the stories is about my love for sweets, which I still enjoy today. My father had always kept sweets from his contract periods. And sweets in a village those days were a scarce and highly attractive commodity. They tasted sweeter, smelled exceptionally interesting and they were something people, especially children, appreciated so much.

My father, after returning from one of his many contracts, had kept leftover sweets, but apparently for a specific purpose.

When I think about this story today, I am amazed at how humans always had the ability of putting anything to good use. If sweets are sweet, and they can certainly do wonders, why not use them as need? This is how my father must have sat back and thought of the best way sweets could become some sort of a solution to a major problem my parents faced at a crucial time of the year. Here, they had this little toddler who did not understand the importance her people held about the cultivation of fields at a specific time every year. Nothing can stop people of northern Namibia from cultivating their fields. Only the rain or a lack thereof, can do so. A mother not cultivating because of a difficult toddler is unheard of and my father was determined to find an amicable solution. After all, I am his daughter, the first child for that matter. Young and inexperienced parents are not quite sure whether crying, is after all, harmful to children. So, my father tried to find a lasting solution, and the sweets came in handy.

Working in the field was, and still remains, an annual routine that had to happen. It did not matter if one had an abundant surplus of produce from the previous year. Every year between December and April, all able bodies must be in the field. Bigger families worked faster and could chat while working; my mother was just starting a family and had to do it by herself for some years. For some reason, my father did not do much cultivating. I recall how he would happily plough the field, but when it came to tending the field, he only checked from a distance to see who was not working hard enough. Otherwise he did some correctional work, especially straightening pathways in the field.

Having cultivated the field for a considerable number of years in my life, I cannot think of any time of the year that I hated more than the cultivating period. Yes, we got used to it as children, but if there was a way of having this part of the year cut out, I would have been a strong supporter of such a move. There is no doubt that this is not an activity one would easily do with a baby on the back, at least not for an entire day.

It is exactly for this reason that my father invented this simple and straightforward solution to a complex problem. My father must have first thought that it would not be difficult to succeed as he, after all, had just the right commodity at his disposal. All he needed to do was to place me in the shade under a tree with enough sweets next to me. My mother would be in full view from where I was sitting. Why then crying, or the urge to crawl to her? Well, I am sure I did enjoy the sweets, but they are only sweets. I am also sure that I would have enjoyed them more sitting on my mother's lap. To my parents' disappointment, especially my father's, it did not take long before I started protesting. And protesting at the age of two years old normally leads to the desired result. My parents' problem remained unsolved and my father quickly had to devise a new strategy. Besides the sweets, the human presence would be an added value. That was not difficult to organise. There were enough older children around who would be interested in playing with me under my tree in exchange for sweets. What my father did not contemplate was that the sweets would get finished, or the children would have had enough of the sweets. In the event of either of the two, these children simply walked away when they had had enough, either of the sweets, or of me. I wonder what else my parents tried out but I am very certain that they managed to have the field cultivated that year. It simply had to happen.

The other story my father enjoys telling is my love for meat. At least this story no longer causes me embarrassment. Butcheries did not exist in the villages, and still today when it comes to slaughtering an animal as big as a cow, one needs to mobilise half of the village. Once the word has spread, a number of people would come around. In the end, everybody would get to eat a piece of fresh meat. Slaughtering a cow in the Oshiwambo culture is therefore an elaborate affair and a social function in itself. The actual slaughtering is considered a man's job and it happens in the kraal. The men, equipped with appropriate knives, do a thorough job. The cow is brought down with an assegai. It is not every man who is precise in this skill. Once the cow is lying lifeless on the ground, all the men would collectively attend to the skinning of the animal, no waste of any edible meat. The skin will be as white as one can imagine, and there is no drop of blood until the cutting of the meat commences. It is understandable that the process takes time.

Normally, well brought up children those days should not bother their fathers when they are engaged in as serious a business as this one, especially in the presence of other men. When it happened, the father would tell the child to immediately stop misbehaving and to return to the mother. Well-behaved children would do so. It was also an embarrassment for a father when his child demanded something as unusual as meat in front of everybody. It was seen as a sign of being spoiled. It was just a norm that children did not ask for meat, and little girls did not normally wander around the kraal when slaughtering was happening.

I, however, managed that, to the biggest embarrassment of my father. One day, news went around that my grandfather had invited a number of men to slaughter a cow. Of course, my father was going to be among them. This news also reached my ears and I made sure I was not far from where it was happening. Once the animal was on the ground, in my eyes, it was already meat. I called out to my father to quickly give me a piece of meat. I loudly indicated to him that it was not necessary for him to go round to the entrance of the kraal, he could just hand it over to me through the wooden poles. My father, overwhelmed with embarrassment, screamed at me and told me to immediately return to my mother. I apparently found that grossly unfair, not so much the shouting, but about not getting my meat immediately. Instead of seeking consolation from my mother, I went straight to state my case to the owner of the house and of course of the cow. Grandfathers those days were different from fathers. Asking for meat at that age was not at all embarrassing.

While my father thought that his instruction to me was crystal clear, he was surprised to see me back in a very short while holding my grandfather's hand, approaching the kraal. As one always does with spoiled children, my grandfather asked me to repeat what I wanted. I did that loud and clear. I cannot recall my father's look at that moment. My grandfather demanded that I be given a piece of meat immediately. One man, of course not my father, cut a small piece from the side that had been skinned by that time, and handed it over to me between the poles. In the company of my grandfather, I walked away with my piece of meat that I threw into the fire to fry shortly thereafter. This episode, besides causing embarrassment to my father and laughter to my grandfather, earned me a nickname Tshandjala, meaning, 'a starving little thing'. After that, my grandfather hardly ever called me by my real name.

Living in my maternal grandfather's house was not going to last. It is acceptable that the newly wed man spent the initial years of marriage in his parents' home, but the expectation is that he uses this period to prepare for the establishment of his own homestead. It is a period to go for one or two more labour contracts, and thereafter find suitable land. After the purchase and clearance of the suitable land, the cutting of enough poles and building of a decent homestead follows. All this sounds physically demanding. Preparing for a wedding was a stressful affair those days, and taking a short break before getting into another mammoth task was only reasonable.

When I was about three years old, it was high time that we moved. My father had put up a homestead very close to where the Eluwa Special Education School in Ongwediva stands today. That is about 5 km from the village of my grandfather. Since we had not known other modes of transport than going on foot, for us as children, that was a faraway place. I still remember walking endlessly behind my parents and wondering how much longer the journey would take. Since everybody else around was walking, there was no point in making a fuss.

I do not have much memory of the two years we spent at our first homestead. Besides the walking episodes to visit my grandparents and back to the new home, I recall something unusual during this time, and that was seeing a car for the first time. Since we stayed very close to the road between Ondangwa and Oshakati, the two first established towns in northern Namibia, my sister and I spent endless hours outside the homestead marvelling at cars without really understanding what they were. They were simply fascinating, and since they passed by so fast, we obviously waited for the next one. At the end of the day we had counted how many cars we had seen that particular day, and how many of each size, shape and colour. I do not know how long we observed cars, but it was an interesting game for the two of us.

Then all of a sudden, there were men working on the road and from one day to the next the gravel road turned black. We did not really understand how these men turned the road black but their action added to our enjoyment. Not only did the noise of a car on a black road sound different from what we had got used to, but it also had a different effect on us. We could hear it approaching from far away. It sped by us so fast and we amazingly continued hearing it after it had disappeared. One day, as we were enjoying the passing cars, something else caught my eye. The new discovery was the objects the workers who were turning the dusty road into a black colour were pushing around. Without understanding what they were being used for, I found the rolling objects interesting and I was certain that I wanted one as well. I picked up the courage and asked these working men if they could give me one of those things. I could not explain why exactly I wanted one but I pleaded with the men to give me one. I am sure these men found me a bit insistent, but they agreed to give me one of the many objects. However, they wanted to know what they would get in return. I offered a chicken and the deal was sealed. I had no problem with chasing and catching up with my payment. In no time, I had paid and was happily rolling over my new toy, an empty steel barrel drum. When my parents returned home later in the day, they were surprised by my new acquisition. I obviously did not feel any wrongdoing with the chosen price. After all, the drum is much bigger than a chicken. In my eyes, that was a real good bargain.

Although a chicken is not a big item to part with, my parents were far from being happy to see me developing selling skills at such a tender age. I did understand that it was not such a good habit and I was made to promise never again to get into such a serious business without the permission of my parents. In any case, it was made clear to me that selling is not children's business. Be that as it may, my drum was to become an indispensable multipurpose household item. Everyone in the family found it to be useful for so many things. My sister and I found in it a wonderful toy, and my brothers joined in the game as they grew older. My father first used it to draw and carry water, similar to the road construction workers. At one point it was out of bounds for quite a while as my mother stored *omahangu* in it. When it was free again, we as children used it as a ladder to reach *eembe* fruit on one of the trees. And one day, one of my brothers found the drum useful to put one of our baby brothers on it, so as to avoid being seen by other boys carrying a baby on his back.

Carrying a baby on the back is normally a girl's job. In our case, out of nine children, seven are boys. By the time my sister and I left for boarding school, my mother did not hesitate one bit to have my older brothers care for their baby brothers, and this included carrying babies on their backs. That particular day, when my brother heard his peers' greeting, he at once took off the baby and placed it on the nearest flat surface that just so happened to be the top of my drum. And off he went to meet his friends before they came any closer to where he was. He went on attending to his friends and there was no hurry to get back to the baby on top of the drum. When my mother heard the story, she was convinced that anything could have happened to her baby including dying. From that date, my drum was banished to the tree where we played. There it brought us in conflict with my father. Not only us, his children, but also other children from the neighbourhood, as well as any other person who passed the tree. We all put the drum to use to rip his tree of its *eembe* fruit. In short, the drum served us in various ways for so many years. It forms part of the family history and it bears testimony to my early creativity.

Besides counting cars and creative games with the drum, my sister and I had also to do some work, and some of that was to look after cattle. Just like my mother did not see anything wrong with boys carrying babies on their backs, my father did not think twice before sending the two of us off to look after cattle. He seemed to have thought to himself that it was not his fault that his two firstborns were girls. We did not protest, neither did it occur to us that we were being asked to perform a boy's task. We happily picked up our knobkerries, and walked behind the cattle in the forest. Those days, forests really did exist in the north of the country. There were very few inhabitants in the area and the danger of having cattle going into a neighbour's field was remote. My parents were therefore not concerned that we might not be able to control the cattle. There was enough grass and the cattle did not put much pressure on us. We could sit under a tree, play something and from time to time lift up our eyes to see whether the cattle were all still there. If one of them went a bit astray, we only needed to whistle or call out its name, and it took heed.

Looking after cattle afforded us also an opportunity to explore and discover the forest. We listened to the singing of the birds and the crying of all kinds of tree creatures. We could distinguish the singing of various birds and as the time went on, we were convinced that we understood the meaning of the songs. We even managed to sing along, but with real words and the songs made sense. One of our famous bird songs was the dove song known as '*aasita yoogoka*'. All kids in our area who looked after cattle knew the song. My sister went to the extent of claiming that she had heard a bird calling her by name in a song. When we went back home one evening, she could repeat the song to my father, which went like this: *Gwamateu-teteu-teuteu*. My father told her that she must be special for a bird to have made a song just for her. For a very long time, my father nicknamed her 'My only daughter who was called by a bird by name'. And for a long time, my sister was very fond of that reference.

At times we got so absorbed in the happenings around us in the forest that we found ourselves following the singing of the birds. We of course took the cattle along and interfered with their grazing in the process. It just so happened that one day we wandered off so far that, all of a sudden, we no longer had a sense of direction. As it was getting late, we were desperate to get home, but in vain. My father, alerted by our not turning up way beyond the usual time had to go out to look for us. After some walking around and calling our names, we finally managed to determine the direction his voice was coming from. By the time he found us, we had done some serious crying and had no clue where the cattle were. He first had to take us home and then return to look for the cattle. After that episode, my father asked one of his nephews to come and assist with the cattle. We were not completely released from looking after the cattle but we no longer did it systematically, and especially much less in the afternoons. We rather went for the morning sessions and when we brought the cattle home for milking, our boy cousin took over. When our two elder brothers were old enough, they assumed their male responsibility and we had to start in all earnest with girls' duties.

After just a short while at our own homestead at Ongwediva, we all of a sudden had to return to Omayanga. By that time, we were three siblings. At one point, my mother had to leave us alone with my father and returned to my grandmother for a while. After a few weeks, she returned with my little brother.

My father was not eager to explain anything about our imminent return to our old village. Were we returning to my grandfather's house? Or would we move in with my grandmother this time? Back in those days parents were not obliged to respond to children's questions. Children too did not bother adults with questioning. Children did as they were told. I don't think we were bothered that our parents decided not to tell us more about the move. We could, as yet, not call the new place home. If we were going back, we were delighted to live closer to our grandparents again. What we did not realise though was that the moving was going to happen soon.

It all started with my father going back and forth to Omayanga. We were often alone home with my mother, and my father would spend the day away, returning only in the evening, just to leave again the following morning. I cannot remember my parents discussing the moving, they certainly did it when we were sleeping. But plans were definitely in place. One evening, we were told that we were leaving. We were happy to move back but we did not expect to do so in the darkness. My father was in such a hurry and he told us that we needed to go quietly. Asking questions at that moment was not the right thing to do. Although I keenly wanted to understand why we could not wait for the following morning, I stood ready to move.

My mother put my little brother on her back. My father placed my sister over his shoulders. I obviously had to walk. Quietly we left our temporary home where we had spent the entire previous year. There was no talk of coming back. It didn't really matter. I hardly knew anybody in the area and a year was not long enough for me to get attached to the place. What mattered at that point was that I was in the company of my parents and going back to a place where I knew a number of people, especially my grandparents. During our one year away, I had not had many opportunities to go back to Omayanga. Firstly, for my parents, I couldn't walk fast enough and I made the journey longer for them. I was taken twice or so to church in Okatana and since it is very close to Omayanga, we could make a quick stop over at my grandmother. The second time, my mother and I got a lift back home from the very same Father Heimerikx, who was nicknamed Pata Kaishara ka Nangombe. Pata Kaishara was on his way to somewhere closer to Ongwediva. Climbing in a car for the first time was quite exciting, but as soon as it started moving, my world was upside down. It was at the back of the pick-up truck and, for the very first time, I was subjected to speed. The highest speed I had known was on the bicycle. The trees sped by and at one point I had the feeling that the car was stationary and it was the trees that were speeding by. It was an awful feeling. The pressure of wind against my face was unbearable and tears were streaming down my cheeks. My mother was pleased that she did not have to walk and we came back home much earlier, but, for me, that was the very last time I wanted to be in a car, an object I had admired from a distance for so long.

As I walked next to my parents without seeing where I was going, I really wished there was some sort of transportation. I knew too well that it was pointless to complain as it was impossible for either of them to take on an additional load. I braced myself and pressed on. Occasionally, I dozed off and tried to walk with closed eyes with a wishful thinking that I was in my usual sleeping place. That particular night I regretted all the many nights I found excuses why I should not go to sleep when it was time to do so. I badly needed sleep. I can't remember when we finally arrived, but somewhere still in the night. Surprisingly my mother and the three of us children went to my grandmother's house where we stayed for a few days. My father told my sister and me to respond to whoever asked us why we were at our grandmother's house that our parents had quarrelled. I cannot recall whether the situation arose, but that should have been our response.

When we finally joined my father, I was surprised by the size of the place. Our new homestead was big and surrounded by a huge field. It had not struck me at that time that this sizeable piece of land would require so much of my labour in many years to come. What was certain this time was that we had found a home. It was a property that many people would have wished for. My father had indeed struck a good deal. The story however as to how he managed the deal, involved an amount of lobbying and manoeuvring. And this was exactly the reason why my sister and I were asked to tell a lie about our stay with our grandmother.

To date, it is still hard for me to sketch out the story but it sounds like the following: My father wanted to come back to Omayanga. Not only did he want to come back, but he wanted to have a good and a well established homestead at a good location. This was not only for his ego, but it was also a sort of unfinished competition with his cousins. In a way, this was a settlement of unresolved issues dating from way before my time.

When my father, as a young man, went to join the household of his uncle who was my maternal grandfather, he found two elder brothers of my mother, and five other nephews of my grandfather. Girls did not pose a threat during those days. These sets of male cousins, including my father grew up together under one roof. To a certain extent, beside the fact that my father arrived much later in this set up, he was also alone in relation to the two sons and the immediate nephews of his uncle, my grandfather. In the process, opinions were formed among the eight young men as to who was the favourite of my grandfather and who could do things better. These types of opinions are common among competing men and in this case among cousins. When the family moved to Omayanga in the 1940s, these cousins were adult men who were literally on their way out of my grandfather's house. They were, however, in a new environment and they all wanted to remain in the same village close to their father and uncle. Finding a decent homestead could only occur if two things happened: either if someone chose to move out of the village, or died. These two things did not happen so often those years. Waiting and being patient was therefore a must.

As these cousins married one by one, they had to move elsewhere, either within the village or to another village, as my father did for a year. He however married much later than his cousins. By the time my father married, my mother's two elder brothers and the three other cousins had married and found good homesteads within Omayanga. Since my grandfather was the headman, they had to 'buy' the homesteads from him. Obviously, there was always talk of who had been favoured and in which way. When my father was married and ready to move out, no good homestead had become available for some years. My father saw this as a lack of interest from my grandfather to facilitate the process for him. As a person, my father holds himself high in society. He is confident of his abilities and, if need be, he can go as far as being confrontational. My grandfather, on the other hand, refused to be challenged. What became clear is that, when my father moved to a different village for a year, he must have vowed to himself to return one day, with or without my grandfather's facilitation. And when he finally did, he did so in big style. My grandfather, as a respectable headman, had no choice but to give in. After all, this was his nephew, his son-in-law and the father of his grandchildren. My father used all these special relations to his fullest advantage.

To get this specific homestead, my father decided to go it alone. When he got wind that a certain elderly man from Omayanga was about to move elsewhere, he engaged the old man directly. The normal procedure is to go through the headman, but this time, my father did not trust the headman. The best would be to do the groundwork first, including reaching an agreement with the old man, the owner of the homestead. The first step was to establish the exact date the old man was physically moving. Due to lack of communication technology that time, all this had to be done verbally. That meant that my father had to visit the old man regularly. When the exact date was certain, my father went practically every day to Omayanga. Of course he made sure that certain people, including his cousins, did not get to know about his regular visits. My grandfather did not suspect anything because traditional procedures were very clear, and thus far, there had been no case of acquiring a homestead in a different way. For my grandfather, when the old man had made up his mind, he would go to the headman to take leave. This would open up negotiations for those who were interested in the available homestead.

While my grandfather was waiting to be notified about the departure of the old man, my father was about to move in. The night when the old man left, my father spent the night in the homestead. And that was exactly the same night that my father made us walk through the night and left us at my grandmother's under the pretext that he and my mother had quarrelled. The reality was that he could not bring us along as he was not fully confident of the success of his strategy. I only understood his strategy much later. My father's strategy was to make his presence in the homestead felt by certain individuals, which would make my grandfather enquire. And these were none other than his cousins with whom he grew up in the same household of my grandfather. So, he made fire every evening and this attracted curiosity from the neighbours. If the owner had left and the race for the homestead had not yet started, who could be making fire in the unoccupied homestead? Some courageous individuals ventured closer to the homestead to establish who the new occupant was. This being an illegal occupation, my father was ready for confrontation. And this is one of the reasons why he left us out of this initial occupation of the homestead. When finally the envoy of my grandfather questioned his presence in the homestead, he responded that he took possession of the homestead because he found it abandoned. But he was very quick to offer more payment to the headman. By the time my grandfather came around to confirm what the envoy had conveyed to him, my mother and we, the children, had joined my father. Obviously, it was difficult for my grandfather to force my father to follow the proper procedures. We were already there and, as it was the rainy season, my mother had already started sowing the field. In the Oshiwambo culture, it is unheard of to leave seeds in the field. Could my grandfather evict us at that strategic time of the year? No.

It did not take us long to settle in. For me, the surroundings were so familiar that, in no time, I could move around on my own. As the time went on, we again became part of the village. My parents were, of course, very happy to be back in their village. We children adapted quickly enough. Very soon I was going to take up my rightful place and role as the first born and daughter in the family.

There was nothing to be taught; everything came naturally. The entire society, my only universe, moved in a specific direction. There is no point in doing things differently; it is simply not done. It is such a closed society and therefore, very homogenous. Everybody does what the neighbour is doing, and life remains similar for everyone. Children rebelling or absconding was unheard of. Girls grew up doing specific tasks and duties, as did the boys. No need for negotiations; everything was crystal clear.

As their first child and a daughter, my parents were very eager to see me growing up in nothing else but a very correct traditional manner. If they succeeded in that, all my siblings would emulate my ways. The thinking seemed to have been: if you get the first child right, all the others would follow suit. For my mother, I had to be a well brought up girl, able to perform all household duties and be a good wife in the future. For my father, I had to be the pride of the family, portraying the goodness and the success of the home I was from. Obviously, these were high expectations from my parents. I made an effort and by the time

I was 15 I was almost the second mother to my siblings. After having worked so hard, following almost all the rules of my parents, my sister, at the age of 16, manifested rebellious tendencies, and she got away with it. If I had only known!

My mother married very young, and when I was about six, she already started the process of introducing me to certain duties. She made sure to progressively involve me in certain household activities. I still recall how I walked next to my mother with my little bundle of firewood or my little pot of water on my head. Of course I could not imitate my mother by not holding the load with both hands. That I learned much later. Next, I had to learn how to pound *omahangu*, initially without the part of sifting the flour. The same applied to working in the field with her. To start off, I had first to learn how to make use of the hoe without chopping off my toes. I was also not allowed to weed as I could not yet differentiate between *omahangu* and the weeds. The big challenge was to learn how to cook *oshithima* (porridge) over the fire. And to crown it all, the cooking is done in a clay pot. First of all, the heat from both the fire and the boiling water was overwhelming. Then it was not easy to keep the three other pots used as supporters of the cooking pot in place. The worst for me was that high probability of the cooking pot giving way to the pressure. There was nothing more horrifying than seeing the contents of the pot running into the fire. Firstly, making new fire after cleaning up the mess was unavoidable, and the worst of it all was to walk up to my mother and explain and justify how a girl at my age could have such incidents so often. At the age of 12, I was fully on top of many household duties and my mother could rely heavily on me, including looking after my siblings. By then, we were already six children.

I was not lazy as a child, nor was I irresponsible. The biggest challenge was to miss out on playing. Since my mother was overwhelmed with work, she seriously did not see the point why I needed to play under a tree with other children or simply run around in the field. From the stage of playing seek and find with my father, my mother wanted to turn me straightaway into her assistant. I happily pleased my mother and assisted her to the best of my ability at that age, but whenever the chance presented itself, I had to sneak out for a quick play. Sometimes a quick play landed one in trouble. At least I had enjoyed the play. I never wanted to give up playing. I had to find a way. When we learned that there was a playground in Oshakati with better swings than those we made with palm leaves under the trees, we had to venture to locate it. Once we knew where this playground was, we did not mind walking 4 km each way to and from Oshakati. Oshakati was not a place where many parents wanted to see their children going to. For the sake of the playground, we devised a number of plans and found ways to get there.

Work was the life of the village. Spending time not doing anything was unusual. And if one was not doing anything, it was because one was sleeping. And sleeping could only happen at night. In short, the working village had an annual structure and pattern. Besides the daily activities throughout the year, there were seasonal activities, especially in the field. During the rainy season, cultivation is at the centre of life. This is accompanied by collecting sufficient wild spinach for storage for the rest of the year. Gradually, we entered the period of *omagongo* when women, after spending the morning in the field, spent their afternoons squeezing the marula juice out of the fruits and, once back home, they prepare *omagongo,* an alcoholic drink made from marula fruit, before starting to cook dinner. Around May, the harvest period starts and this means collecting *omahangu* by breaking them off one by one, picking beans, and all kinds of melons and assembling them at one place, *oshipale.* This is followed by a process called *okushwa* when *omahangu* grains are separated from the waste. This is all very hard work as everything is done manually. After storing the harvest, there is one month where there is not so much work in the field. Women make use of this short period to make baskets, clay pots and produce marula oil. By early September, the clearing of the fields starts in preparation for the following rainy season, and the whole annual routine begins all over again.

As a girl, one sometimes has a fuller day than others. The day starts with the pounding of *omahangu* before sunrise. At sunrise, I was required to join the rest of the family in the field. Around midday, I had to prepare lunch. After lunch, we could still go back to the field. In the late afternoon, I went to collect firewood and water. Back home, I started preparing dinner and all that went with it. By the time I went to sleep, I had hardly had time to sit down doing nothing. The following day would be another day. The routine was such that I naturally accepted my duties as part of my life. I could not imagine my life differently. The other girls in the neighbourhood did exactly the same.

Then there was the task of looking after my siblings and I often had to perform some of my duties with a baby brother on my back. As one was never still, the movement made babies sleep. It was sometimes hard to find a reason why I wanted my mother to take the baby back. Walking up to her and telling her that I was tired was out of the question. Certain duties for me were just too hard to be performed with a baby on my back. I had to find a solution. The first solution I found was to pinch the baby so hard that it cried. My mother had no problem taking back her crying baby. When it became too frequent and when it only happened when I was performing certain duties, my mother must have suspected foul play. I was not careful where to pinch the baby. As she sat with the baby on her lap, she noticed marks on his legs. When you pinch a white child, the child would have a red mark. When you pinch a black child, you cause a greyish mark on the skin. When my mother saw the grey marks on her son's skin, I got a serious warning. I was however not relieved from carrying babies on my back. So, I had to find a different solution.

The second solution worked so well that my mother never suspected anything. My brothers were only spared when I outgrew the practice. What I did was to hit the forehead of the child with the back of my head. I mainly did that when I was too tired or to find a reason to go and join my mother at a celebration. When my mother left home for these types of things, I knew very well that, when my little brother woke up and cried, I should take him to her for breastfeeding. I would time the waking up and the crying in such a way that it coincided with the time people were about to eat at the celebration. These things were easy to guess in the village. When I left home, my little brother would be sleeping peacefully on my back. When I got closer to the venue of the celebration, I sharply pushed my head backward and my poor brother would pull together before releasing a loud scream. I would hurry straight to my mother before the pain subsided. Otherwise I would need to push my head backwards for the second time, which was not as easy, as the baby I was inflicting the pain on was after all my little brother. As my mother consoled and breastfed her son, I enjoyed food and a drink. After we both had our fill, I would put my baby brother on my back and we peacefully returned home.

Despite these little mishaps, I lived up to the challenge of being a firstborn and a daughter. My mother could count on me for almost all daily household duties. She had however to give up on some specifics and what I, to date, consider technical responsibilities for women. These include how to make baskets, homemade brew and marula oil. Besides those three activities, I excelled in the rest. This does not mean that my mother did not try hard enough. I too did try as hard as I could. I think these were just beyond me. My mother had always made sure I was next to her as she made the baskets. I was provided with everything and I was encouraged to make my little baskets. My mother could not comprehend why I was completely unable to produce anything that came close to a basket. One day, at the age of thirteen, my mother prepared all I needed and sent me off to a tree where I was to remain until I could show something that looked like a basket. By late afternoon, I had various little samples, but none of them could be described as a basket. That saddened my mother as this was a potential reason for a girl never to get married. And if, by odd chance I would get married, my mother would never find peace in her grave as my husband would constantly remind me that I had a useless mother. I sympathised with my mother and I wish I had known then that there were so many other societies where the baskets were not decisive items for girls to be happily married.

I went through the same agony with making *omalovu* (traditional beer). My mother was determined to have me acquire that skill. One afternoon, after some training over years, it was time for the test. She measured all that was needed, how long the whole mixture should cook, how often I should stir, explained once more how I should tie the sieve and how I should place it. As the entire process was being repeated to me I confidently repeated that I understood. My mother left to visit her mother. I am sure it was an excuse that I had no chance to call on her, should something start going wrong. I bravely started the process. The mixture started boiling and I stirred as often as I was told. I watched out for the changing of the colour of the mixture from pale to dark brown. Then it was time to tie the sieve and turn it inside out. Yes, I also knew that the sieve had to be turned inside out. I placed it exactly where and exactly how my mother normally placed it. I got out the pot which should be the yardstick for the amount of flour my mother measured out. Not only should it be filled but there should also be a quarter left over to top up in the morning when the immediate family members would have taken the first sip. When the neighbours would arrive in the afternoon to taste my first *omalovu*, they must be presented with a full pot.

All prospects looked good. I was on my way to surprise my dear mother and to make her proud in front of her neighbours. I took the first container of boiling mixture and put it in the sieve. From my observation of my mother performing the same gesture, the smoking orange liquid would immediately pour in the pot underneath the sieve. In the case of my first attempt, no single drop came through. It was certainly because I put too little. I added more and more, the sieve was getting full, but nothing was getting in the container under the sieve. I thought of giving it a hand. I stirred in the sieve. Nothing! Then I waited until the sieve had cooled down, and I pressed it on the sides with both hands. I had never seen my mother facilitating the process that way, but if it could help, why not? After a real struggle, I got out a quarter of what my mother said I should have got. Out of disappointment, I no longer followed instructions. The end result was that there was no *omalovu* the following day, and there was no next time. My mother was not prepared to waste her produce. She, in the end, did not bother about other duties such as making marula oil which was more elaborate than making *omalovu*. From my observation whenever my mother made the marula oil, there was nothing as complicated. From the marula nuts in a basket, the end product would be the marula oil, similar to cooking oil. What was required was minimal: the marula nuts of course, the wooden pounding container, a pounding stick and a bit of hot water. But the process to get the oil was meticulous. The nuts needed only to be pounded so much; the lukewarm water must be of an exact temperature measured by a dip of a finger; the number of water drops added to the crushed nuts at a time must be precise; the time to stop crushing the nuts and switch to turning the mixture around with the pounding stick and pressing it must also be precise; if at this stage one realises that one has put in too many drops of water or that the water is slightly warmer, one needs to immediately blow a bit of cooler air on the mixture, and the process just goes on. Seeing how complicated the marula making was, my mother did not waste her time.

We each have our shortcomings. Mine is that I am simply awkward with my hands. And awkwardness doesn't translate into laziness at all, and my mother knew that too well. Just as I could not make a basket at that time, I can't sew or do needle work today. I just do not have that in me, but I can do so many other things. When I later went to the hostel during my school days, I watered the plants or washed the dishes while other girls went for needle work. Such is life!

I nonetheless had my humble beginning like any other girl of my generation from the part of the country I am from. From that village girl, running barefoot, constantly carrying babies on my back, using my head to carry heavy loads, I was to grow up to leave my village for the bigger world. When the time was right, I stepped out of my village to school, 3 km away from my village.

ᔕ

My memories of the outside world go back to when I was six. This only outside world was the Okatana Roman Catholic Mission Station. Although not far away, the station stood out as a different place compared to everything that surrounded it. And we went there for several reasons: Holy Mass, school, hospital, shop, selling, and the only thing we sold at that time was *omahangu,* although my mother in the end also sold guavas to the kitchen there. Going to the mission station was an elaborate action in itself. One never just got up to go to the mission station. You had to first wash, change clothes and look presentable. And next to the hospital there was a place we called *eembisiningi,* certainly an amazing Oshiwambo coinage of the English word 'business' and that's where we bought bread. This bread was originally made and sold by people of Angolan origin, and it was baked in a flat fish tin. Although those who baked and sold bread lived in the villages around the mission station, there was no way one could buy bread in the village. Bread had to be sold at the mission station. And to get bread, we had first to go to church, hospital or school. All these things belonged together; it was a package.

The first wonder for me was the church. Just to step inside that huge long building with colourful windows was amazing. Then, the man who stood in front and spoke to us was white. As going to church became a routine, so did the happenings inside the church and the gestures of the priest. The priest though remained a distant figure, not only because of his different colour, but mainly because of what he represented. Not much was explained and people were left to form their own opinions. Nonetheless, priests were seen as people from far away. The only thing we knew about them was that they were from *Ondowishi*. We had not the slightest clue where that country (which turned out to be Germany much later, derived from the German name *Deutschland*) was, nor did we have an idea how things looked there. But at least that country produced priests and nuns who came all the way to Okatana. In any case, in my mind, by then, all priests could only be white and German. And priests performed tasks that were sacred in nature. Somehow they could not just be ordinary people or human beings like us. They must be between us and God. They spoke their special accented Oshiwambo language and we got used to their way of speaking. After all, we got to hear them only on Sundays.

Next thing I took note of was the hospital. The only doctor there was also white, a German nun. Her name was Sister Franceska and to make life easier for ourselves, we called her Sesta Fara. Sesta Fara was either overwhelmed by work or she was just a fast person by nature. She spoke very fast: an Oshiwambo word followed by a German word and the sentence ended with an Afrikaans word. Whether those to whom she spoke understood or not was not the issue, one just had to move on. People took and swallowed whatever she gave. As children, being taken to the hospital was not something we happily did. As we sat in the queue, we were terrified by the thought of what Sesta Fara would do with us. If your mother was shown to take you behind a curtain, this was a complete certainty that an injection was ready, just waiting for you to be seated in the right position. How could something that hurts so much make you feel better? Unlike my grandmother, I did not want this sharp object anywhere close to my bum. My grandmother trusted nothing else than an injection. The fee to be paid for each visit to the hospital was 20 cents. If she went to the hospital and didn't get an injection for her 20 cents, there was no genuine treatment and she would talk of the ripping off for the entire following week.

My second brother was the first one among the four of us to be born in the hospital. When my mother left home, I did not understand where she was going and why. Later that evening, my father took me along and there was my mother, wearing the same clothes as other women sharing the room with her, and she had a baby! The most fascinating thing for me was the light. It was dark outside, but in the hospital, it was brighter than in the middle of the day. The white walls were even whiter than usual. All this, with my mother seemingly comfortable in this place, was overwhelming. A few days later when she came home, I had so many questions to ask her, but she did not have all the answers either. When she went back two years later, the hospital became the place where my mother had to go now and then to return home with a baby.

⤳

By the time I started school at the age of six, the mission station was just the place we went to. I ended up going to school quite accidentally and not because my parents thought it was important for me to go to school. One day I happened to have gone along with my uncle, my mother's youngest brother, who was a teacher at the Okatana Roman Catholic Primary School. He was, of course, an unqualified teacher by today's standards, but he taught children who eventually went far in life with their education. My uncle did not take me along because he was convinced of anything, but because I asked to go along and he thought it would be fun for me. I cannot remember any formalities; I just remember sitting in the classroom not having a clue as to what was going on. I nevertheless continued coming back for two more years until I realised I was learning a few things. What I can remember to date, though, is my many miserable afternoons I had to spend in one big room alone with an old man. This old man was a teacher who had to make sure that I wrote with the hand all other children were writing with. In those days there was no compromise on the hand with which children had to write. Left-handed or not, that was simply not up for discussion. It was much later when I was studying in Europe that I came across people writing with their left hands. But since it was instilled in my head that one may not write with a left hand, it did not appeal to me, neither did I bother to try it. The second thing I remember about my early school life was punishment. I have never understood the kind of trespasses that warranted a teacher to pull on children's ears as punishment, I sometimes just happened to find myself going through this anguish. And this happened to me again and again.

School also became an accumulative activity, just like going to church every Sunday, except school had to be every day, except Saturday and Sunday. In fact Sunday did not count much as we had to return to the mission station for the Holy Mass. The Okatana Catholic Mission Station was an addition to my village and became a part of my universe. I no longer felt strange being in a brick room, nor did it amaze me any longer when I turned the tap on to fill a bucket with water to water the plants in the school yard.

In 1972, I was 14 years old and was in what we called Standard 6 in those years. This corresponds to Grade 7 of today. 1972 was the year when it rained so much. There was water all over and a number of schools had to be closed down except for Standard 6 learners as we were going to sit for the end of primary school examinations. A decision was made that all Standard 6 learners should move to the hostel at Okatana Catholic Mission Station. By then, the purpose of hostels at the Catholic missions had evolved. They were to accommodate learners who lived far from the school. Needless to say, the learners had to be Catholic without any exception. Initially, however, hostels were built to keep children away from their cultural environment, which missionaries considered to be heathen and would therefore interfere with their efforts to convert young people to Christianity.

During our youth days, hostels were to a certain extent attractive. Those of us who lived closer to the school admired the learners who lived in the hostel. They seemed to have an easy life; they seemed to have better bonds with each other; they looked neater and smarter, and above all, they lived in those brick rooms. I wondered how it felt to live in there and not do as much work as we had to do at home before and after school.

When the decision was made for all Standard 6 learners to go to the hostel for a few months, this was a dream come true. Although it was clearly said that this was only until the water subsided, I managed to stay in that hostel for close to a full year. And I was the only one to have managed that.

Going to the hostel was exciting but I soon found out that the routine was a bit harsh for me. Things had to happen at certain times and no longer according to the position of the sun. All of a sudden I had to go to bed at a specific time, and once that time came, no one moved or spoke. Even whispering was forbidden. In the morning getting up was also part of the hostel programme, and twice a week, we had to go to the holy mass as early as 6:30 in the morning. This was not what I thought was an easy hostel life. The difficulty was that the same German sister, Sister Harthmar, who was the school principal and my teacher, was at the same time the hostel matron. Every evening, she would come around to make sure that we were in bed and quiet, and in the morning, she would come around to make sure that we were up, that our beds were neatly made up and, when it was a Mass day, that we were all in church.

It so happened one day that I simply did not hear the other children getting up and getting ready for church. When I was still deep in my sleep, I felt my blanket being pulled off my face and as I opened my eyes there was the sister asking me something. As I had an upper bunk bed, the sister's eyes were right at the same level as mine. I couldn't understand anything of what she was telling me. She certainly wanted to know why I was not in church. In my panic, instead of pretending that I was not feeling well, I answered that I was not sick. The sister stood in the door waiting for me to get dressed and follow her to church. As I was rushing to the corner where I kept my clothes, a very bad reality came to me. The previous day, which was a Sunday, an older girl had borrowed my only church dress to go for her stroll. Of course for me, it was some sort of recognition for this older and senior girl to deem my dress worth borrowing for a stroll. With such a newly acquired status, I did not think of asking her to return my dress when she came back the previous evening. Now I had to deal with the sister, the hostel matron and the principal of the school. There was so much at stake here for a borrowed dress. I cannot remember how I resolved the issue, but I think the sister must have thought that I was not in my right mind and that she rather went to church than trying to understand why I could not get dressed and go to church. I had other mishaps during my stay in the hostel, including falling out of the bunk bed, and almost drowning during one of the swimming expeditions in the nearby river, but I gradually mastered the hostel life.

The hostel life stimulates the brain for survival. One of the things hostel kids had was money to buy bread and sweets. I had all that during the period I was legally in the hostel. As soon as the water subsided, other learners from the surrounding area went back home. Not me. I started enjoying and appreciating the hostel life. I did not need to help with work at home, I did not need to take care of and be in charge of my siblings. It was not really that I no longer wanted to be my mother's assistant or replacement whenever she wasn't at home. I just wanted to be in the hostel, and for that, I had to invent a number of stories. The first one was that I was doing much better in school as I had enough time to study and that the sister had asked me to stay on at the hostel till I had completed Standard 6. My mother did not take that lightly and asked me to tell the sister that she needed me at home because she was pregnant. I had seen my mother pregnant several times and I knew when she was pregnant and when she was not. I walked in the direction of the mission station, sat under a tree for a while and returned home, and told my mother that the sister had asked to see her. Seeing that she was not really pregnant and that she had no means of communicating with the German sister, she gave up for a while. A month later, when I went home for the weekend, my mother simply decided that it was the end of my hostel life. Of course the sister did not mind: I was very close to school, and normally I should attend school from home. But because of my cunning, but sweet personality, she did not mind one additional child in the hostel, as long as I did not give too much trouble.

My mother had however decided that I had overstayed at the hostel and it was high time that I returned home. After all, why should my younger sister and brothers attend school from home while I was in the hostel? I had no choice and I stayed at home. One day, by sheer luck, but by really sheer luck, I came late to school. Since I was in the final primary school year, the sister was unhappy with my coming late and she threatened that, should it happen again that I came late, she would as a punishment, make me come back to the hostel. I started coming late straight away. The following Sunday, the sister said something to my mother mentioning my name and my mother just had to say, 'Eewa sesta,' meaning 'Yes sister'. The language and cultural barriers were so absolute that my poor mother had no possibility of putting her case across to the sister. The sister was only interested in my being in school on time. For my mother, well, it was good that I went to school just as other children did, but she had a full programme for me at home but no means at her disposal to convey it to the smiling sister in front of her. The sister, after having stated her case to my mother, took leave of her and off she went.

The following week I was back in the hostel. My sister was, of course, very furious with me. She felt that I was shifting the entire responsibility to her. Such was life. I had had my fair share. After all, I was not at fault here, but Sister Harthmar was. Since then, I was in Catholic hostels till I was close to 18. Although the hostel life meant falling in line with every single rule, I had no problem. We all had the same upbringing, a very traditional rural way of life, mixed with very Catholic teachings, and the two made us perfectly well-behaved young people. Just dare to do a little thing in the slightest different manner, and you were on your way out. Negotiation or discussion was simply not on; there was no time for that, and language barriers on both sides were quite considerable. To make life easy for everybody, we accepted and respected rules as rules.

⤾

In January 1973 I set foot in Secondary School. I was one of the few Catholic youngsters accepted to the newly created Catholic Secondary School in the north with a curious name: Canisianum Secondary School. The school strictly admitted only 30 learners per year, ten from each of the three main Catholic mission stations in the former Ovamboland. The school started off in Okatana for one and a half years while the permanent school buildings were being completed at another Catholic mission station known as Anamulenge.

You can imagine the big eyes I had when I first heard the two girls from Anamulenge in my class speaking. The curious thing was that I could understand everything they said, but their intonation indicated that they were definitely not from nearby. For six months, I was convinced that only children and youngsters could speak the way they spoke. There was no way that adults could speak in such a melodic fashion. A few months later when we moved to Anamulenge, I understood that this was how the people in this area chose to speak. I also started wondering whether they found my intonation peculiar. Little did I know that this was my starting point of discovering the outside world, and other people as well.

Canisianum School was based on exactly the same principles as the Döbra Roman Catholic School in Windhoek. As a matter of fact, the retired principal of Döbra, Frater Gregor was the founding and only principal of our then Canisianum School. Catholic schools operated on strict rules. To date, I cannot recall these rules being read out to me. I might have heard them from others, but we were all crystal clear from day one. It was a question of taking it, or leaving it. These rules somehow overlapped with the rules from home, making us perfect learners under this environment. This did not mean that there were no cases of mischief and cunning, but if ever detected, that was the last day of the culprit at the school. There was no avenue for apology. The attitude was that of 'You should have known better'. And the famous last sentence of Frater Gregor in the Afrikaans language was: '*Hoe minder, hoe beter*', in other words, the fewer learners there were, the better. Once you have heard that pronouncement, then you knew that there was no option of returning. That was definitely your last day at this particular school.

Anamulenge was 100 km away from Okatana. I vividly remember my first trip to the new school on the back of a truck. The journey was endless. And when we reached our destination, I knew I was far away from home. For the first time, I had to spend months on end without going home, or seeing someone I associated with home. Hostel life taught us to find new ways of living together and life went on. In those days in the north, attending secondary school meant living in a hostel. It was unheard of to be in a secondary school and not to be in a hostel. It did not matter how close one lived to the school. This put us all in the same boat and exactly on equal footing, be it in the classroom, the dining room, or the dormitory. We all had the same challenges, and of course, the same opportunities.

Shortly after arrival at the new school, we all fell into line with the routine. Things happened exactly at a certain time, not one second earlier or later. We had neither watches, nor alarm clocks, but we were always there where we were required to be at the prescribed time. We started the day with the Holy Mass at six o'clock, followed by breakfast at seven, and we were all at our desks at eight. Meals were as important as the Holy Mass or the classes; it was compulsory to eat. I wondered what would have happened if one just decided not to be hungry? None of us tried that. The day always ended with an evening study followed by a prayer in church after which we quietly walked to the dormitories. No noise and straight to bed. The hostel matron, a German nun, would walk up and down until each of us was in bed. She was also one of our teachers. As soon as we were in bed, the entire generator went silent and the sister walked back to the German nuns' house by the light of a torch. At the same time, a brother, whom we called Frater, was also finding his way from the boys' hostel.

This was our lives for a period of three years for most of the learners at the school, while some of us stayed close to five years. The majority who left after three years went straight to Döbra. There was a change of surroundings, but life was exactly the same. It did not matter where we found ourselves, such was our school life. And we made the best out of it. It was really not hard, just different. After a few weeks, we had adjusted and we went through our daily routine without lifting an eyebrow. Failing was rare those days; everyone made an effort to pull through. The school authorities repeatedly reminded us why we were there, and, during our weekends and holidays, our parents did exactly the same. School authorities were more concerned about sufficient space for the next intake, while our parents were concerned about the R4 they had to pay a term for the school, hostel and meals. Since not everybody believed in school, failing could easily confirm the conviction of those neighbours who were convinced that school was not good for their children.

Anamulenge and its surroundings became my second home. In no time, I moved around comfortably and even went for weekends with friends from the surrounding area. All of a sudden the language intonation became natural and I hardly noticed the difference. In my entire stay of four years, it happened only once that I could not guess the meaning of a word and only that one time did I need to ask for an explanation. Otherwise, I was perfectly at home and at the age of seventeen, I had not ruled out the possibility of marrying in the area in a few years time.

3

My world opens up

The year 1977 started just like any other year. After spending Christmas holidays at home, I returned to Anamulenge for my final year of secondary school. I had no idea what I would do thereafter. It did not really matter. There was no rush. We settled in our respective forms (grades). I was now in Form V, the equivalent of Grade 12. There were only seven of us, quite a small class. As senior students, we no longer needed supervision during the study hours. We were seen to be responsible enough.

Shortly after the start of the academic year, everything was going on as usual except for one little detail: there were more young men moving around the Anamulenge Mission Station than usual. The mission station was already full of young boys. Some were primary school learners while others were our colleagues in the secondary school. Those years, boys were always the overwhelming majority in schools. But, in the blink of an eye, there just happened to be these young men who were moving with ease around the mission station. They were slightly older than our school boys. Although we clearly took note of them, their presence did not strike us as unusual. Firstly, a road went right through the mission station. Secondly, there were so many reasons why people came to the mission station. Besides the four hostels for learners, there was a hospital, a nurses' home, a store and a parish office. The mission station was therefore a busy place with people moving in all directions on a daily basis.

But something was different about these young men. They were on bicycles, wearing shorts and long thick socks. They initially kept to themselves, but after a short while they did everything to draw our attention whenever we passed them as we went about our routine activities. They stood by the church bells as we went to the dining room or to the classrooms. They would cycle around and stop for a while to watch us playing netball. We were not quite sure whether they were the same persons we saw the previous day. All that we knew was that there was always a group of them hanging around somewhere and our paths just happened to cross. Amazingly, we never asked them who they were, and neither did they seek to strike up a conversation with us. They were content with short greetings and smiles. One thing was certain: they were friendly young men.

Some of us who were not from the area somehow assumed that these young men were home from labour contracts. The mission station was also a possible social meeting place and maybe these young men were there to try their luck. Any assumption was viable. As things normally go, we gradually got used to seeing these young men around. After a while, their presence just became a normal occurrence. We would greet them when we came across them and gave them very short answers to their short enquiries. They minded their own business, whatever that might have been, and we too minded our own. But one thing that amazes me to this date is that we were not able to recall their faces so that we could tell whether we had seen them before or not. We had no individual faces for the group. In our eyes, these were just a group of young men. Did we not look at them closely although we saw them so often? Were we not really interested to get to know them? Were they perhaps playing a trick on us to not allow us to get to know and recognize them? Or were there just so many of them that every day there was a different group? Whatever the answer is, they managed to conceal their identity while engaging with us on a daily basis for a period of time.

Not far from Anamulenge, at the town of Outapi, there was a big military base of the South African Defence Force (SADF). The white South African soldiers were a common sight at the Anamulenge Mission Station. They wore uniforms and were always armed, even when they attended the Holy Mass. Their military vehicles were on constant patrol and their thundering rolling could be heard throughout the area, including during the night. All at the mission station and the surroundings were aware of their presence, their military power and authority. We were therefore always careful with them, and attracting their attention was the last thing wished for. Should anything happen at the mission station, they were there within two minutes. One Sunday the kitchen of the school caught fire and they were there in no time to play the role of fire fighters.

Just as the SADF soldiers became part of the normal occurrences, so did this group of young men. In the end, we were not really bothered. The attitude seemed to have become that anyone was free to be at the mission station. Why not them? Little did we know that their presence was far from being just a casual hanging-out. The day we understood the reason for their presence marked the start of a major change in our lives.

But before that, we had our usual one week Easter holiday and we all went home. After the holiday, we all returned to school. Our friends were still around; this time in bigger numbers than before the holiday. Had they always been here, or had they also stopped coming during our absence? Well, it didn't really matter what they did when we were gone. Their presence at the mission station certainly had nothing to do with us.

⌁

One evening, during the study hour, something unusual happened. And this happened in all four classrooms. We had all seen the same thing and as we stepped out of our classrooms, we were very eager to share our experience. What we did not know was that what we had seen, the others had also seen. We had all seen a mentally disturbed man in our respective classrooms. Between the classrooms and the hostel, we stood around in small groups telling each other exactly what this mentally disturbed man looked like and what exactly he did and said. He obviously looked the same to all of us – very dirty, bare chest and with shabby shorts. In my class, he said a number of things in Oshiwambo that did not make much sense, and he threw in some Portuguese words, or at least they sounded like Portuguese.

After a few days, we had forgotten about the psychiatric man and we went on with our lives. Mentally disturbed persons exist everywhere and can turn up anywhere and at any time. By then, we were also much used to the presence of these young men who didn't have much to do other than hanging around the mission station. That was their business. We were here for schooling and nothing stood in our way. If they had nothing else better to do, let them hang around at the mission station. After all they were not troublesome and we had no monopoly over the mission station.

We slept in two long dormitories with another similar room accommodating bathroom facilities and a dressing section separating the two. Once Sister Baptista, a German nun who served as our hostel matron, was satisfied that we were all in bed and quiet, she would whisper to the head girl to lock behind her. This was the standard practice for the four years I had slept in that place. The night of 19 April 1977 should not have been different. Yet, that very same night, just after we had slipped into our first hour of sleeping, we were awoken by heavy footsteps and whispering male voices. The footsteps and whispering voices were not reaching us through the windows; they were right in our midst.

First, it all sounded like a bad dream. You know the type of dream which would not make sense the following morning? That was exactly what was happening to us. How could these men just appear in front of our beds? There was no time to find an answer and most of us swiftly glided under our thin beds. Being under the beds did not deter these men from their mission. They were moving energetically and purposefully around us and they portrayed a sense of urgency. Their first recognisable communication to us was to establish whether we were scared of them. I guess it is hard to tell someone straight to his face that one was really scared. So one of us, Marina, responded from the refuge beneath her bed that we were not scared. And she quickly added that we were in that kind of state simply because we were ripped out of our sleep.

Since we claimed not to be scared, the men offered to shake our hands as they were meeting us for the first time. That was not too difficult and many hands emerged from under the beds. After greeting us they asked us to come out from our hiding places because they wanted to talk to us. They explained that we needed to get dressed and to follow them outside. Oh, why could they not just tell us and then leave us alone? Well, that was not going to happen and none of us dared to suggest it to them. We emerged from our hiding places and started moving in all directions. There was, in any case, limited space to move around. And we had these men who were just mingling with us. They were everywhere. Walking across to the other dormitory was not fruitful as our colleagues there were also in the company of the very same men. Those who attempted to go to the toilet outside the hostel could do so, but they also bumped into the same men in front of the toilets. Our dream simply had no end.

Finally, some of us got to the dressing section which was just five steps away from our beds to try and put some clothes on as instructed. The logic would have been to take off the nightdresses and put on other clothes. But this was not a night of logic. We had to get dressed, and do it fast. The men saw the confusion and issued clearer instructions: 'Put on a dress, a jersey, shoes, and carry a blanket.' More than that was not necessary, they repeated. They showed us to our shoes with their electric torches.

As I tried to put on my clothes, I happened to come closer to my friend Claudia and we managed to whisper to each other, and we came up with a brilliant idea. We squeezed ourselves between the cupboards and shielded ourselves with the doors of the cupboards on either side. We pulled our feet close against the wall so that they did not stick out. We hardly breathed and we were certain to have managed a good hiding place. We stayed in our hiding place for a while until we heard the others leaving the building. We could still hear a few men who were making the last round of inspection. As we were about to be the lucky ones, Claudia recalled a story she heard from somewhere that in similar incidents, armed people had burnt down the buildings after leading everyone out. We had to make a decision there and then, and the choice was between burning in the building or going with a group of unknown people to an unknown place. We rushed out and joined the others who had by then assembled next to the church. The two of us were part of the group again and we were set to be part of the group until the end.

Claudia and I were not the only two who quickly devised a quick clever survival strategy. Elizabeth and Celine came up with one too. Theirs was more elaborate and Celine managed to fall out of the group for good. Right at the beginning, the two of them bravely walked up to one of the men and explained how important it was for both of them to go to the German Sisters' home to collect their money which was in the care of Sister Baptista. It was the first time that any of us got to know that Sister Baptista rendered services of looking after students' money!

Of course Elizabeth and Celine could go to Sister Baptista, but two of the men offered to accompany them. The two brave girls did not despair yet as they were sure of finding another solution between our hostel and the Sisters' home. As the whole mission station was up, the four met Sister Baptista on her way to come and check on us during this chaotic night at the mission station. Things were happening so fast for everyone to the extent that neither did the Sister react when she saw the two girls with their two companions, nor did the two girls give the slightest sign that this was indeed the same Sister who was supposed to hand their money to them. The Sister continued on her way and Elizabeth and Celine proceeded to go and fetch their money. Finally, they stood at the entrance of the Sisters' home and the unexpected happened. The two gentlemen were well aware that they may not enter the nuns' home. Under normal circumstances, with the exception of the cleaning ladies, only the inhabitants were allowed beyond this point. One of the men suggested that only one of the two girls may go in to fetch the money. Whoever was going in was required to return as fast as possible as time was of the essence. Celine was faster and Elizabeth had to wait with the two men. After a moment, there was no sign of Celine and the two men decided that they could not wait longer. Next thing, we saw Elizabeth joining us, but still in her yellow nightdress, and no jersey. Could she return quickly to the hostel to put on other clothes? The position was crystal clear: we could no longer afford to lose more time. It was now time to move.

We were swiftly moved through the mission station, passing by the school kitchen and dining room, then towards the classrooms and the boys' hostel. As we were moving through, we met a sister here, and a priest there. Nothing was said, neither by the strong German authority of this Catholic mission station which we had known for years, nor by the newly in charge companions. As we went past the boys' hostel and saw no movement, we quietly thought that the boys were damn lucky. These men were not aware that boys slept here! No one spoke. Everybody seemed to mind their own business. The men whose company we were in definitely knew their business and it was evident that, whatever their business was, it was time bound. We had no clue. As we moved on, and finally left the mission station, so many things were going through our minds: Is this a one hour business? Is it for the rest of the night? Is this just about a meeting at a certain venue? Would we be back tomorrow for classes? There was no time to ask. Neither could we share these questions with each other. At a much later date, when we reflected on this happening, many of us had identical questions.

On the outskirts of the mission station, we found another crowd of people, and soon realised that these were our school boys. They had moved faster than us. They certainly had no money to fetch from the Brother. As soon as we had joined them, we were organised in an amazing pattern. To explain it in a simple manner, we needed to move in an orderly manner. Moving from one side to another was simply not part of the arrangement. For the first time I realised how perfectly disciplined we were. Nobody complained. Compliance was and became absolute. It first appeared as if the movement pattern was only meant for us. As we adapted to the new order, it suddenly became clear that we were not moving in a haphazard manner. There was certainly a plan, but a real serious plan. And these men were not ordinary men, somewhere and somehow, they were accustomed to this kind of moving and way of doing things.

Right in front of us were a few lines of these men, as well as right behind us and on both sides. It was clear that there was no way that any of us could break out of this solid wall, nor could an outsider reach us so easily. Although the whole arrangement was scary, there was, at the same time, something that inspired a sense of admiration. These men, who had turned up from nowhere, seemed to be well organised and were on top of their mission. They moved energetically, despite their load. What were all these pipe looking things they were carrying over their shoulders, some of them neatly trapped around their waists and across the upper parts of their bodies? We quietly observed them, listened to the steps of their heavy shoes and the squeaky noises from their equipment. Who could they possibly be? What was their mission? And what exactly did they want from us?

One of the two German priests who were posted at Anamulenge at the time, Father Adolf Volk, decided to come along. One of the men, probably the leader, tried to persuade him not to as their mission had nothing to do with missionaries. Father Volk insisted. Clearly, these men had no time to negotiate and it was left up to Father Volk to decide. He went a distance with us and as the walking was going too fast for him, he turned back. We moved on for the rest of the night, keeping pace with these energetic men.

All of a sudden, a whispering voice ordered us to halt. One of the men spoke softly to us, explaining how important it was for us to do exactly as told. The first thing was that for the next thirty minutes or so, there was an absolute need to move together and at the same pace. Secondly, should we hear a gun shot, we must lie flat on the ground, and most importantly this was not the time to be stubborn or difficult. The explanation really sounded as if it was a question of life or death. I for one took this as a golden opportunity to get out of this incomprehensible affair. Although I could not share my thoughts with any one, my mind was made up. Should there be a single gun shot, the sensible thing to do was to run. Lying down here on this seemingly dangerous terrain was out of the question. Before I could finalise my escape, I heard the cutting of wires. We were ordered to move fast in the direction the noise came from. Once on the other side of the fence, we had to run for a while. The running did not change our moving pattern. These men kept to their lines. The spacing between them was exactly the same. We ran for a while and we were ordered to slow down back to our previous pace.

At dawn, after what appeared to be a long march, we could rest. We sat around, and as it became lighter, we managed to make eye contact with each other. There was not much to say. None of us knew any better, and speculating under these circumstances was just not possible. It was a matter of wait and see.

～

We finally managed to take a close look at our new companions. In the darkness, we could see that they wore similar clothes. We now could see that they wore uniforms, army uniforms for that matter. They had rifles, pistols, and huge pipes, which later we learned were sophisticated weapons. They each wore well-arranged chains of things around their waists and chests. Well, clearly, these were indeed soldiers, but from which army? From the looks of things, a definite answer was not yet within our reach. We were very unclear on a number of things: Why did they bring us so far away? Just to tell us something as they said the previous night? And when would they do so? And the biggest question was: What would happen after they had told us? Would they just simply tell us to go back? It was hard to imagine that they would accompany us back.

Then I took a look at my school mates. I had never seen such blank faces before. One could not deduce fear, anger or anguish. There was just no emotion of any kind. It all happened so fast that the events between the time we went to bed in one country and the time we woke up in a different country completely derailed us. Emotions were very far from catching up with us and the attitude was that this was completely new and there was no point in wearing ourselves down with prediction. There was no basis for prediction. Then, our dress code: We had changed from neatly dressed school boys and girls, to dishevelled, gangster-like youngsters. The boys' appearances were somewhat acceptable. We, the girls, looked really bad. Almost all of us still had our nightdresses on, showing from underneath our short dresses. Since we were ordered to put on jerseys, we each had a jersey on except Elizabeth. And since this was the age when girls wore very high heels, well, those were the shoes we wore. The combination and the layers of clothing just made us look like motherless children. We looked funny, but it was not the time to laugh at such things.

As we sat there resting, the uniformed men sat a little away from us, with a few of them dozing off. I heard some of my fellow learners asking for permission to go behind a nearby bush. That sounded like a genuine and understandable request and they were allowed to go. I quickly joined them and off we went. We were hardly behind the first bush, and the others started running in all directions. Emilia made a quick attempt to pull me along but she had to give up. Before I could realise what was happening, I was alone. I hesitated to follow and soon it was going to be too late. More confused, I found myself walking back to the rest of the group and I sat down with the others. I kept what I had just seen to myself and silently wished good luck to those who took the chance. After a short rest the armed companions decided that it was time to proceed. We got up and took our positions in our newly established walking pattern. As we did that, all of a sudden, there was a sight of shoes without owners. Yet, each of us had our shoes on! The soldiers did not require any explanation. The new rule from now on was clearly spelled out: Whoever wanted to go behind the bush, must do it close by. I deeply regretted not having gone when the chance was still there.

After another fast paced walk, the soldiers appeared to be satisfied with our progress. Now was the time to give us a bit of information. By now they were fewer men and we were not even sure whether they were the same ones we started off with. Amazingly, as we moved on, there were always new men appearing from behind bushes. They hugged each other and mingled with the rest of the group. Now that they were fewer than before, that meant that as we progressed, some of them must have left the group. Things were so incomprehensible for us, but these men did all this in a seemingly easy way. They acted in such a way that one could even conclude that this was their daily life. Until this point, after having been in their company for the last 12 hours, we had no clue who they were, where they were from and what they were supposed to do in the bush on the other side of the border. There was no doubt that they were somehow linked to us. They spoke the same language as us and they knew about us. But we knew very little about them.

Finally, we were briefed. They told us, "We are freedom fighters of the People's Liberation Army of Namibia. We are PLAN combatants. We are fighting for Namibia's independence. It is a challenge, but victory is certain. That is why we need reinforcement, and you are that reinforcement". They enthusiastically sung a few songs, which we later understood were revolutionary songs. This was the way for a big number of them to take leave from us, saying that they were returning to the border to prevent the SADF soldiers, who were hot on our heels, from getting closer to us. They hugged each other, energetically lifted up their fists and in the blink of an eye, they disappeared behind the bushes.

What a story! This was after all not a one day business! But if not, then how long would it take? And why were the Boers pursuing us? What did we do wrong? It was only a few months later that we managed to understand the whole story. Before that, we simply could not make logical sense of the whole thing. Confused as we were, the journey had to continue, and with fewer companions this time. Two hours later, we stopped in thick bush for lunch. To our biggest surprise, there was lunch, just exactly as we knew it from home. A number of civilians sat around, undoubtedly from the nearby villages. How did they know that we were going to be here for lunch on this specific day and at this time? The food was freshly prepared and brought to the venue just before our arrival. And how could they prepare sufficient food without knowing how many we were? From their conversation with our companions, it was clear that this was not their first encounter. These were, in fact, their acquaintances. But how did they fit together? These were armed soldiers, and the others were regular civilians. Yet they chatted freely and laughed together. The puzzle was getting more complicated. We ate as we were told and kept to ourselves. None of us joined in their conversations or laughed at their jokes. Although they could speak the same language as us, we simply could not follow. For some of us, our minds just shut down and nothing made sense anymore.

To our surprise, one of my classmates, Rosalinde, recognised one of the civilians as her brother-in-law. He was the husband of her elder sister. She tried to gather from this supposed brother-in-law what all this could be. But the man calmly responded that we were amongst the luckiest youngsters to leave the country under the protection of the PLAN fighters. Others had to cope on their own, which was risky. It was clear that this man was not sympathetic to our distress. In his opinion this was the best thing that could have happened to us, so why could we not see that?

After our tasty lunch, it was time to hit the road again. I cannot remember any of us thanking those who provided us with food, nor did we say goodbye. Maybe this did not matter to them, as providing food to groups such as ours seemed to be a standing arrangement. How far we walked no longer mattered. We did not know our destination or how far it was. If we reached it that same day, or only a few days later, that also did not matter to us. We would see when we got there.

By now we were going through thick forests. When some girls complained about exhaustion, a suggestion was made to get a car to pick them up. Getting into a car and being separated from the group was not safe at all. We would rather all walk and keep together and face whatever was ahead of us as a group. I felt tired, and carrying my blanket was even more tiring. So I decided to drop my blanket. One of my good friends, Marina, urged me not to leave my blanket behind as I would need it at night. I did understand her point, but I was determined not to carry a blanket beyond that point. I would be able to deal with the cold when that time came. Poor Marina picked up my blanket and carried it along with her own. Her gesture did not move me at all at that time. Later that evening, though, when we stopped in the bush for the night, I felt indebted towards Marina. And I would remain forever grateful to her. It was a cold night, and the first one I had spent outdoors. The following day I neatly folded my blanket and put it safely under my arm for the rest of the journey. I do not recall what we ate the following day or even feeling hungry. I remember spending the second night again in the middle of nowhere, and, just before lunchtime on the third day, we reached where we were to spend the following two weeks.

I must open a parenthesis here. Armed men deep in the bush are normally considered as being reckless with women. Here we were in the bush for several days and nights with these armed men whom we had just met a few days earlier. Of course we naturally had our misgivings. We were surprised. Whenever we stopped for the night, all that these armed men cared for, was our security. They ensured that we were well positioned (as they called it) and they took their strategic positions and slept. The following morning they woke us up, of course very early, so that we made the necessary progress. We, as women, felt safe with them, and when we reached the final destination, again in the bush, we had the courage to ask the leadership the pertinent question, 'What do I do when an armed man approaches me?' The answer was straight forward, 'You do exactly what you would do at home.' I would like at this point to take my hat off to these young armed men in whose company we were and who carried out their mission to the letter.

⌣

Three days after leaving Anamulenge, having walked endlessly and finally reached somewhere one could call a destination, we no longer worried about what would come next. This was a new situation, a new environment and, therefore, whatever was ahead, we would survive. What we needed most at this stage was our togetherness. We knew no one else other than ourselves in our group. Together we stood in front of an office to have our names recorded and to receive blankets. We received our blankets and were led to our part of the place. We were shown to a tree and we were left to settle in. We put our blankets down and sat around. We looked around and saw that there were very few structures. From what we saw they were very new. One accommodated the office, the other one a clinic. There was another one called *omangandjina*, from the French word *magasin* (a storehouse where provisions, usually including food and clothing, are kept) and sleeping quarters for a few leaders in charge of the camp. Everyone else slept under the trees, and so would we.

We later understood that the camp, known as Vietnam, was established a few weeks before our arrival. Camps such as this, being close to the border with Namibia, were not supposed to be permanent. That was easy to understand for those who understood military affairs, but not civilians and newcomers like us. We could have protested about sleeping under a tree, but to whom? We were not being denied anything. That was how things were for everybody else! So our complaints did not go beyond our group. After the first night under the tree, and after a few tears that appeared every time I opened my eyes and saw stars glittering through the branches, I knew that this was not a short time business. I was not the only one who went through this; quite a considerable number of girls shed tears. Boys put up brave faces, but the eyes of a number of them displayed anguish. They were after all also children like us. One thing was becoming clear to us, although we had no details, we were sure we had just joined a liberation movement.

We had to fall in line with the routine of the camp. It was made very clear to us that our mere presence in the camp exposed us to danger and the word 'vigilance' was repeated to us. The sooner we started with the training, the better. We needed to be fit for all the eventualities, certainly for our own benefit and survival. This was war, and we had to be prepared. The following day we started with foot drills early in the morning. We returned to the camp straight for the political class, then lunch, and, in the mid-afternoon, it was time to go and bath in a pond not too far from the camp. Before sunset we ate dinner, followed by a singing session. Our days became regulated although there was no printed program hanging anywhere. All was interiorised and it was surprising that we all just went along.

The PLAN combatants were people who came from home and as we spoke to them, we could recognise some of them. Or we knew at least someone who knew them or the villages they were from. We, however, had not yet understood why they had come specifically for us. But one thing was becoming clear; a few of our colleagues, especially a number of boys, knew something. We were surprised that Onesmus handed us a bar of soap and a pot of Vaseline every time we were about to go for our bathing session. How come he had packed all those items? Why was the door of our hostel not locked that night of 19 April? Anyway, finding answers was no longer necessary, we were now here in the new environment and life had to go on.

By the way, 19 April is also a very significant date for SWAPO. We got to know much later that on 19 April 1960, SWAPO was founded to liberate Namibia from apartheid and colonialism and to achieve the independence of Namibia. I am not saying that it is the case, but it is significant that what happened to us happened on 19 April 1977. Was this a coincidence? Or was this part of activities to mark the celebration of the foundation of SWAPO in 1977? Maybe the latter is more probable.

〜

A few days after our arrival at our new place, a cow was slaughtered in our honour. What a treat! We had to divide ourselves into platoons and sections. Some were in a platoon of collecting firewood and others in the platoon of meat that was divided up further into sections of cutting meat, making fire, getting water, or whatever else was needed. What mattered to the combatants was that we were getting this army vocabulary into our heads. As for us, we did not bother what they called our little groupings, as long as we got fresh meat in the end. After we ate our fill, the soldiers who were with us encouraged us to sing, and, to our surprise, we had picked up quite a few songs during the few days we had been in the camp. In the middle of all this, three of our colleagues who had run away from the group after going behind the bush the morning of our exodus, turned up. We were delighted to see them, and they were even more so. During the next few days, others rejoined us. Only a few who fled managed to make it back home. They all had a similar experience. After having landed up in the homesteads of the people in the area, the soldiers caught up with them. Obviously the soldiers and the surrounding community were good friends. That was, of course, the reason why the soldiers did not panic when they realised that there were shoes without owners.

We enjoyed the meat, the singing and the reunion. It was however time to go back to our respective trees to sleep. Before going to sleep, a password was given every night. We never asked why we needed a password, but we understood that if we were asked for the password, we had better know the right one for that specific night. These were not times for stubbornness. One simply had to do as told, and asking questions was really not part of the game. A high level of discipline was the motto. We were told several times that we were there for a purpose. And the purpose was a noble one. To achieve this purpose was not easy. But through hard work, self-sacrifice and discipline, we would make it. This was about the liberation of Namibia. We had no details then, but well and good, if we could make a contribution, why not? We first found the camp routine complex and unnecessary, but we managed to fit in within a week. The day started with foot drills and physical exercises very early in the morning. Then we returned to the camp for a parade where the day programme was spelled out. For us newcomers, the parade was followed by political lessons and occasionally by military training. The initial military training was to make us aware of the prevailing war situation and the need to observe certain precautions. After lunch we had a short break that was followed by some household activities (collection of firewood, cooking, cleaning the surroundings, etc.). We then had a bath. I do not know whether the bathing was compulsory, but when it was bathing time, we all just went.

After two weeks in the Vietnam camp, it was time to move on. We were not told where we were going but we just knew we were leaving. There was nothing to pack and in no time we were at the office to give back the blankets. Once we had handed in the blankets, we had to get into a big Scania truck. Some of my friends knew the driver as he came from the same village as them. So they stood around and chatted about home. He enquired about a number of things and he clearly appreciated fresh news from home. He had been away since 1974. I thought that was a long time to be away from home.

I was not well as I had swollen tonsils. Somewhere I got to know that if I did not get better, I could not travel on with the others. I needed to recover before I could travel for a long distance. I had some medication from the clinic and I thought that although I was not that well, I was going to be better soon. Remaining at this place without the group was just impossible. I therefore joined others in the queue to hand in my blanket. When it was my turn, I just heard the officer saying, 'You are not leaving. Next person please!' I was not sure if I heard correctly. I also wondered if the officer knew what he was saying.

Soon everyone I knew in the entire camp was in the back of the truck. I looked on incredulously as the driver closed the back of the truck. He made another round to ensure that all doors were closed. A number of armed soldiers jumped on the truck as well. The driver embraced some of his comrades who stood around and he jumped into his seat. I heard the door closing and the engine starting. One puff of smoke and the truck was moving. With eyes full of tears, I looked on as my friends were moving away from me, leaving me alone amongst these people. Although I had begun to admire them, I did not know them. And I definitely did not want to face them on my own. We had managed this far, but in a group. As the forest engulfed the truck and the sound of its engine faded, I found myself in untold confusion. My heart just made me believe that I would not be able to survive without the others. And I definitely wanted to survive. My composure, and all those aspects that make a person a human being, deserted me.

I felt so empty and helpless, and gave in to the tears. I do not ever remember crying like a child as I did that day. And I did it right there at the office. Those who saw me could hardly believe their eyes. At first they seemed not to care. So many other people had gone through this camp and they were never exposed to such a noisy and unusual scene. After a while of non-stop, solid crying, some people started paying attention. I wonder what they thought of me, but many of them started to be sympathetic. These were trained soldiers who had gone through hardships over the years, and here was a girl who had left home just two weeks ago and was crying her head off, and all this simply because her friends had been transferred to another camp. After all, the intention was to keep me there until I was better and only then would they take me where my friends had gone to. It sounded logical, but how could I know that? I had no clue about their set up. I did not know how they operated and who decided what would happen and how and when. I had too little information. When I later understood the system of SWAPO camps and settlements in neighbouring countries, I became embarrassed, and still am, about that scene.

Just before lunchtime, they had had enough of my crying. If I was going to be in misery, and I had been that particular morning, it was hard to imagine that I was going to recover from whatever I was suffering from. As I stood at the same spot where the truck had left me, some soldiers came around and all indications were that they were in quite a hurry. It was clear that they were getting ready for a trip. What were they up to? They quickly spoke to each other, nodded and walked away in different directions. I kept to myself and to my crying. Shortly thereafter, they were back. This time with more ammunitions and each of them carried a small khaki bag. I was not sure whether they were the same guys who came around a while ago. To me, they all looked alike. All of a sudden, a smaller military car pulled up near the office. I was ordered to hand in my blanket, which I still had in my hands, and I was shown to the car. Without hesitating, I got into the back of the car. About six soldiers, including two females, got in next to me. They saluted the others and the car drove off. But how sure was I that I was being taken to the same place as my friends? I did not dare to pose any questions. It was clear that these guys were not happy to have dropped whatever they had to do just to accompany me to some other place.

As we drove through the bush, they were talking about things I could not understand. They spoke about UNITA, one of the two largest political parties in Angola that was led by Jonas Savimbi, and the number of skirmishes they had had with its military forces. No wonder I was one person but being accompanied by so many armed personnel. And I now remember when the others left early the same morning they were sitting in the inner part of the truck and the soldiers were standing at the outer side. From a distance, all that could be seen was a truck full of soldiers. At one point, another car came from the opposite direction towards us and we stopped. The soldiers got off and were speaking to the occupants of the other car who were elderly men. What struck me was that, not only did these people know each other, but it was also clear that they knew that they were going to meet at this particular point. How did they know about each other's movements? From the body language of the soldiers, I could also deduce that the elderly men commanded some sort of seniority. They somehow spoke about me as part of a group of school children recently assisted to cross into Angola. The elderly men greeted me and asked me where I was from. I gave them brief answers and they decided not to bother me any further. It was only much later that I got to know that one of the men was the SWAPO Secretary for Foreign Affairs. How could I have known that? At that time, I did not even know what 'Foreign Affairs' was all about.

At sunset, we came to a gate that looked like the entrance to a big settlement. Those who manned the gate inspected the car and asked me a few questions. Permission to proceed was granted and we had to travel for another 3 km or so before coming to an actual settlement. It was a huge place, with some solid buildings, but mostly with a lot of tents. We stopped in front of a building that looked like an office and I was asked a few questions about my identity. Here I did not hesitate to provide whatever information was required. The distance I had covered since leaving home some two weeks earlier was so huge that it was high time to give up any hope I harboured to find my way back home. The moment to look solely forward had come. Once the officials were satisfied, I was led through a number of tents to where I was supposed to stay. As I approached the big canvas tent, I could clearly hear familiar voices. So these were honest people. When they told me earlier in the day that they were going to take me to my group, they meant it. I entered the tent and all the girls of my group were there. I looked from one face to the next, it was unbelievable, but I was finally among the people I knew! It was pure joy. Here we were again, together, this time in a tent, and not under a tree. One thing was certain, we were very far from home, and were now part of an amazing undertaking, whatever it was. We knew it would take us time to understand, but we also knew that together we would make it. Our togetherness was critical.

⌒

The following morning I looked around in the tent. It was quite big as it could accommodate twenty-five of us. Improvised beds were neatly arranged in straight rows. They were made in a creative way. Four simple poles were erected from the ground and four others across. That alone provided the frame of the bed. Then there were two vertical ones, also solid, and many small sticks arranged in the horizontal direction. The beds were not perfect, but at least they could do the job. Mattresses were not part of it. Nor did I see a single pillow during my entire stay in this place. Since we all had equal treatment, it did not even cross our minds to request things we had not seen being made use of in the settlement. How would you start your query? Why should you feel you needed special treatment such as having a pillow? And, if for argument's sake, one could be found, what about the 3,999 other people?

The next day we woke up in the new settlement. It was enormous and there were people all over the show, mainly women and adolescents. There were a handful of soldiers in uniforms who constantly carried their guns. Many other people wore uniforms too, except the new arrivals like us. We were then told to go to the office where we each received a greenish uniform with military boots. I can't recall whether we also received socks. As from day two in this camp, we wore uniforms. It was not clear at the time whether it was easier for everyone to have similar clothing, which in fact would make life simple for everyone, or it could also be that since this was a war situation it was therefore appropriate to wear military uniforms. What was amazing is that none of us raised any questions. We just did as told. There was no unhappiness; this was simply a new life for us, and from now on, things would be different. The same day we found out that we would only have one meal a day. It was not due to lack of food, but cooking for 4,000 people could only happen once a day. When our turn came to work in the kitchen, we understood the logic. Again, none of us saw anything wrong with cooking once a day. We accepted it as a norm and we just found a way of keeping part of the daily meal for later in the evening. Food was normally served around 15:00 and if we kept some of it for later before we went to bed, we were perfectly fine, especially us girls. Boys took some time to get used to this eating once a day business. They particularly found the waiting time for the dishing out of food too long. Everyone knew that food was only ready by 15:00, and a signal in the form of a bell was given, yet some boys preferred to wait around the kitchen.

As we walked around the settlement and listened to people chatting, we picked up that this was the Cassinga camp. It was therefore not just a settlement but a camp. In the middle of the camp, there was a kitchen, which was always busy. Cooking started early in the morning and by the evening, the washing up was not quite finished yet. Understandably, one could not work in the kitchen two consecutive days. It was a one full day shift. Next to the kitchen, there were rows of huge orange trees. For the first time, I saw oranges on a tree and not in a plastic bag in the shop. How could oranges possibly hang on a tree like the marula fruits back home? Oranges were not items that one easily came by and one always had to spend money to enjoy one. And to explain to your parents that you had spent five cents on an orange was not easily defendable. Here they were, on trees, and no one seemed to take note of them except us, the newcomers. But this was camp life; you did what you were told to do. And since no one walked up to those trees to pick an orange, we could not be an exception to the rule. I cannot recall anyone telling us that this was not allowed, but our instinct just kept us away from those trees. Not far from the kitchen was a big building whose doors were always closed. We later found out that that was a prison. On the western side was another neat building, a big clinic or a health centre. A little bit further, on the north-eastern side was the home for those who were in charge. There were three important leaders I got to know a few months later. On the left of that house were smaller houses where some other important people in the camp stayed. On the northern side towards the river was a huge field of maize. The set up and organisation of the life of 4,000 Namibians, 200 km or so inside Angola, was amazing.

As days went by, we also became part of the camp. Soon we had our own platoon with various sections and the relevant commanders including the platoon commander. I recall that Claudia, my friend who tried to find her way back home, was our platoon commander at one point. She was one of the toughest commanders I was to know. Yes, the same Claudia who hid between the cupboard with me on the night of 19 April.

The first thing we had to learn was how to march. Within a few days, we arrived at the morning parade marching like all other platoons. We turned in the right directions as we were instructed, lifted our feet higher when passing the senior officials, came to a halt when it was time to do so and stood at ease when the Commander called, 'At ease!' But we remained in an orderly pattern, attentive, not moving or looking around. Discipline was setting in. We stood there, platoon after platoon, listening to a number of things. The first item that we listened to was the news. Very quickly we got to understand that Mr Kalimba had the responsibility of listening to the news and briefing the camp about issues related to Namibia every morning. Of course this became the highlight of the day. At the beginning we had some adjustments to do to get into the right mindset. To start off, we had to get used to the name Namibia. What exactly it represented was to come much later. Back home, we spoke of our respective villages, churches, schools, and that was almost it. And specifically for me, my world started at Oshakati and its surroundings and ended at Anamulenge and surroundings. What was beyond these two places, irrespective of which direction, was foreign.

So we were here to fight for the independence of Namibia! Just as I was struggling to understand the structure of the Cassinga camp, I also had to struggle with the understanding of the structure of the South West Africa People's Organisation (SWAPO), the liberation movement of Namibia. The first part of the structure was obviously the People's Liberation Army of Namibia (PLAN), the military wing that was waging war against the South African army. The very existence of PLAN finally helped us to make sense of the presence and the deployment of the huge South African military machinery in our areas back home. White South African soldiers had become a common sight in the northern Namibia rural communities as they drove or moved up and down. So they were there to fight against SWAPO, and I was now part of SWAPO. It was then really in my interest to get these things in perspective and to understand them in the correct way. But it was complex.

Then Mr Kalimba would talk of the United Nations (UN) that was trying to find some kind of solution for us and, once this solution was found, we would go back home. That sounded interesting and it was worth understanding as well. Then there were those countries that were our friends and others who were friends of South Africa. Now many countries that I had heard about back home as being the good ones, were now said to be friends of South Africa. How could this be possible? Concepts were getting ever complicated and I am sure I only got the right picture two years later. In the meantime I had to battle within myself about all these many things and new concepts, including the UN, the liberation movement, independence, communism, socialism, and so many others. I am sure I was not the only one going through this dilemma. Moving from a very limited perspective to something worth the meaning of understanding takes time.

Besides the news in general, we were also presented with the news within Cassinga that included things like the reporting of people who slept during the guarding, those who were caught selling blankets to Angolans, the number of people who did not go for physical exercises the previous day, and so forth. Such things obviously are common everywhere among groups of people. Finally, the daily duties were read out and we sang a few freedom songs to boost the morale for the day. The parade would not last long as we were told not to assemble in big numbers. That was dangerous in a situation like ours. Whatever that meant! We would then march back to the camp and disperse for our various daily activities. Besides the household activities, this was the time for political instruction and induction to military training. Here again the emphasis was laid on physical fitness, vigilance, commitment and discipline.

The political instruction was given by Commissar Greenwell Matongo, the Political Commissar of SWAPO. This was the person entrusted with the responsibility of politically guiding the cadres of the party and boosting their morale. He was good and tried to guide us through all these complex concepts. He explained how important it was for SWAPO members to be disciplined as we were going to be faced with many challenges, including life-threatening dangers. The issue of self-sacrifice was also persistently highlighted. Part of the instruction was also to acquaint the cadres with the manipulation of the gun, the AK47. To start the process of being militants, we were first allowed to walk around with guns, but of course without ammunition. Once we were comfortable in the company of the weapon, we were trained to learn how to dismantle it, reconstruct it and, in the process, we learned the names of its various parts. Then we moved on to how to clean the gun, while taking special care about the direction it should point as accidents could happen during the cleaning process. Scary stories!

As I listened to Commissar Greeni, as we called him, be it at the parade, during the political instructions or whenever I met him in the camp, he struck me as a nice and kind person with a fatherly care. He spoke so well in Oshiwambo, but somehow there was something peculiar to his intonation. Why did he put intonations in the wrong places? And why did he say a few things not quite the right way? Whatever his problem was, I could not figure it out at that time.

Cassinga became home and we eased ourselves into the routine of the camp. Each day started with physical exercise. There was no specific explanation why this should be the case, or more specifically why on a daily basis. Somewhere it was mentioned that physical endurance was important in our particular situation. Under the circumstances, we should be fit to be on the move as long as necessary and to survive until reassembling. Again it was said that when camps were attacked by the enemy, it was usually during the morning hours and it would be safer to go out for physical exercise. Whatever the real reasons were, we had to go for the physical exercise. When one was new, one tended to do everything as required. After a certain period of time, we came to know about some tactics for missing some days of physical exercise. The exercises were not that hard, but getting up so early in the cold weather became challenging for some of us. We were woken with a certain signal and responsible individuals went around to make sure that we all went out of our tents. Somehow some people managed to remain behind. I must have tried my luck a few times too, but I cannot recall where I found a hiding place in the tent. But I did go most of the time. When we returned to the camp after the physical training, we immediately lined up for tea. And it was just tea, nothing else, but it became some kind of incentive. It tasted so good and gave us some warmth.

Human beings have the capacity of devising ways and means to corrupt any system, including ones to their own benefit. The physical exercises are good and, in our specific situation, it was for our personal well-being and survival. Yet, some people found ways not to go for the physical training, but still managed to join the queue for tea. The camp authorities detected this very fast, although we were convinced that we could keep this to ourselves. The surprise would catch up with us pretty soon, and it happened on one of the many days I went for the physical training. After two hours or so of training, we were called to a halt for an announcement. The announcement was that we should each tie a tiny string from a tree branch, around our right wrist. It was also explained that when we went for tea, we should slightly lift up our shirt sleeve to show it. We did exactly that and back at the camp we lined up for tea. As usual, the clever people slipped into the queue straight from their beds. All of a sudden, beyond the tea distribution point, there were two huge groups: one of those who had tea and the other one made up by those who had none. Those who had no tea looked perplexed. Since they came from different tents and joined the queue at different places and times, they could not figure out why they were shown to that group without tea.

That day, I learnt something significant. Those of us who had tea proceeded to the parade as usual and received our daily instructions. As disciplined party cadres, we marched off to our respective duties. The group that did not have tea was allowed to spend the day not doing anything. Since they found physical exercises so difficult, they would also find work difficult. They should be allowed to spend a restful day. When we returned around 15:00, the resting group sat under trees in the vicinity of the kitchen. We lined up to receive our daily meal and returned to our tents to eat. A message went around that we could go back for a second helping. As we were getting the second helping, the resting group was dismissed to return to their tents. Later in the evening, it became clear that the resting group had no food, just as they had no tea in the morning. Nobody scolded them. They decided to skip physical training, and similarly, they were allowed to skip tea, work and the meal. Although there was no discussion on this episode, a lesson was learnt. The following day, the entire camp population was at the physical training. That was only the first learning experience I had at Cassinga.

The second one involved almost everybody in the camp. One morning, it was announced that we would not be going for our daily work that day as we were expecting visitors. All that we were supposed to do was to clean our tents and the immediate surroundings. Out of pure laziness and playfulness, almost nobody did any cleaning. After all, nobody was really going to check. We all went back to our tents and hung around comfortably. Commissar Greeni must have observed this boldness and a bell rang. As soon as that kind of bell went off, we all knew that we were to assemble in the shortest time possible. In no time, the entire Cassinga population was ready to receive instructions from the Commissar. Everyone was summoned, including the team that had a shift in the kitchen. The Commissar had not much to tell us and his short message was, 'The instruction given this morning was to clean. I went around, and did not see much cleaning going on. Since you are so tired that you cannot even clean your own tents, you have permission to sleep further. And the permission is for all of you including the team in the kitchen.' As soon as the order 'Dismissed!' was uttered, we all turned around, and walked quietly to our tents.

We spent some time in the tents and wondered what was going to happen about the one meal a day. At one point a friend of ours, Annascy, picked up the courage to leave the tent. Her destination was the kitchen to quietly check whether there was really no cooking going on. She of course first checked whether the Commissar was moving anywhere as far as her eyes could see. Seeing no one, she concluded that the Commissar must be back in his house. She carefully made her way to the kitchen, inspected the place, and since there was no one manning the kitchen, she decided to try her luck to find food. Who knows? There might be food. Although the cooking was nowhere close to the final stage at the time the cooking team was ordered to join the resting camp, the food might still be edible. These were no times for tasty food. It was a matter of having a filled tummy.

As she was about to be the only lucky one in the entire camp to have discovered food that specific day, she was interrupted by a voice that came from a parked truck under a nearby tree. It was the well-known voice of the Commissar. When you were caught in an act such as this, you could not go unpunished. Punishments were not always harsh, but they were such that one hardly ever repeated the same thing. Even your friends and your colleagues would have the benefit from that one experience and would not emulate the act. Our silence in the tent was interrupted by the gaze of our friends fixed on the entrance of the tent. Annascy was back, entering the tent crawling. She left on her two legs, and she was now returning on her knees and elbows. This kind of movement was our new acquisition. But it was meant for certain circumstances when there was the need to avoid being in the range of the fire of the enemy. In fact, this was a war zone posture during actual combat. What the hell was Annascy up to? As she assumed her vertical posture and finally sat on her bed, we all stood around her to hear why she did not walk back into the tent. She first dusted both her knees and elbows, cleared them of little thorns, and wiped sweat from her forehead. She then explained how she came very close to finding food before her encounter with the Commissar. On the instruction of the Commissar, she approached the truck. She was not asked to explain, she was only ordered to crawl back to the tent and to remain there like everybody else until the next order was issued. Annascy did not find this story funny, but we all had understood by then that when an order was given, we complied until otherwise ordered.

Discipline was setting in and this was to our advantage. We did not really know what lay ahead of us, but we knew we had to keep going on. The next thing we had to go through was initiation to military training and guerrilla warfare. A month earlier, I would have been scandalised if someone would have vaguely suggested something like that to me. So much had happened in such a short time of just over thirty days. Thirty days ago, we were school children, and here we were, embarking upon military training.

We started with long walks over difficult terrains, going up and down hills, and sometimes crossing rivers. Then came the part where we were divided in opposing armies. Of course, no one wanted to be a member of the SADF, but for the sake of the training, it had to be done. Each side was divided into various sections with specific responsibilities. What I did not like at all was to be part of the reconnaissance. Even if we knew this was for acting, we always had a chill when we went to explore the territory of the enemy. To be part of the communication team was not very easy but at least one remained within the platoon. Then there were those with bigger guns and those who should run behind in the event of retreat. We had a whole list of sequences, step by step, of a combat, and so many other things to memorise. As for the movement, we had to learn how to walk in columns, making sure that, should we come within the firing line of the enemy, the entire platoon was not wiped out. We had to also try to step in the same footprints so that in the case of pursuit, the enemy could not easily estimate how many we were.

Laying an ambush was also something critical to the whole exercise. Here one needed time and a lot of patience. Sometimes the enemy took a long time to pass our way. So we would lie under bushes for hours just waiting for the enemy to be there. As soon as the first person at the beginning of the ambush had seen the enemy entering within the ambush range, he or she gave a signal. The very same signal had to be carried through the entire ambush from one person to the next. One of the signals, which stuck in my mind, is the breaking of a dried twig. We were each hidden behind a bush, well spaced by counting steps from one person to the next. We lay there, well concealed, somehow in a straight line, each of us with a dried twig in our hand, ready for action. As soon as you heard the breaking of a twig from the person on your left hand, you immediately broke your twig, and the person on the right hand did exactly the same. At the time the person at the far end of the right broke his or her twig, the Commander would immediately issue the firing order. This was followed by firing sounds sang out for a pre-determined period of time. At this stage, depending on the outcome of the battle, the platoon was ordered either to retreat or to capture the enemy troops. Although we all knew this was only training, we were so submerged in this exercise that it was not a nice feeling to be captured.

Depending on our performance, sometimes we were required to repeat the battle. That was quite hard. But one day it was worth repeating. After about two hours of ambush and everything else, we were ordered to go back to our very same positions, as we had not done the exercise to perfection. As we settled in our respective positions, one of us discovered a colleague who missed out completely on the entire exercise, as loud and animated as it was. He was peacefully enjoying a nap with his gun next to him under his bush. Neither did the artillery sounds nor the orders 'Retreat' and 'Forward' wake him up. This was real sheer luck for him. We could have done well and would have returned to the camp. We did this kind of training very far from the camp and unless one was familiar with the surroundings, it was not easy to find one's way back. But as is always the case with fate, these were really times when our protecting angels were right next to us.

~

As surprising as it may seem, we were in the process of embracing SWAPO. Mind you, by then, if someone would have seriously demanded from us to define SWAPO, we were certainly not in a position to do so. These were really trying times for us. We were battling within ourselves with so much conflicting information. To start with, these very same people were part of those we greeted from underneath our beds a month ago. A few weeks later, after having raised within ourselves so many unanswered questions, we realised that these very same people were not likely to harm us. Here we were now being trained, yet we had not understood the full story. We still had a lot of questions, but how would we ask them? Would these people have all the answers? The first question would be about SWAPO itself. Some of us had heard very little about SWAPO, and what we had heard was not comparable to what we were experiencing at that particular moment. Yes, we all had heard about SWAPO before, but the only person we had heard about being associated with SWAPO was Sam Nujoma. Where was he? How come we had not seen him yet? And who were these other many people?

Our memories on SWAPO, at least for many of us, were non-existent. As a child, I had vaguely heard people talking about the Verenigde Volke Organisasie (VVO), the Afrikaans translation of the United Nations. I recall that occasionally after church in Okatana, people stood under one tree and a few things were said about the VVO. That VVO, pronounced 'FIFI' in my language, became the synonym of SWAPO during my childhood. The prominent person of the FIFI in my area was Kaxumba Kandola, but I could not fix that name to anyone's face. It was just a name. A group of people, led by Kaxumba Kandola, came around to give some FIFI talk after church, but this did not last long. The FIFI talk came to an abrupt halt after a certain young Leo Shoopala from the Okatana surroundings was killed. We understood that he was part of the FIFI, but who killed him and why he was killed, I had not understood.

The death of Leo was followed by a time when we saw so many helicopters and white soldiers moving around our villages. We called this period *ethimbo lyomadhagadhaga*, the times of helicopters, because of the noise these flying objects made, especially when they landed. Some neighbours were interrogated. Why them and not others? I also did not get it. Everything sounded so serious and of course so dangerous to the extent that there was talk of *assamane yeli meethelela*, men who disguised themselves as women by wearing women's traditional attire.

Amidst these events of the mid-1960s, a stranger appeared in our village and stayed with one of our immediate neighbours. In the village, we knew all the residents, and their relatives who occasionally came for visits. But with this particular man, it was certain that this was his first visit to the village. Certainly, he could be a relative of our neighbours, but how exactly he was related to them, was never explained. It was also not clear whether he was there for a short visit or was staying for a while. He also did not have a proper name. His name sounded like a nickname. He did not mingle much with the rest of the village. We saw him occasionally. Otherwise, he kept the profile of a visitor. We were aware of his presence, but he did not participate much in the life of the village. But as things always go, we got used to seeing the man, and gradually, his presence in the village became a normal occurrence.

One morning, as we were working in the field, a number of the SADF military cars stopped at this specific immediate neighbour. For the first time, we saw many white soldiers at a place. Everything happened so fast. A bit of commotion with the arrival of the military cars, some running around and some shooting, then it was quiet again. I don't remember anyone from the village going closer to the neighbour's house to enquire what the matter was. Adults might have had more information than us children. A few days later, however, a strange story was circulating in the village. The first thing was that the day of the commotion was also the last day we ever saw our neighbour's visitor. And he never ever returned to the village for another visit. The second thing was that, seemingly, the man was not killed in the shooting. This would have been a big story in the village.

Whatever the case was, the disappearance of this particular stranger from the village made everybody in the village understand that this man was the reason why the soldiers came to the neighbour's house. The shooting was also directed at him. Why? Nobody really wanted to speculate, and obviously not in the presence of children. The man however found his way out of the homestead. Some people claimed to have seen him running towards and disappearing behind an anthill in the neighbour's field. But no one saw him beyond the anthill. Neither was his body found anywhere close by. Only a donkey was seen grazing around the anthill by those who dared to inspect the place. What could be the explanation? Did this man, who had been with us for months, disappear into the anthill, or alternatively, turn himself into a donkey? Nobody bothered to find out whose donkey it was. One thing we children never dared to do as from that day was to go close to that anthill.

In Cassinga, I could not understand how the FIFI evolved into SWAPO, but it became clear to me that the two certainly had something to do with each other. Those who spoke of FIFI after church, I could establish later on, were the same people who had something to do with SWAPO. But it took some time from the time we last heard about the FIFI to the time we started hearing about SWAPO. There was some gap and by the time SWAPO emerged in our lives, the information we received was so disconnected that we could really not figure out the identity of SWAPO. So, SWAPO, for a long time, remained a mysterious entity. We were left to speculate. Then, with the spread of the SADF by 1974, a number of scary things were said about SWAPO. First, the scary notion associated with SWAPO was *eendume dhomuthitu*, literally meaning huge men or monsters of the forest. For us as children, this description gave a picture of people who loomed in the forests who could not possibly live in homesteads. We had not ruled out the possibility of their feasting on children. Somehow we were aware that initially these *eendume dhomomuthitu* were people like us, because we all knew of someone who was said to have gone to SWAPO. But there was always that conception that these people went through a transformation that turned them into monster beings. One of the things that were blatantly repeated to us by the SADF was that they had been cooked. This 'cooking' enabled them to be invisible and to turn themselves into animals and objects. This could be the only explanation how the visitor of our neighbour could have disappeared.

As time went by, words like 'communism' were thrown around as something SWAPO would bring to the country. Communism was defined as total chaos and the South African Apartheid system worked very hard, as part of their campaign against SWAPO, to instil this chaotic image of communism into the minds of the black population. I recall my father saying that once communism had reached us, we would not have individual homes. My father could not possess a single cow or goat. Even wives would be shared. That was the worst set up one could imagine. And all these things were associated with SWAPO, and were more or less the perception that I personally held in regards to SWAPO. So I had every reason to mistrust them, and I am sure that many of us held that perception when SWAPO appeared in our lives in April 1977.

ⸯ

Two months after I had been assisted to join SWAPO, I still could not claim to understand SWAPO, but this did not mean that we were not starting to embrace SWAPO. The embracement, however, first came about through admiration. There was a huge difference between what we were told back home and the hard reality we were experiencing. The fact that these people could plan the operation to bring us all the way to Angola was amazing. Not only did they plan and observe us for months, but they turned up in huge numbers, fully fledged soldiers, and took their time to get us out of that Catholic mission station. No one at that well-established mission station at Anamulenge suspected anything, and when it happened, no one could notify the South African army next door in the town of Outapi. After we were moved out of the mission station, we walked for a good number of hours before we crossed the border, yet no one caught up with us. Then we were taken to a new camp, which, as we figured out later, was one of the many SWAPO army camps along the Angolan-Namibian borders. We were then transported by a truck to Cassinga camp, a transit settlement with an amazing structural set up and organisation. Little did I know that more surprises, bigger ones for that matter, were still to come.

I finally met people from my neighbourhood back home. They were all three from the same area as me, attended school in Okatana and disappeared some time in 1974. Here they were, all three members of

PLAN, serving at different fronts, including a girl. I first met the girl and recognised her immediately. Except for the military uniform and her energetic movement, she was the same girl I had known for years. She was at Cassinga just for a few days for a short mission. She proudly told me about her experience as a soldier. I somehow admired her courage, but also wondered how easy it was for her to be part of an army that fought against the powerful South African army. It all sounded so simple for her, and she was absolutely certain that what they were doing was doable and manageable. She kept her hand firm on her AK47, and it was clear to me that this was a habitual item she did not part with.

As I listened to her, I recalled the day she disappeared into thin air. Leaving the country to join SWAPO in exile those years was an extraordinary event. It literally happened every day around us, but unless you were part of those who were getting ready to leave, you would not get to know until those who were leaving were way on the other side of the border in Angola. The night that this particular girl disappeared with two boys, she had been at a wedding celebration of one of the girls in the village. We were all there, and as far as I could recall, she did not look any different on that particular evening than any other day. She chatted and laughed as everyone else did. The first thing everyone in the village heard the following morning was that she had left for Zambia, as people said those days. I hardly could believe it and I went around to her house, just to confirm what was being said. She was not home and her family were going about their household activities as usual. They were quieter than the way I knew them, particularly the mother. Obviously I could not ask any questions; these were not things people in the villages discussed openly. The parents were quietly going through untold pain and the fear of the South African army was constantly looming, especially over the homes of those whose children had left. With time, wounds healed as more young people continuously left for exile. It became anguish for parents as each of them had one or two children, if not more, who had left for Zambia. The anguish was that no one really knew what was along the so much spoken about route to Zambia. No information was available on whether these young people had reached their destination, and above all, they had not the slightest idea if and when they would come back. As the Oshiwambo saying goes

Dhoyendji kadhi ehama okulila, the distress shared by many is bearable. Parents kept the fire lit for the safety of their children in an unknown place and for an unknown period of time, and they would keep the fire going for as long as it took.

A few weeks later after my encounter with the girl from my village, I met the two young men who had travelled with her. They had no uniforms on because they were on their way to the Soviet Union for further military training. They were in Cassinga on transit, whatever that meant. We spoke a bit about home, one of them gave me a coat as it was cold, and they both gave me all their money, as they would not need it in the country where they were going. Meeting my village people had an empowering effect on me. If all three had managed for the last three years, I would also manage.

The togetherness of the group from school was still vital for our existence away from home. But we gradually became aware of constant departures of others from Cassinga. We really wondered where they were leaving to and why. Since we didn't know them, we didn't ask them, nor did they seem to find it necessary to tell us. The constant arrivals and departures became part of our camp life.

We certainly were not going to be an exception to the rule. One day my good friend Marina, the girl who helped carry my blanket the first day on the way, rushed into the tent and told us that she was leaving for Jamba. She was not going alone; Benedict and Leopold were also leaving with her. They were going to teach at the school there. Marina had wished that one of us girls was going with her, but there was no time for such requests. Marina quickly put her few belongings together, murmured a few words of goodbye and she was out of the tent. When next would we see her? These were not times of appointments and promises – Marina was about to board a truck to Jamba. We remained in the tent and wondered how long we would still be here. When another friend, Rosalinde, got sick and did not get better after a few days of treatment at Cassinga, she was also sent to Jamba for further medical treatment. What next? We had now been in Cassinga for three months. We had by then understood that Cassinga was a transit camp receiving newcomers from various camps along the border with Namibia. We also had understood that sooner or later, it would be our turn to move on.

One morning, a group of us were instructed to go and meet someone under a big tree. In no time, we were under the tree ready for instruction. Commissar Greeni, in the company of a neatly dressed man in civilian clothes joined us. We were told to sit down, and paper and pens were handed over to us. Since April earlier in the year, this was the very first time that we came closer to schooling again. This time Commissar addressed us in English, and so did his companion. It turned out, from the little we could understand, that we were there under the tree to write a test. We couldn't really link what was about to happen to the actual situation we found ourselves in. No prior warning, no preparation and for the first time we were writing a test in English. Our understanding deduced from the happenings of the last three months was completely different. School was over. We were now in Angola, part of SWAPO and the mission was to liberate the country. How and by what means, that was not yet explained to us. Now we were required to sit for a test, something we thought we had left behind us. We looked for comfortable dried tree stumps and sat down. We looked at the paper and it was explained that we only needed to pick the right answers. I never had such an exam in my life, but since it was only a matter of ticking it should have been easy. We started ticking, but I soon realised that identifying the correct answers by ticking was not that easy.

One of the challenging questions on which I spent a considerable time was: 'Which one of the following languages is not Namibian?' Among the possible answers listed were: Rukwangari, Otjiherero, Oshindonga. Oshikwanyama, Nama/Damara, Afrikaans, Swahili, Subia. I went through the list several times and I was not at all sure about the correct answer. As a last attempt, I looked at each listed language and subjected each of them to my very simplistic criterion: Have I ever heard about this language before? Although I hesitated about both Swahili and Nama/Damara whether or not they were Namibian languages, I somehow had an impression of having heard a bit about them before. How and where, I wasn't sure. But one language I had never heard about, and this beyond any reasonable doubt, was *Subia*. In any case, the word Subia had not crossed my path before the day of the test under the tree. So, I confidently ticked it off as a non-Namibian language.

The man who served as invigilator was none other than Commissar Greeni, the man I had known, listened to and admired for the last three months. As we compared our answers way later after the exam, I discovered that Subia was spoken in the former Caprivi region, and that region was part of Namibia. I also found out that Commissar Greeni indeed came from Caprivi and that Subia was his mother tongue. No wonder I found his Oshiwambo accent peculiar. Although I felt embarrassed towards the Commissar about this mishap, I was far from being worried about the outcome of the test because I had no understanding what it was for. It was just one of those things one had to do.

After the exam, we went on with our lives. The neatly dressed gentleman who had come from wherever with the question papers, had collected them and had long gone. We attended more political instruction classes with Commissar Greeni and we furthered our military training. At no point did he mention anything about the exam and the answers provided. We had the exam behind us and there was no turning back.

We finally became useful members of the camp. We participated in the cooking shifts; we did night guarding in the camp. We were simply normal members of the liberation movement. At one point, I was even Secretary to the Camp Council. We explained to the newcomers about life in the camps. We felt so great when we stood there being in possession of information in front of a group of students who had just arrived from Oshakati Secondary School. We knew them from netball and football tournaments. Here they were, unsure of the whole situation, and we boasted around with confidence. Of course we still had our reservations, but we would not show it. We had by then been around for about three months and we were now playing tough and committed cadres. We had improved on our marching skills and arrived at the parade just like any other platoon. We knew already about some of the news within Cassinga even before the announcements at the parade. Our understanding of events outside Cassinga was however still very minimal. Although words such as the UN, the Frontline States, the Group of five Western countries, negotiations, etc. were familiar vocabulary because they were so often repeated, they were still far from meaning much to us. Yet, we felt part of the whole thing and we were convinced that sooner or later, things were gradually going to become clearer.

One morning, the parade became very lively and more interesting than usual. We had all taken up our usual positions. All of a sudden a huge platoon entered the parade marching high but with fast strides. There was no doubt that these were real professional soldiers. They were all young, energetic, and enthusiastic. They were certainly on their way from somewhere. Although there had always been a number of soldiers in the camp, such a group of young men was a novelty. The marching we had seen so far was of slow motion. This was apparently a style from an Arab country. The style of these impressive young soldiers was said to be Soviet. So these were soldiers returning from training in the Soviet Union. I do not recall seeing them again. They were there that specific morning just waiting for their transport to the next destination. This was certainly why this place was called a transit camp, and not home as we initially took it.

⤷

The time of our group in the camp was also going to be up. A word went round that a number of younger members of our group were going to Jamba. A day later, they were gone. Not long after that, a group of us including myself was called to the office one evening. The instruction was that we should be ready the following morning and return to the office immediately after the parade. Back in our tent that evening, we stood around scratching our heads. What do we pack and in what? These were times of instinctive innovation. One of the girls had an idea how to solve the dilemma. We each had two or three dresses and a few pairs of underwear. All that was supposed to happen was for each of us to destroy one of our dresses, sew the sleeves and seams closed and find a way of running a thread through the neck part. After a few hours of cutting our dresses apart and passing a needle and thread from one person to the next, many of us had travelling bags. Those who wanted to spare their clothes were advised to look for boxes.

The following morning, when the call came for us to report to the office, we were ready for the journey. By now we had accepted that we would be departing without knowing the destination or how long we would be underway. It did not really matter. Beyond our respective villages and the few Catholic mission stations where we had been before, the rest of the world was unknown to us. Our knowledge of geography was so minimal there was no point in speculating! We would find out when we got there. We boarded a big truck. We already knew that we were supposed to remain seated and the soldiers accompanying us stood all along the edges. Whoever saw the truck passing saw a truck full of armed soldiers. The journey was long and rough, the roads were not the best. We slept for the most part of the journey, as there was really nothing to look at in the truck. After eating, chatting and giggling about a few silly stories, we fell asleep. From time to time we passed through towns and we were allowed to stand up. It so happened that we passed through towns at night. The lights were impressive. Never before had we seen such a colourful illumination.

After travelling an entire day and night, we stopped at a settlement for lunch. This was Lubango, SWAPO Military Training Centre. We ate, stood around, and soon it was time to proceed again. Next, we arrived in a huge town and we were dropped off at a big building called *Omangadjiina*. Only much later would we understand that we were in Luanda, the capital city of Angola. We spent one or two days here. We were allowed in a big room with a lot of clothing, and we were told to select a few things, whatever could fit us. The room was so huge and everything was in massive piles. We selected all kinds of pieces of clothing, including shoes. It was hard to find things that fitted together, let alone in the correct sizes but it was not a time to be fancy. The issue was to find clothing to replace our military uniforms with which, we were informed right there, we were about to part. Wherever we were going, we were going in civilian clothes. At least it sounded so. The word *Omangadjiina* would be part of our vocabulary in all our camps and settlements. This was a big storeroom that each settlement had, where civilian clothes and food supplies were kept. These items were supplied by the friends of SWAPO around the globe, especially the Scandinavian countries.

The following day we were ready to move on. We had our newly acquired outfits on, right from the piles. No chance to have them ironed. I still recall my black dress with little white dots. Although our looks were not that sophisticated, we were picked up by a very decent car. We got in with whatever little belongings we had. The car started and we were again on our way to the unknown place. That is how we had been living for the last three months. We were either in a camp where we fitted in with the rhythm of things, or we were on a vehicle moving somewhere else. We always found out where we got to when we got there. There was simply nothing to worry about. The car moved through this huge town. It stopped when some lights changed to red and moved when they became green. There should have been an explanation why it had to be that way, but that was none of our business. Ours was to sit in the car and to get off when we were told to do so. We could observe things on the way, but since most of them did not make sense to us, we did not bother to ask or comment on them. We had no clue about all these things, how could we comment? And even if we did, none of us knew any better. The idea seemed to be that we would get it one day and, for the time being, it was not worthwhile to explain. And I think that assumption was correct. There were thousands and thousands of us in the same category, the explanation would have been insufficient and would have had no end. For most of us, the new world had absolutely no similarity with what we had known back home. So, tough luck, we had to be blindly dragged along.

The car stopped in front of a huge building, and we were asked to get off. Obediently, we took our luggage and stood in a group looking at each other. The driver left and the man, who had travelled in the car with us but next to the driver, indicated that we should follow him. Inside the building, there were many people moving in all directions. Some were going really fast as if they were late for something. Others strolled on as if they were killing time while waiting, whatever they were waiting for. We moved through these many people. The most important thing was not to lose sight of the man we were following. We didn't know his name, neither did we really know who he was, but he was the only person we could claim to know in this huge place. If we lost him, that would be the end of us. The language that was spoken in this building did not sound any closer to either Oshiwambo or Afrikaans. So there would be no way of asking for any direction or assistance.

We kept pace with this man until he stopped in front of one of the counters. We also stopped a little distance away. Here, he put down a piece of paper in front of the person standing behind the counter. He explained a few things and pointed at us from time to time. It was clear that whatever he was telling this person, it was about us. We were not worried about their conversation, whatever was being said, it was fine with us. It no longer mattered whether we spent days in this building, or if we were about to leave the place. We took things the way they came. The nodding of heads signalled the end of the conversation and the man hurried back to us. It was time to proceed and we closely followed him. We had not gone far when he stopped in a corner to explain something to us. We were now joining the queue and at the next counter we would be asked a few questions. We should not worry because the interrogator spoke Oshiwambo. We were at liberty to answer any question but to whether we had Angolan money, we should answer 'No'. This having been said, we joined the queue. We gave very brief answers and we were in unison to the question regarding money, except Claudia. Either she had forgotten what we had just been told, or she wanted to test what would happen if she responded that she had money. That was a mistake.

After the questioning, we, except Claudia, could proceed. She was asked to stand aside while someone else was going to attend to her. I wondered what went through her mind at that time, but her eyes displayed a real panic. None of us could offer to assist or remain with her. One did not know what was beyond the next door. It was better to remain together and go through this building together, even if it meant walking to the other end of the building and going right back where we came from. We had no choice but to proceed and left Claudia to go through her test by herself.

At one point, other people who moved in the same direction as us had to show booklets of different colours. We had none, nor did anyone ask any of us to show them. Why the others had them and not us, and what exactly they were for, we were to find out only two years later. We finally emerged from the big building and found ourselves standing in front of a colourful big bus. The man who was leading us got on the bus and we quickly did the same. Once all those who were supposed to be on the bus were on board, it started moving. I was not sure where to look. There was so much movement and we just looked on without grasping what we saw. The bus came to a halt and we all got off. When I looked up right in front of me, there stood a huge creature with writing in green: ALITALIA. I looked at the thing, and those who were with us, in a very natural way, went towards the stairs and started going up. We looked at each other as our chaperone went straight for the stairs. What was inside this thing and what was it that we were going to do in there? Once inside this hollow creature, our companion directed us where to sit. When we were all seated, he also took his seat. Now it was time to sit and wait for the next happening. What a discovery! There was no description about this new place in which we all of a sudden found ourselves. It was not exciting as we had no clue why we were there or what was about to come. And there was a big question mark about Claudia. How would she find us in this place? Would she be allowed out of the building? And if she were, would she be shown to the bus and finally climb into the right creature? Mind you, there were many others.

All of a sudden, Claudia walked in. Her big eyes showed her relief to see us. She excitedly called out to us and all the glares of other people were on her. We didn't see anything wrong with her loud calling of our names! Next, Claudia was about to sit at the first free seat, but she was shown elsewhere. What we definitely did not understand was why they had to disperse us all over the show. Was it really difficult to make us sit together so we could at least try to make sense of the situation? I was seated next to a white lady. Traditionally, we greet everyone we come close to, but I think I never greeted that woman. Everything happened so fast and unexpectedly. And the fact that we sat apart, made us more miserable. We tried to make eye contact with those closer to us, but there was not much communication. A voice came through explaining something I didn't understand and a few ladies in neat uniforms came around to help us to be tied to our seats. Some seats were given pushes and some signs were given. Whatever was being said was not meant for us. This was a completely different world. Did we really have to be here? Other people looked so clean and elegant. In our case, there was not much difference compared to our looks in Cassinga. No decent clothes, let alone proper shoes. Annascy did not manage to find the same shoes. She had a sports shoe on one foot and a flip-flop on the other. This was our haphazard dress code.

Later when we knew better, we wondered what the other passengers must have thought of us. But for that particular day, we were just there as we had been at other places before. Suddenly, the whole place was noisier. It was not quiet since we got in the thing, but now it was really noisy. And then, the big thing started moving. What followed was really indescribable. Everything went so fast, the noise was unbearable, the speed was disquieting and I was sure not to survive whatever we were going through. Air was being sucked through my ears. My whole being was devoid of its strengths and abilities. I could not even turn around to look at the eyes of others. How did they feel? This was beyond us. If only someone could explain to me what all this was all about. The lady next to me was not going to be helpful, that was already clear from the time I sat down. She was deep in her book as if nothing was happening. How could one read in this abnormal situation?

Next thing, Annascy was unwell. Some of the girls in uniforms came around to give her a khaki looking envelope. She looked terrible, which confirmed that this was not a normal experience. Later I saw her sucking an orange, apparently that helped to make her feel better. People around us started discussing and laughing. They were having a real conversation. Of course we could not understand anything. If they were laughing, there was maybe no problem after all. For me, the earlier this was over, the better. I was surprised that other people did not show any anguish. Some stood up and walked around. The girls in uniform were going up and down with big smiles. Then when I lifted my head up the next time, they were handing out drinks. When it was my turn, I blankly looked at the girl and she understood that I had no preference. So she gave me some drink and I drank it. Next thing, they were handing out trays of food. Again I couldn't answer any of her questions, and she found a table right there in front of me and placed the tray on it.

The food looked good and colourful. Coming from a place where we ate once a day, this was a welcome gesture. I literally ate everything and drank everything that was edible and drinkable. Only one little black thing did not taste nice, but I managed to swallow it. Ten years later I learned that it was an olive. Next, I opened a little packet, placed sugar in my hand and threw it in my mouth. And the meal was over. These girls came back again and they were taking cups to pour coffee in. I tried to swallow my coffee, but there was no sugar in it. How can one prepare coffee without sugar? At home, coffee or tea, when available, was always served already sweetened. It was unthinkable that sugar could just be displayed for self-service. Here I was now with my coffee in an amazing place, but no sugar. But I had just eaten my sugar. So the sugar I ate was meant for the coffee that was supposed to be served afterwards. Although I could not finish my coffee, I at least learned something about sequence in this kind of place.

After the meal, I felt better but my many questions still lingered on. What is this thing in which we were? Why was it moving so fast and where to? How long were we to be here? This was again one of the things we had to get used to. If others were sitting calmly, chatting and laughing, it was maybe not as dramatic as I was thinking. So, it was maybe better to sit and wait. As I sat there, I tried to reflect. So this was an aeroplane. The tiny thing which we saw in the air passing over our village can be so big when one sits in it? And how did it manage to lift itself up and keep itself up there without having its weight resting on a solid surface? I really did not know what to think. I rather rested my brain, sat as usual and waited for the next episode. Who knew, the next one might be even more dramatic!

As I sat there and gazed at whatever crossed before my eyes, other people started standing up. I remained seated. The woman next to me gestured and I understood she wanted me to make way for her. I stood up and waited like everybody else. People started moving forward and I followed. All of a sudden, I saw some sunshine. We were again in the outside world. There were the stairs and we started going down. Finally I had my feet solid on the ground again. What a relief! But where were we? Definitely not in the same town where we got into the plane. This meant, the plane took off, travelled for some time and landed somewhere else, and this was where we got off. My short stay on board was not at all helpful for me to understand what I had just experienced. I could not make any connection between the planes I saw passing over my village a few times and the big, well-arranged and organised space I had just left. The concept was just too complex for me to understand. In any case, there was no point in trying to make sense out of what I had just experienced at that time. I had just to move on, just as the others were doing. It was only then that I grasped that we had moved from Angola to Zambia. Since I was never good in Geography, there was no way that I could position myself in relation to my village. What mattered at that time was that I had ground beneath my feet and air to breathe. The rest,

I would survive, as I had been doing for the last three months, and just as I had done on my first flight.

As we stepped off the plane, we were greeted by two men. They only spoke English. They said whatever they said and pointed us to the bus. Only after a few weeks did we get to know that they were Hage Geingob and Stanley Shana, the Director and the Registrar of the UN Institute for Namibia respectively. When they met us at the airport, we had no clue who they were, what their titles stood for or what institution they represented. Neither did we understand what any of this had to do with us.

4

Exile becomes a normal way of life

We got on the bus and drove off. We arrived at some big premises, queued up and at the end of the queue each of us received a blanket, a pillow and two very white neatly folded bed sheets. Next, we were taken through long corridors to some rooms. There were four of us in a room. We did not have many belongings and we settled in very fast. Soon we were moving around the corridors and we started talking to some people we found there. We were relieved to note that these people also spoke Oshiwambo. How and when they had arrived, we were to find out later. My two friends ended up in the bathroom and came back perplexed. They told us that they found two ladies deep in conversation in the bathroom saying many clicks one after another as they spoke. We all ran to the bathroom to hear for ourselves. We left being convinced that the two ladies in the bathroom were just pretending to impress others. After a few days, we were really perplexed to see some others also not speaking Oshiwambo. What was going on here?

What impressed us first in this new place was the dining hall, a huge hall where one was allowed to sit wherever you wanted to. No school regulations were applied here. You could even say what you wanted to eat, but in English. We initially managed with some sign language. In any case we had to learn to appreciate the food and learn the names of new dishes. Where on earth had we eaten salad before? When it was put on our plates, we just ate. What was new and impressive was that we had more than enough food and we ate three times a day. We did not need to cook, other people did. But we were required to speak English to them. They were after all Zambians and not Namibians.

After a few days, we found out why we were brought here. We were here to learn, and to learn in English. There were so many other people besides us at this school. Some were to join our class but they did not come from Angola on that plane with us. They came from elsewhere but all were apparently Namibian students, speaking a variety of languages. It was also difficult to figure out where the people in charge were from. They spoke English to us and among themselves. They were of all colours and from all nationalities, including those I had never heard of before. They did not speak English the same way. For the first few days, we managed quite well, simply avoiding being where they could have contact with us.

Very soon, the situation changed, and we had to come face to face with those in charge of the place. We were there to learn, and learning takes place in the classroom. In this confinement, there was no way of escaping. We were all exposed in front of these teachers. There were a few fellow learners who could understand and speak relatively good English. Or at least they made us believe so. There were those who knew just a bit of English and those of us who could hardly put a few words together to make sensible sentences. Initially, the teachers underestimated the diversity of levels of our understanding of English.

Notebooks per subject were handed out and teaching started. Many of us would look up at the teacher and then at the person sitting next to us. One thing we certainly didn't do was note taking. At the end of the second week, our notebooks were as clean as the day we had received them. As soon as the classes were over, we rushed out of the classroom to share our frustrations. We had no solution and the next day would be classes again. By now, those who were in charge of this place had understood that many of us were far from following what was happening. They had to find a solution.

The first thing was to determine exactly how poor our English was. This was done through Sunday meetings with Hage Geingob, the Director, and it appeared he wanted to find out if it was solely a language problem, or a language problem combined with a lack of understanding of concepts and notions. In most cases, it was everything. I still remember how dependent we were on the others. When the Director said something, we would laugh or clap hands but only a few seconds after the reaction of those who understood. I am sure if I was asked to explain why I was laughing or clapping, I would not have had an answer. One Sunday, the Director asked us a question which remains unforgettable to me up to this date. The question, which he posed with ease was, 'Who is the SWAPO Representative in Cuba?' No answer was forthcoming. For many of us, there were two difficult words and they turned out to be key to the question. What was the meaning of 'representative'? And what was the meaning of 'Cuba'?

To strengthen the effort of the Director, a proposal was made that we should try to listen to the radio in English, especially the news. We were encouraged to join some colleagues who had radios and try to listen to the news. Most of us joined a group that listened to news at 13:00 under a tree in the yard. Sometimes the Director would come around to listen to the news with us. That was the time that we pretended that we were paying full attention and we were following what was being said. After the news, the group would debate about what was said on the news. Those of us who could hardly follow wondered how the others managed to get all this information together through whatever was said over the radio. Day after day, we stood under the tree and tried very hard to identify the words we knew. I recall how attentive we became once we heard words such as Namibia, SWAPO, UN, Sam Nujoma, and South Africa. But what exactly these wordings had to do with each other, we did not know. With such a situation, there was no doubt that if we were to learn anything, something serious had to be done.

Suddenly, a team of English teachers arrived. Everything else had to wait. We repeated words, sentences, went through dialogues, and after three solid months, we were speaking English. We felt comfortable to hang around anywhere without fear of bumping into a teacher and being engaged in English. We finally understood clearly that we were at the United Nations Institute for Namibia (UNIN), the institute created by the UN to train future Namibian public servants. We were still to find out about the functions of public servants but we knew that we were to perform those functions in Namibia one day. Complex explanations were provided as to why exactly the UN had to create such an institution. We gradually also found out the nationalities of the staff including a good number of Namibians. One of the Namibian staff was Hidipo Hamutenya, the man who came to Cassinga to make us sit for an admission test under a tree. Despite my wild guesses on the Namibian languages during the admission test under the tree, I made it to UNIN.

We were to stay there and to study for the next three years. The first thing we needed to do was to get used to town life. It was surprising that none of us were run over by a car. Crossing a road was real guess work. Why cars were coming from every side and why others stopped and went again when the traffic light turned this or the other colour, we had not the slightest clue. We just loved to go to town, and when we started off on our trips to town, we didn't think about the traffic lights. When we were about to cross the road with streams of cars, it was time to improvise. Somehow we had to get to the other side of the road. One place we had to go to almost on a daily basis was the Kamwala market to buy mangos. Mangos were a new discovery and all the coins we managed to get were spent on mangos.

After a while at UNIN, we started getting a monthly allowance. This was great. Instead of us paying for attending school, accommodation and food, we were paid 25 Zambian Kwachas a month. This was when budgeting became difficult. Never before in our lives did we get money on a regular basis, and there were no parents to advise or to back you up when the monthly allowance was finished. We could easily spend money on mangos and sweets before thinking of buying soap and other toiletries. And little did we think about clothing, despite our precarious situation. Our minimal clothing did not go unnoticed, and our group became popular: those kids from Anamulenge. One day we were told to assemble at the gate of the Institute. Here we met a tall and good looking lady who asked us to follow her. We did not even ask where she was taking us, we just followed. After all, this had become a culture. In town, we went from one shop to the next and the instruction was clear: each of us may get a dress and a pair of shoes. I am not sure what the boys were allowed to get. Back in our rooms, there were four of us with exactly the same dress and shoes. The selection was not that big. We were nevertheless very grateful. For the first time in the last six months, we could look at ourselves in the mirror with admiration.

As time went on, we started the emancipation process. We started appreciating what was happening around us. Over the weekend, we had lessons on the SWAPO Constitution. We were taught about the SWAPO party structure and how everybody else fitted into it, including a number of the Namibian staff at UNIN. So, these Namibians were not only employed by UNIN as administrators and teachers, they were also part of SWAPO. And they had not only been SWAPO cadres over a long time since the early sixties, but most importantly, they were part of the SWAPO leadership. Hage Geingob was in charge as a Director and we all ended up calling him Comrade Director despite his protest pointing out that he did not call us Comrades Students.

By now, we had been in SWAPO for more than half a year, but we had not yet seen Sam Nujoma. We had heard so much about him, his name was mentioned in so many liberation songs and speeches, but where was he?

Word went around that Sam Nujoma was going to address the Namibian community in Lusaka and it was going to happen one Sunday at UNIN. We looked forward to this day. Finally, we were going to see the man who was leading SWAPO. That day, we waited for his arrival. When a number of cars arrived and people got out, there was nothing particular that could indicate who Sam Nujoma was among all these people. Nonetheless, we went to the hall known as the auditorium. The hall was packed. People excitedly exchanged greetings before they took their seats. We didn't know people who came to the meeting from outside UNIN, so we remained seated and waited. Once everyone was seated, we took note of the people seated at the podium facing the audience. Among them, I could still not see anyone I could associate with Sam Nujoma. Although I had not seen Sam Nujoma before, nor his photograph, I just happened to be convinced that none of the people in front could be Sam Nujoma. Was he still coming?

The meeting was about to start. We stood up and sang the SWAPO anthem. Thereafter one of the men in front called out the SWAPO slogans. He was soft spoken and his power salute was not as energetic, neither did he lift his fist up high. He rather went horizontally. This was

Sam Nujoma. He was not a giant as I expected and did not at all fit the South African description back home. He was a humble, soft-spoken man. He smiled, just a normal human being like any other person. In his speech, he gave a run down of recent events on the Namibian liberation struggle. The speech was delivered in such a way that the audience, and more specifically the newcomers like ourselves, got the needed hope that the liberation of Namibia was very close. For the first time during my short stay in exile, I started seeing the purpose of SWAPO. I started understanding and believing that the liberation struggle was doable. Of course, I also started seeing the hope of going back home in the not too distant future. During the speech, especially when a significant event had been mentioned, slogans were interjected and the whole audience would stand up and respond vehemently while thrusting fists high. Slogans were so powerful that we responded in unison and with big excitement:

SWAPO! *Will win!*

Namibia! *Will be free!*

Victory! *Forever!*

This was followed by songs of meaning for us under the circumstances, such as 'through the barrel of the gun we will liberate, Namibia our country to be ever free…'

These types of meetings were going to be part of our lives in exile and they somehow propelled us onward. They strengthened our sense of being in an unusual situation, with a unique mission for a noble cause. We were to carry this sense of belonging and responsibility wherever we went in the world. It drew us closer together and made us feel a deep and huge responsibility, not only for securing the independence of our country, but also towards each other wherever we found ourselves, be it in small or big numbers.

More meetings of this kind were to come with different leaders of SWAPO. They wanted us to know what was happening, but without raising doubts in our minds. When we were new, we were always told that things were moving in the right direction. Statements such as "we will celebrate the next Christmas in Windhoek" were made. These were jubilant moments for us. We counted months before the next Christmas. In our very naïve minds right at the beginning of our life in exile, the period between the time such speeches were being made and the next

Christmas was manageable. It was just a matter of months! When this same message was said to us a second and third time and the following Christmas we were still in Zambia, bringing the total of Christmases I had been away from home to three, I then understood the purpose of the statement. Others were certainly told the same thing back in 1975. In 1977 and 1978, it was our turn to be told the same. We knew that the independence would come because that is what we were told but at one point, we also realised that it would take some time. It was not really harsh on us as this was done progressively. While we were being told of celebrating the following Christmas at home, we were also gradually becoming politically mature to understand the complex issues related to the liberation of Namibia.

This started with the talks at the UN to negotiate a settlement for the independence of Namibia. We came to know and understand bodies and concepts such as the United Nations Council for Namibia, the Western Contact Group, the United Nations Security Council and its Resolution 435 and so many others. In our naïve minds at the time, there was no way that a big organisation like the United Nations and the powerful five Western countries (the United States of America (USA), the United Kingdom (UK), Canada, France and West Germany) could be defied by South Africa. After the first collapse of the talks in 1978 I realised the cruelty of the world. How could they do that to us? Namibia's case was crystal clear; what was it that they could not do? Didn't they understand that we wanted to be back home, just as they were in their respective countries? We were still to understand the complexity of the Namibian question, well blended with political and economic interests of those who had the power and the capacity to make things happen, and this understandlng was what made my 12 years in exile bearable.

The adaptability and capacity of humans is amazing. We were barely at UNIN for a few months when we started feeling at home and doing just what was expected of us. As early as 1978, we were effortlessly taking notes, engaging lecturers, asking questions or seeking clarity and spending hours in the library, a concept that was not part of our world until our arrival at UNIN. During the lunch break, we would hang around some lecturers, either those who taught history or any others who also belonged to liberation movements, South Africans and

Zimbabweans, and listened attentively to their analysis of issues. The most interesting thing for us was to hang around the Director or the Namibian lecturers, as here and there we managed to get more details on our own liberation struggle and to appreciate the challenge of the SWAPO leadership. During weekends we had specific discussions on the SWAPO constitution and some ideological talks. The attendance of the orientation on the constitution was compulsory though. Some evenings, there were film shows on the Korean revolution. We went regularly, but what was more attractive were the snacks that were served before the film shows.

With this inclusive package we gradually managed to put most pieces of our liberation struggle puzzle together. In a nutshell, this was a struggle we were prepared to fight, no matter what. Both military and diplomatic fronts were ready and mobilised. Whatever succeeded first, that was the route we would take. This was a firm decision and was clearly demonstrated by the concluding remark of the SWAPO President after the collapse of one of the series of the UN talks, 'If the Boers are not prepared to agree with us around the table, we will meet them at the battlefield.' With this specific remark, it was clear for us that SWAPO meant business and we were part of this business. And the business required determination, discipline and self-sacrifice.

Slowly but surely, we glided from the naïve, narrow minded and traditional human beings to vibrant members of a liberation movement. We were prepared to live according to the motto: Everything for the struggle! We kept our fighting spirit high through meetings, discussions and songs of the liberation struggle. We were aware of the complexity of the situation, the superiority of the South African military capability and the support South Africa enjoyed from the powerful western governments. Yet our conviction of conquering one day was absolute. Andimba Herman Toivo ya Toivo's words in the Pretoria Court back in 1968, before his imprisonment at the notorious Robben Island for sixteen years constantly spoke to us: 'I know that the struggle will be long and bitter. I also know that my people will wage that struggle, whatever the cost.' In the face of such a challenge and responsibility, each of us felt that obligation to do his or her part. We knew that we could not all attend to the same thing. Whatever assignment landed on our lap, we picked it up and carried it forward. The task ahead of us clearly did not allow preference. Once a task had been assigned, all that was expected was an appropriate execution. The time this hit us, we were students. To study, although in English, could not be comparable to other heavier assignments. With this vigour, we plunged ourselves into our studies. It was repeated to us that we would be public servants once Namibia was liberated. We repeated the same to ourselves, but it was only after the independence of Namibia that the term 'public servants' started making sense to us.

As time went on, UNIN became our community and home. The advantage was that we were many and amongst our own. We finally understood that being Namibian meant so many things. We did not speak the same language. Neither did we share the same culture. The struggle was our unifying factor. During the holidays, we went to the Nyango Health Centre. This was a similar set up to Cassinga; the only difference is that Nyango was slightly bigger, and in addition, there was a kindergarten and a school. So, we were at UNIN for studies and we went to Nyango for holidays. It was a life pattern that was somehow familiar.

Our first visit to Nyango in December 1977 was eventful. It was a new environment, a big settlement with a large population. While Cassinga had many tents, Nyango had more permanent structures. The structures did not consist of walls as we knew them. They were unusual and impressive frame structures. Although they did not look permanent, they were made to last. The set up was the same as at Cassinga, a kitchen, a clinic, a huge *magasin* (a French word we *massacred* and referred to as *omangandjiina*), a garden and of course the parade grounds, a large area for gathering. Besides the school and the kindergarten, there was a vegetable garden and chicken farm. The chickens were only there to lay eggs for the patients and kindergarten children. The clinic, the kindergarten, chicken farm and vegetable garden were the creations of Dr Libertina Amathila, the first black Namibian woman to be a medical doctor, trained in Poland in the 1960s. She expanded these facilities and services to all SWAPO settlements in Zambia and Angola for the well-being of Namibian women and children in exile.

While at Cassinga almost everyone went to the kitchen for their meals, at Nyango, a considerable number of people cooked for themselves. A ration of food items including sugar and salt was distributed from the *magasin* on a monthly basis. This lessened the burden on the public kitchen and provided a homely feeling for those who cooked at home. In reality, those who went to the kitchen were newcomers and visitors like us, the students.

During our first stay, we took note of a large number of young men who, in a certain way, lived in a big community but at the outskirts of the settlement. They had their own kitchen, and contact with them was not that obvious. Although their presence in a big number was not that unusual, we grew curious to know who they really were and why they were there. After chatting to a few people, we got to know that these young men were soldiers who were associated with the Andreas Shipanga rebellion in 1976. Andreas Shipanga himself and his close collaborators were in jail in Tanzania and the majority of the group was accommodated here while SWAPO was assessing them and finding a way of reassigning them. I personally did not know any of them, but some of my friends recognised a few of them. I recall visiting one of them with a friend and chatting to some of them. We really did not know what to ask them and they did not seem to trust us. But the little we found out was that after a rebellion in a SWAPO camp in Zambia where 26 people were killed during a military attack by South Africa, the rebellious soldiers were handed over to the Zambian army and kept at a refugee camp. After some had indicated their wish to return to SWAPO, they were offered to stay at Nyango until they had made up their mind. Those who really wanted to leave for good went as far as Sweden for political asylum. However, those who were in Nyango expressed their remorse and wanted to be reintegrated into PLAN. During our second holidays in April 1978, we witnessed the colourful reintegration of these young men back into PLAN and their moving departure for Angola. They finally received their uniforms and weapons back and we were treated to a professional military parade as they marched to the waiting trucks. They were under the command of SWAPO Secretary of Defence, the late Peter Nanyemba. The soft rain that fell that day did not shorten their march nor did it delay their departure for Angola. Once they were all on board, the engines of the trucks started one by one, and soon thereafter, Nyango Camp was waving goodbye to enthusiastic members of PLAN.

The convoy of the trucks rolled on and the settlement at the outskirts of the camp was completely empty.

Being on the move had become part of our lives. For the next three years, Lusaka was our base. But others were moving on. As we got used to our new base and pattern of life, some of our friends whom we had left in Angola and members of our famous Anamulenge group, turned up in Lusaka. It was exciting to meet again. There was so much to talk about and we had to catch up on news before the next move. It was again time for some of them to leave for studies in Ghana and others to the former German Democratic Republic (GDR). By now we knew that a bigger group of our younger colleagues had left Angola directly to Cuba. The older boys went for military training in Lubango. Our group was no longer intact; we had to go in different directions. What mattered was that we would keep in touch. We had understood that there was no way we could stay together. We were happy to have a few old friends around. When we bade each other farewell, there was no sadness. This was our new life and we knew we would make it. Those who were leaving did not seem worried and that was good. There was an unexplained but natural understanding that while the others were physically fighting, we were the studying contingent. And we were to do so wherever in the world opportunities were offered to us.

One day I found out that French was being offered at UNIN. It was not compulsory and those who were interested could attend classes during lunch or after hours. Without really understanding how French would sound, I found myself registering. There was no explanation why I wanted to learn French, I guess it was out of pure curiosity. Classes started and we found ourselves confronted with this nasal language. First I thought the teacher had very narrow nostrils. In no time, we were hooked on the story of the lessons. It was about two young people, Pierre and Mireille, meeting in Paris. Every day, the story ended up at a critical moment that gave us the desire to know what came next. Obviously we returned to the classes to find out the next happening in the story. The pictures helped us to follow and to guess the meanings. While the story was getting more interesting, the language was getting more difficult. Then it was time to be exposed to writing. Looking at the words and listening to what was being said and being told that what was being said was exactly what was standing on the blackboard or on paper in front of us, sounded like a pure lie. The written and spoken languages had nothing to do with each other. And this was in addition to the grammatical challenge. Our interest was the story, but the teacher could not go any further until certain grammatical issues and pronunciation were well assimilated. For the sake of the story, we made an effort to please the teacher, so as to get to the next part of the story. Unconsciously, we were learning the language. As it became more difficult, fellow learners started dropping out, claiming that they wanted to use their lunch hour for something else. Too bad for the story! At the end of three months, out of the 20 beginners, there were seven of us left.

Unexpectedly, tragedy struck. In the early hours of 4 May 1978, the SADF attacked Cassinga. What a shock! This was a home to me and so many others not long ago. I vividly remembered the set up of the camp, its surroundings and the nearby river. The news of the attack was hardening. The South African military planes unleashed bombs on a Namibian civilian population far away from their natural home. Those who survived the attack spoke of a black sky all over Cassinga. Many were killed. Others were injured and marked for the rest of their lives. The river that provided bathing and laundry water to the camp became a trap that particular day, and contributed to the death toll of the attack. Those who headed in that direction, if not drowned as they desperately tried to flee the hell in the camp, were met with the fierce South African bullets at close range. The South Africans knew too well that these poor civilians would run in all directions including towards the river, and their ground troops were mercilessly waiting for these distraught civilians to emerge from the river. Getting any closer to safety became a real challenge for the trapped population of Cassinga. Why did this have to happen? The pain and anguish were unbearable.

We were vulnerable after all. Did refusing to live under occupation and merely leaving the country warrant death? Did the South African army have to travel hundreds of kilometres into Angola to inflict death on us in such a merciless manner? And the irony of it all was that they carried out this hideous act during one of the numerous times when the negotiations on a peaceful settlement for Namibia were underway. It was hard to comprehend how they could inflict death on hundreds of Namibians under the care of SWAPO while the SWAPO leadership was sitting with them in New York in the presence of the UN and the five Western Powers. What a coincidence! The SWAPO leadership had no other option, but to abandon the peace talks, and rush back to take care of the survivors and to bury the dead. We were all shaken.

It was then said that Cassinga was attacked with the French manufactured Mirage jet aircrafts. This was going to affect our learning of French. Out of anger and pain, UNIN students staged a demonstration against the French teacher. We, his students, were also disappointed. Why should politics be so complex? Certainly, this man was not aware about the South Africans using French Mirage jet fighter aircrafts to kill Namibians. That did not matter, he was a French national and at that point, Namibians were mourning their comrades and whoever smelled of being close to those responsible for their killing, was made to understand our pain and anger. After a week or so, the French teacher was back and we were advised to return to our French class. Boycotting classes would not bring back our comrades. We needed to continue where they left us. They could not die in vain. Their blood would sustain us. We returned to our French class, but some of our comrades and friends were unhappy with us. How could we continue learning French, while the French had a stake in the attack of Cassinga? Why did we accept that the French offered us education while offering weapons to South Africa? Would the French stop selling weapons to South Africa simply because seven Namibians at UNIN stopped learning French? The French teacher might have shared his experience at UNIN with his Embassy in Lusaka, but how much of it would even reach Paris? These and many more questions were tormenting us, not only those of us who were learning French, but the others as well.

As time went on, we resumed our French classes. Three months later, some survivors from Cassinga joined us at UNIN among the new intake for 1978. Besides the trauma, the pain and scars of the attack were clear on the faces of many of them. They told us the story. It was a horror. Most of them were very new in the camp and were unprepared for such an act. We understood them, as during our own stay in Cassinga less than a year earlier we were also not prepared for such an unfortunate happening. In fact, the attack was unthinkable. Yet, here we had these young people who went through the unthinkable, something that would mark them for the rest of their lives. Whenever they heard a banging noise, their first reflex was to look for a hiding place. Hour after hour, they spoke of their experience, how they managed to survive and how they felt a few days later when survivors had regrouped. From their stories and my own recollection of Cassinga, I could not imagine how I possibly could have survived.

I did not realise until much later how much I was absorbed by the story of the Cassinga attack. The story already affected me before I heard the live stories of these youngsters. Through my imagination, I could live through the attack. The story from the survivors confirmed my imagined story and sharpened the feeling of our vulnerability. Suddenly, I was seized with the fear that what had happened at Cassinga could also happen at UNIN. I spent sleepless nights, and lay awake in my bed. My imagination pulled me into an unrealistic world.

One night, something unexplainable happened to me. I am sure this was not a dream. As I lay in bed, I all of a sudden heard white male voices, right in the corridor in front of our room. Since they were speaking Afrikaans, I could not understand what was being said, but one thing was certain in my mind: the other students were also awake and moving along the corridor. They were being taken away. I wondered when someone would open the door to our room and discover the four of us. Nobody opened the door. No one seemed to have noticed that we were still here. I held my breath and waited. There was no way that I could check with my roommates to establish whether they were also scared as I was. Moving or whispering might compromise our safety. I chose to remain dead still. Who knew, the four of us might be the only survivors of this ordeal. Gradually, the voices faded away and the night went silent. So, we survived. Motionless, the rest of the night dragged on. I waited to look into the panicky eyes of my three roommates and share our anguish.

At the usual time, I heard Claudia getting out of bed, and so did the other two. I sat up and looked at them with expectation. Claudia reached for her towel and was about to go to the bathroom. I asked her what she was doing and she shrugged her shoulders and left the room. I peeped through the window and saw everybody moving about as they did every day. What was that I experienced through the whole night? How come I was the only one to have heard male voices speaking Afrikaans? After telling the story for a few days, I gave it up. Apparently nothing happened that specific night. I was going to experience such imaginative life and death situations for a few years to come. I must admit, this was a personal weakness.

Despite this weakness, I was determined to become a useful member of the liberation movement and succeed in whatever assignment was given to me. UNIN was the first testing ground. Although I was not among the best students, I was well above average. As soon as I had the English language under control, I started enjoying my studies.

↪

During my second year, I came to hear that one could write home. Just the feeling of writing home and stating that one was doing fine was quite exciting. Even putting the name of the recipient on an envelope and walking to the post office to send off a letter was an awesome experience. My first letter finally left and the long wait began. My mother was only going to believe that I was still alive if she saw some visual proof. So I included some photos. I sent the letter via a teacher at Döbra. After some weeks, I received a letter with a Windhoek post office stamp. Receiving letters from Namibia was after all possible! I nervously opened the letter and this was not my letter. This was a letter addressed to us from one of our former teachers, a Belgian religious man known as a Frater. The letter went from one hand to the next and we were just overwhelmed to hear from a person we knew well and from home for that matter. From the letter we got to know that after our departure, the school closed down. The teachers together with the few left over students moved to Döbra in Windhoek. A few of the students were the successful ones who left their shoes behind, and managed to cross back to Namibia on 20 April 1977.

As we reread the letter and chatted about it in the corridors, the UNIN administration came to hear about it. It, of course, became a source of concern, especially for the Namibian staff including the Director. We obviously did not see any problem in receiving letters from home. And we were about to send a collective response. Just before we drafted our letter, we were informed that there was a general meeting to be addressed by the Director. These are opportunities to be briefed about significant happenings, both at home and within the liberation movement, so we were always eager to attend. There were quite a number of issues to be discussed and unexpectedly, 'writing home' was one of the agenda items. As much as it is natural to feel like sending and receiving news from home, it was not appropriate to our peculiar situation. Not only did it pose a danger to our families back home, but also to ourselves. We might compromise the security of our families, and there were enough examples of letter bombs among liberation movements. From that point of view, writing home was really not encouraged, unless letters were hand delivered by specific and trusted individuals.

'And a message specific for the kids from Anamulenge. The Catholic authorities from Windhoek have written to express their joy at the news that, "our former students are at UNIN."' No doubt, the Director and his colleagues had irrefutable evidence that some of us had indeed written letters home. At the same meeting, we were told of the visit of both the Catholic Bishop Rudolf Kopmann together with the Vicar-General Father Henning to UNIN, prior to our arrival in Lusaka. They wanted to check with SWAPO about our whereabouts. So, the highest Catholic Church authority came to see SWAPO and enquire about us. Although caring was always a pleasant thing, it can also be embarrassing in certain circumstances.

The collective response to our letter was now hanging. Would we write back or not? On one hand, we appreciated the security concerns. On the other hand, writing home was a real joy. Would we now give it up? We thought hard about it, but one thing was certain, we would not want to be faced with hard evidence about this delicate matter. We also, honestly, did not have sufficient understanding of the danger posed by writing home. I cannot explain it, but at that point, the unclear events of the large group of soldiers who lived at the outskirts of Nyango came to my mind. The location of their living place in the camp in my mind sounded like a temporary suspension from the liberation movement and a period to rethink one's dedication to the Namibian cause. Although in the end, all went well for them and they were reintegrated into the People's Liberation Army of Namibia (PLAN), I sensed that it was not a pleasant experience. The rebellion itself, and the subsequent events, were big things in our small minds. They were after all not told to us in chronological order and our limited experience of the struggle was not sufficient for us to fully understand what exactly happened and why. It was simply too complex for us, and as it always goes at that age, we tried to analyse the situation among ourselves. You can imagine the conclusions we reached. Was writing home comparable to a rebellion?

This may sound unbelievable, but we went to the extent of confiding in some older comrades. Was the Director really upset with us and could writing home land us in trouble? The response was quite comforting. After a loud laugh, the late Tate Shoombe re-explained the danger of writing home and the concern of the Director. He underlined the importance of responsibility of the party cadres and that care was to be taken not to worsen the security situation of those back home. It was not about writing home per se, it was purely a security matter, both for those in exile as well as those who were in Namibia. He also consoled us by stating that the Director was quite aware that as newcomers, we had not known any better. The explanation was crystal clear. Writing home excessively was out of the question. Sitting around a table and drafting a collective response to our teacher was definitely out, especially after the general meeting. We finally gave it up and left it up to individuals. We understood that this was part of growing up in the liberation movement. We were fully part of it and we were prepared to play our role.

∽

Every day we bumped into new people, new ideas, new happenings and we expanded our horizons. One day, by mere coincidence, I bumped into a lady who would become my mother in exile. Although I consider myself as having had a number of 'exile mothers', this one was going to shape my life in exile, and my future to a certain extent, in a very significant manner. There was really nothing extraordinary about our meeting. It was one of those banal happenings. She was a young mother and one of the senior students at UNIN. On this particular day, she came to UNIN with her baby son. Out of respect, she didn't want to go up to the Director's office with a baby. I happened to be seated nearby and so she asked me if I didn't mind holding her baby while she was quickly seeing the Director for something. Obviously, I didn't mind. Being a big sister to so many siblings, holding a baby for a while was really no big deal. And since I had not had a chance to do so for some time by then, I enjoyed that short moment. When she came back, I asked a few ordinary questions about the baby and the conversation was over.

After a few days I again took note of the lady; she was not one of the quiet students. From a distance, she looked friendly and easy going. I decided to strike up another conversation with her when the opportunity arose. When it happened, I asked about her son and she remembered me as the girl who had held her baby one day. She was probably impressed that I had shown interest in her baby and so she asked me whether I wanted to go home with her one day to visit her son. I happily agreed and the following weekend I went home with her. After what felt like a long time for me, I was finally in a home again. There was the lady, her husband, her baby and a friend who lived with them, along with her one-year-old son. I shared the room with her friend and her son. What struck me most that weekend was the fact that this house had a homely ambiance. I spent most of the time looking after her little boy. The following Monday I had to return to the hostel. But it so happened that whenever I bumped into this new mother, she asked me whether I wanted to go home with her for the weekend. Although I had no clue who she was, I never declined a single offer.

As I got to know her better, I also came to know a few of her friends. They were also students at UNIN, but I could not clearly recall who they were. One Saturday afternoon, there were four of them. As I played with the baby, I also observed them and vaguely followed their conversation. They played music and from what they were saying, this was South African music, Ipi Tombi. As they moved around (it is only later that I found out about dancing), they sang along and laughed happily together. I wasn't sure what they found funny. From that encounter, I realised that there is a huge age difference between a twenty-year old girl and twenty-six year olds or above. I simply could not connect with them. Their long stay in exile made them different in my eyes. One thing was certain: they had known each other for a long time. It also became apparent to me that they didn't meet in exile. They spoke exactly the same language as me. I understood perfectly everything they said, but from their intonation, it was clear they were not from close to where I was from. And I had definitely not heard that intonation before. Which part of northern Namibia were they from?

Although a number of my questions about my newly discovered relationship remained unanswered, I instinctively knew that I had found a new home. I had of course still my room at the UNIN hostel, but on Fridays I naturally packed up and went home for the weekend. When it was convenient for me, I also found a reason to spend the whole week 'at home', and attended classes from home. Gradually I moved out of the hostel altogether. For all practical purposes, I became the big sister to the little boy, Shafa. My new parents found my being around useful as I could take care of the little boy, especially in the evenings or the weekends. Soon they came to discover that I was an anxious person and staying home alone with the baby in the evenings was a major challenge for me. After some convincing, we agreed that they would drop the two of us at UNIN on their way out and they would pick us up on their way home. I knew it sounded funny that I had to drag the boy along to UNIN and look after him there, but, under the circumstances, I had no choice. He was taken care of, not only by me, but by so many other students, and I felt secure. Shafa was a lively little fellow and it was not easy looking after him among so many people. He needed a constant eye on him. Something that was peculiar about him was that he wouldn't sit on a chair or on a bed as we did, he always sat on the window sill, and some windows were quite high. And since our whereabouts were not always predictable, I was also not sure how to handle him in certain environments.

One happening that would mark me for a long time happened during the period that was known as 'ready' in exile. These were periods when all of a sudden, for security reasons, we couldn't sleep at our usual homes or camps. For this specific period, the two parents had to sleep elsewhere and the boy and I at a different place. Not much was discussed with me. All that I got to know was that for an unspecific number of days, the boy and I would be dropped at a certain house in the evenings for the night. For the first night, I packed our few belongings and we were dropped off. To my discomfort, this was Ms Diallo's house. Not only was she my English teacher, but Ms Diallo was American. And she was not by herself, she lived with her husband and their two sons. All of them were Americans speaking American English! It was not only a language problem, but a cultural one as well. No one thought of my dilemma in that environment, but what mattered most was that the two of us, the boy and I, were safe. Never in my life were evenings and nights that long. I felt so relieved in the mornings when we were picked up. Since the days became so short for me, soon we were back at the same house again. As with all other events, one had no choice but to get used to all eventualities.

⌒

1979 started off like any other year. I was now in my second year at UNIN, and to a certain extent, comfortable with my studies. The problem of the English language was long solved. I wasn't sure how long I was going to continue with French, but I still found it interesting and I attended classes on a regular basis. Although I still had a room at UNIN, I was for all practical purposes attending classes from home. I had even convinced my friend Lydia to come and stay with us as I started feeling lonely. I have known Lydia since the age of six and we had so much in common. Things could not have been better.

Writing letters home was really not encouraged, but a number of us did write from time to time. I for one felt a sense of relief with a bit of news from home, even if it was old news. Just a little sentence saying 'your parents are fine' would have made my day, if not my month. If my parents were fine and nothing was said about any of my siblings, they were obviously fine too. It was normally a Catholic priest, Father Franz Houben, from the Okatana Mission Station who wrote from time to time. Getting a letter to me was not a straight forward arrangement. He would find a way of getting the letter hand delivered to Windhoek from where it was posted to his sister in Germany. The sister would then post the letter to me in Lusaka. I would take time to respond as one had to choose one's words carefully. Should the letter be opened on its long route to its destination, it shouldn't compromise anyone's security. I did from time to time send some photos, but it was not unusual to get a response back indicating that the photos I mentioned were not received.

In August 1979 I received a letter from Father Houben, and to my pleasant surprise, he had enclosed a letter from my mother. Two years after I had left home, my mother found the courage to write to me. I reread the letter many times. What a joy to hear from my mother! Her writing was not that good, but these were her own words to me. She wanted me to know that they were fine and that they were glad to know that I was fine wherever I was. Clearly, she had no clue where I was, but the fact that I was somewhere and fine, was consoling to her. She further told me about the work they had to do with the harvesting and how much longer it would take them to finish this particular year. Alas, I was far away, and couldn't help. She concluded by expressing her deep conviction that we would certainly meet one day, and she signed off. Although I didn't talk much about my mother's letter, I certainly portrayed a radiant face for a number of weeks. If only I could hear from my mother again one day.

It was not long before the next letter came. Although it was already early November, I somehow felt it was a bit too early to hear from home again. For the last two years, Father Houben had not written so often. The practice was that every weekday, we went around the matron's office to check whether we had any mail. I was surprised to receive a letter so soon. I took the letter and took note of Father Houben's handwriting on the envelope. The red sticker on the envelope did not at all mean anything to me. I had never seen one before; why should I know its significance? Since it was break time and one should always read this kind of letter quietly, I neatly folded the letter and slipped it in my skirt pocket and continued the day's routine. By lunchtime, I had completely forgotten about my letter from home. After the afternoon study, it so happened that I went to the bathroom and while there, drew a toilet paper from the pocket of my skirt. Here was the letter I had received earlier in the day. The toilet was also a quiet place and since there were enough toilets, I could as well read my letter without any disturbance.

I opened the envelope and there were two letters, a very short one from Father Houben, and another two-page letter written in Oshiwambo. The long one could certainly wait, I thought to myself, and started to read the very short one. I read and reread the short letter, yet, I couldn't get the message. After having expressed the difficulty of writing to me this specific time, the line read: '*deine liebe Mutter is gestern Abend gestorben*'.

I had learned German during the five years of my secondary school, and Father Houben had always written to me in German. This time, however, the message, written in a very simple German, was simply not sinking in. My mother had just written to me, and I was looking forward to her next letter. How could she just die? I did not bother to understand the cause of her death. Father Houben wrote that my mother had died the previous night, and he could not possibly lie to me. Not with this type of news! I put the two letters back in the envelope and back in my pocket. What I needed at that time was to get to my room, bury my face in my pillow, and to quietly absorb my loss. This was too sudden, very personal and too difficult to share with the others.

From the bathroom, I had to go up the corridor, past the washing area and down the stairs, cross the corridor from the dining room before going up the stairs leading to our room. The distance was not at all long, and I had walked it up and down several times each single day during the last two years, and never did I find the passage challenging. The challenge was that I had to pass a number of colleagues who were moving around. I knew I would have to keep my head down and not at all make eye contact with anyone. Once I had reached my room, I was certain to manage the rest and keep my loss to myself.

I had hardly started off my walk when I went past one girl by the name of Teckla. Teckla decided to stop and ask me something. I pretended not to hear her and while proceeding, she decided to grab me by the arm. There was absolutely nothing unusual about that. At that age, we spent hours hanging on each others' arms, just to get the full attention for whatever silly story one wanted to tell. Teckla did not expect anything different this time. My breaking into tears caught her by surprise. Why should her grabbing me by the arm this time cause such an outburst? With big eyes, she followed me and when we both entered the room, I was uncontrollably in tears. The other girls in the room were perplexed and looked at each other. Poor Teckla did not know better either. I was inconsolable and the others could not guess what could have possibly gone wrong since they had just seen me a short while ago. They helplessly stood around my bed and the more they asked me what the matter was, the more I cried. One of them thought of Pendukeni, my exile mother. As it was knocking-off time, one of the girls rushed out to see whether she was still outside. Luckily enough she had not yet left and she hurriedly came to my room. As everyone tried to make sense of my despair, Maria remembered that she had seen me receiving a letter earlier in the day. Could it be the cause of my misery? The search for the letter started.

When the letter was finally found in my skirt pocket, Maria did not bother about Father Houben's letter. It was in German and too short. Whatever was written in the four lines could certainly not cause the huge pain I was going through. She went straight for the long letter. As she mentioned the name of the author, I recognised the name of the nun. She had taught us in the primary school and she was well known in Okatana, and since Maria was also from Okatana, she was the right person to read the letter from Sister Eufemia. Maria read how mother got hit by a car during a wedding celebration of one of her nephews. She did not die on the spot but was transported to the Oshakati Hospital. There, Maria read further, she had to undergo an operation as she was five months pregnant. The letter gave a number of details of events and I finally heard Maria reading, 'Your mother unfortunately could not wake up, and the twin babies could not be saved either.' And Maria's voice went quiet.

What first started like an unbelievable story a while earlier in the toilet, had all of a sudden become a reality and my friends stood around, some speechless, some trying to whisper words of sympathy. I did not know what to think, I felt empty and robbed. So many questions went through my mind. Why did my mother go to the wedding? Did she not see the car coming? There were certainly so many other people at the wedding, why her? Why such a weird story? Be that as it may, that day I clearly understood that once the word death is mentioned, there is no going back. And I knew too well that as much as I did not want to believe it, my mother's death was real. When Pendukeni suggested that I go home with her, I obeyed. Lydia also came along. After two days, I gathered my strength and I could chat again with Lydia. This was after all my personal loss and affair. It would be unfair to overwhelm poor Lydia with my sadness. She was very sympathetic with me, and I will remain grateful to her. Just a year earlier, she had lost two siblings in the Cassinga attack. These were hard moments, but we had to overcome them. And I made an effort to do just that.

I had no choice but to learn to live with my new status. I accepted that I no longer had a biological mother. I was blessed to have so many caring friends, and Pendukeni really played that perfect mother figure to me. At that level, I felt sorted out. My association with her really comforted me. However, I constantly reminded myself that my siblings back home had no mother. Out of eight, seven were boys and four were under the age of ten with the youngest only two years old. This thought was going to haunt me for a number of years. Seven young boys those years in a rural setting without a mother could only be a mess! My sister, who was slightly younger than me, would certainly not be able to stand in for my mother. Such was life. These were the days of the struggle. Somehow, and some day, we would overcome. At that time it was certain that there was no way I could be of any assistance to my young siblings. It was not only due to the distance. In all practical terms, this was simply out. But one day, I may just be able to do something for them! With that thought I consoled myself and continued my life in exile.

⌇

Somewhere in the middle of 1979, there was talk of the students who attended French classes going to France. As unbelievable as it might have sounded I was one of the students who were going to France at the end of the year. Although we were not sure why we were going to France and for how long, we were just excited about the story. But it was made clear to us that we first had to sit for our end of year exams. At that stage, we were no longer worried where we would go, how we would get there and how exactly things would turn out there. By then we knew that nothing unusual would happen to us, and that we would always manage whatever was assigned to us. We only needed to wait for the assignment, and once the time was right, we would pack up and go.

The story of going to France was really taking shape. Even our French teacher, Mr Jean Gandy, had informed us. Initially, we were supposed to have gone during summer, but some papers he referred to as visas were not ready. Whatever those papers were, we would see them when they gave them to us. We wondered what their purpose was and why on earth they were so important as to delay our departure to France. We however were not concerned about the delay. If we only went in December, that was also perfectly fine. We did not really understand why Mr Gandy repeatedly expressed his concern that we had to go during winter. What was wrong with going to France during winter? We had been cold before in our lives so what was his problem?

The day of our departure for France was approaching. We had written our exams and we were informed that our visas were ready. We had not seen them though. It didn't really matter, as long as the French Ambassador to Zambia, the UNIN Director, and Mr Gandy knew about them. The Director, Comrade Geingob, had explained at length to us how important it was for us to look after the little booklets which would be handed to us before our departure. Our famous visas were apparently in there. But Comrade Geingob also reminded us again and again that we should not pack these booklets in our suitcases but rather keep them on us as some people may require to see them. We promised him to keep them within reach and to show them when asked to do so.

The date of our departure for France finally came. We did not realise the importance of it that time, but Mr Gandy, Comrade Geingob and the French Ambassador to Zambia accompanied us to the airport. We were nine students. At the airport, we hung around and our three companions chatted among themselves. When the time of our departure came, the Director walked with us for a while and said goodbye to us. This time, we knew better than our departure from Luanda more than two years ago. We knew by then that the huge building where we had to wait for the plane was called an airport. And this time, we each had a famous little booklet we had observed from a distance in the Luanda building. We also knew that the little booklets were officially known as passports. And that they were a must at an airport. We thought that we had been lucky to have gone through the Luanda airport without passports. But the truth was that we had gone through many check points without anything.

Confidently this time at the Lusaka airport, we followed the other passengers. When they showed their booklets, we did likewise. Soon we were sitting on the UTA flight to Paris, with a stopover in Douala, Cameroon. We could catch some meaning from what the air hostesses were saying in French and we felt proud of ourselves. When the flight took off and dinner was served, this time we knew what to eat and what not to eat. It was quite a long flight. I cannot even remember the stopover in Douala. When I woke up, we were about to land in Paris.

⤚

To date, I still remember the date we landed in Paris, 4 December 1979. When I approached the door to step out of the plane, I was engulfed by cold air. My cotton dress stuck on my body, my naked legs were exposed and my sandals did not in any way offer protection to my feet. My other eight colleagues were no better off. While we thought we behaved better this time on the flight and the other passengers had nothing to wonder about us, they undoubtedly must have wondered how much we knew about European winter as we were disembarking from the plane. But they had no time to stand around and wonder further, they hurried on to do whatever they had to do. We looked at each other, unable to understand the kind of cold we were experiencing and how we were going to manage during the six weeks ahead of us. Although we were always certain to manage whatever the circumstances, we definitely had our doubts this time. As we followed the other passengers, shivering but putting up brave faces, we all of a sudden noticed someone carrying a sign with the name 'Namibie'. Was this referring to us? As we approached, the lady smiled. She was confident in knowing how to identify us. There were not so many black youngsters on the flight, but most importantly, everybody else on the flight, except for the nine of us, knew a bit about the European winter. So, she came straight for us.

As soon as we had collected our little pieces of luggage, this lady took us straight to a department store. We were requested to select a coat, a jersey, a pair of trousers and a pair of closed shoes. My goodness, these French are organised! Whoever had this idea of bringing us to Paris this time of the year was pretty aware that we would turn up unprepared. After our mass shopping, it was time to go to these huge offices where we needed to complete a number of papers, just for six weeks' stay here. In these huge buildings, we completely lost our direction. One could no longer tell whether one had already been in this particular part of the building or whether one was entering it for the very first time. It did not really matter for us. It was a matter of following the guide and doing exactly as told. Reaching all the places we were supposed to go to was going to take forever and use up the little energy that was left in us. So, we were led to these little rooms that moved up and down. We could not all fit in one go, and when my turn came to depart, I stepped in and off we went. I can't recall with whom exactly I was, but we had no clue where we were going, or what we were supposed to do once the thing had stopped and its doors opened. The thing had gone up to several places, new people came in and left again, but we remained put. At one point, when the thing opened again, there was our companion and the other colleagues we had left behind. How did they catch up with us? The French woman said something to us as we tried to free ourselves from the little room. We did not understand what she was telling us, but it was clear from her intonation that we hadn't done exactly what we were supposed to have done. From her body language, we were supposed to remain in that little room, which I learned a few years later was a lift. It must have been hard for her to get us to do whatever we were supposed to have done in that place. The filling in of forms for the nine of us must also have been a nightmare for her.

After our endless visit to what could only be part of the Ministry of Foreign Affairs, we were taken on a tour of Paris. I remember this endless moving around to places without understanding why we had to do all this driving around. But I cannot recall what I had seen and what I had not seen. Everything was so complex, new and there was no point of reference. So, we looked at all these things and left again. On top of all this, we were so tired.

Finally, our companion took us to another place. She made us sit somewhere while she stood in a queue. Very soon thereafter she handed us little tickets and pointed to one of the long, but really long trains. Clearly, our paths were going to part here. Before she left, she explained a number of things to us while at the same time pointing at the clock on the pole not too far from where we were standing. And with her hand, she insisted on the importance of the time. Although I did not get the whole story, something stuck in my head. And the others seemed to have understood the same thing as well: We were going to a place called Vichy. The train did not stop long at places. So, when we heard the name Vichy, we had to get off very fast. When she was satisfied that we had understood, she shook our hands and smiled broadly, indicating that we should get on board. As soon as we were on the train, she disappeared in the sea of people around our train. After a full day with some young people who had no clue about most of the things which she had to have us accomplish, she could at long last take leave of us. It must have been a hard day for her. She was kind though, and it was hard to see her go, leaving us with these total strangers.

The whistle went and the train started moving. As we pulled out of the station, a few things were announced, but none of us understood. At this stage, we were not yet worried. The name Vichy was not mentioned, so maybe whatever was said, did not concern us. It was dark and there was not much to see. Soon the train was moving really fast. Few colleagues who had been in towns in Namibia spoke of slow trains. I had never been in a town in Namibia and my travelling so far had not involved any train, so I had nothing to compare my first train experience to. I sat back, observed people on the train. All these were new things to me, the day was too long, and all this after a night on the plane. I wished I could sleep. But what if they called out Vichy? And I had no clue at what point the train would reach Vichy. It would be better to stay awake and sleep in Vichy, whenever we reached there.

The train sped off through the night. We sat there, rather calm and looked at each other occasionally. Others didn't look worried and that was reassuring. We certainly did doze off from time to time, but once the train came to a halt, we were all wide awake and attentive to hear whether we were finally in Vichy. At every stop, with our eyes fixed on our luggage, we were ever ready to dash for the door. After all, by now, we were trained to be ready for any eventualities. If the announcement for Vichy came, we would be prepared for it. And indeed it did come, just over three hours after our departure from Paris. When the announcement came through, I must have slept. I woke up just to see Maria going over me and reaching out for her luggage. She did mutter the word 'Excuse me' but I could not quite comprehend where she was going and why she was leaving me there. When it turned out that this was indeed Vichy and we were getting off, I didn't find Maria's attitude quite right. When was she going to wake me up and alert me that we were in Vichy? The lady in Paris said loud and clear that we must get off in Vichy, and fast.

I do not know how many times I reminded Maria how irresponsible she would have been, if the train had proceeded with me still in it!

As we got off, there was a group of young men smiling at us. Who could they be? They spontaneously came towards us, shook our hands energetically and enthusiastically called us comrades. All of a sudden they spoke to us in Oshiwambo. Are these Namibians? What were they doing here and when had they come here? How come no one told us of the presence of other Namibians in Vichy? Their presence here must be known in Lusaka! Even the lady in Paris didn't mention a word about them! Or did we miss that information due to our limited French at the time? Be it as it may, they were here and we were pleasantly surprised to meet them, especially at this hour of the night and in a town where we believed we knew no one. They were six altogether. They each took a suitcase and we happily allowed them to lead us wherever they were taking us. It was cold though and we hurriedly followed them. Just around a corner out of the train station, we entered a big building. According to them, this was our hotel. They said it so naturally that they could not guess how perplexed we were to stay in a hotel. Well and good, if this is how people live in France, then we were ready to stay in the hotel.

The young men were also organised! As soon as we had put our luggage in different rooms, they led us to a kitchen. Two big pots stood on the stove, and a pile of plates were neatly stacked on a table in the corner of the kitchen. These young men not only knew of our arrival but had also prepared dinner for us. They had not met us before, but they knew that we were Namibians and comrades. That alone was enough for them to organise themselves. They had bought the food and had asked the owner of the hotel whether they could cook here for their comrades arriving later that evening. I really found that amazing. I personally would not have thought about that. I would have been excited to hear that some countrymen and -women were coming, but I do not think I would have gone to the extent of doing shopping and cooking for them. But these young men did! And they had no clue who we were. They asked whether we were hungry and they started dishing out food for us. It was spaghetti served with mutton in a very red sauce. The red was somehow shocking, but it did taste nice. From their reaction, this was their daily dish. It was simple, one could cook for many people, and once you had emptied two or three tins of tomato paste into the boiled lamb stew, added a bit of salt and pepper, you had sufficient sauce for a whole lot of people. Although I initially found the sauce too red, I was going to spend the following six weeks frequently eating and enjoying this new dish. I think this was also my first time to eat spaghetti. There is always a first time for everything.

The young men politely took leave of us and told us that they would see us the following day after classes. We went to our rooms. We badly needed sleep. Above all, we needed to be ready for our classes the following day. I shared a room with Lydia, and as the two of us got into our beds, we had not the slightest idea how to find the place where we were going to attend classes the following morning. Nor did we know what time we were expected to be there. All we knew was that the following morning, we were to attend French classes in this town Vichy at some language centre. We somehow knew the name of the language centre, *Centre Audio-visuel des Langues Modernes* (Audio-visual Centre of Modern Languages) or CAVILAM. So, we went to bed and left the where and the how for the following day, and we simply slept well. After all, by now we had learned perfectly how to worry about tomorrow when the next day came.

We saw to it that we were all ready for our classes at the same time. All nine of us walked out of the hotel in search of the venue of our French classes. In Africa, if you can't find a place, you stop and you ask for directions. That is exactly what we were going to do, if we failed to find the place. We confidently started off, walked for a while and we were certain that we were going to bump into the place. We randomly turned into streets and expected this CAVILAM to just appear. But to our dismay, we found out that in Europe, things do not just turn up. You must know their locations and exactly how to get there. But from our little experience, we were still convinced that we would find the place. We only needed to search harder. Finally we decided to ask. We stopped an elderly woman, tried out our very best French and waited for an explanation. The French woman rushed through her explanation, pointed in some direction, and continued on her way. We hardly understood what she said and I am sure, should she have turned, she would have shaken her head as we must have done exactly the opposite of her explanation.

After having senselessly walked for a distance, we started arguing and finally splitting up. It was now time to find this CAVILAM according to one's own instinct. We were after all now late, but we knew we had to report the very same day, at least before the end of the business of the day. Discipline was part of our routine. We hurriedly went into different directions. I wonder whether some of us had not blindly passed in front of the very same CAVILAM several times during our search. We somehow ended up finding the place and before the end of the day, we all managed to get registered.

Once registered, we each got a piece of paper with a name and a number. We were directed to a classroom and once inside, we realised that the name on the paper was the name of the teacher, and the number corresponded to the classroom number. For some reason, many of us found ourselves alone in our respective classes. No other Namibian was placed with me. I bravely knocked on the door, handed over my piece of paper to the teacher and waited for further instruction. The teacher, a certain Madame Madeleine Sauvanet, politely smiled at me, took the paper and showed me to an empty seat. I timidly took my seat and lifted up my head to look at the others. From their faces, they had been here for a few days and they enjoyed learning French. They were not many, about fifteen at the most. Madame Sauvanet, after having introduced me, asked the others to introduce themselves, stating their name and where they were from. I looked at them as they introduced themselves, and I particularly paid attention to their nationalities: Spanish, Italian, Korean, Indian, German, Nigerian, Palestinian, Iranian, Iraqi, etc. I did not know what to think! Never in my life till this point had I had an opportunity to sit in the same room with people from so many different countries. What a variety! Not even in Zambia did this happen to me. By now I knew that not everybody in Namibia spoke my mother tongue, but those who were with me were more or less the same colour as me. Here I was, far from home and Africa, and it was not only the issue of colour, but also the look and everything else. Some names of countries I had only heard in the Bible. Did this mean that these countries really did exist and people really did live there? What a discovery!

Very soon I was going to find out that despite our differences, none of us had an advantage above others. According to the assessment of the French authorities in charge of the language institution, all of us were equals as far as the French language was concerned. The only difference was that we each added a bit of our language flavour to the little French we knew. Although there were new arrivals and departures now and then, a number of us remained in the class for a number of weeks. Gradually we got to know each other and the learning became interesting as we took note of each other's little accents and challenges specifically linked to our own languages or any other language we spoke. Our Iraqi colleague seemed not to make a difference between the letters 'p' and 'v'; both sounded like a letter 'b' for him. When he pronounced a small sentence like, '*Je vais à Paris*' (I am going to Paris) it sounded like '*Je bais a Baris*'. Our Nigerian colleague could not manage to get any closer to the French rolled letter 'r' and he replaced all the 'r's with something that came close to the 'g' in the Afrikaans language.

∽

Learning in the classroom was not a challenge. The challenge was practising French in real life. We had no choice but to do shopping, order a drink in a bar, or things of that nature. Or a French person might just think of having a conversation with you. Good heavens, it was hard. Of course there were things one could avoid. But shopping had to be done. That involved selecting the right items, paying and receiving the right change. And the French like to ask if one did not have the exact amount. The main challenge was the numbers in French. To make life easier for ourselves, we decided to pay only with notes. Even for a single bar of chocolate, we paid with a note of a 100 French Francs (FF). There was no reason that the cashier should insist on anything. In our view, the amount was certainly far more than enough. To any question asked after handing over the note, we decided to give a '*Non*' (No) answer. And all we had to do was to stand there and wait for the change. Once back in the hotel, we emptied the change into a huge container and we replenished our purses with the next notes. We soon ran out of notes but we didn't get worried. The way we received our first money was very straightforward. On our first day at CAVILAM in Vichy, we were sent to a certain office where Mademoiselle Fradin handed over to each of us an envelope full of money. Now that we had run out of money, the obvious thing would be to go back there and we would simply receive more.

Before we did so though, we were sensible enough to mention our intention to our countrymen. They were amazed that we had spent so much money in such a short time. In fact, they explained, the amounts we received were meant for a month. We could only return to the office for new money for the last two weeks. We told them that we had only coins left. And since most of these coins were copper, they could only be useless. In Namibia and Zambia, one could not buy much with copper coins. In any case, we did not want to subject ourselves to counting copper coins in front of a cashier in a supermarket.

Our countrymen decided to count the coins and at the end of the count, they declared that we had a lot of money. The copper coins were FF 10. Although our assistants put these coins in piles of ten coins to make up the equivalent of a FF 100 note, this did not help. If you were asked to pay FF40, but in French without seeing the figure displayed, how would you know that you were supposed to give only four of the coins? Impossible! Up to date, I ask myself why a simple figure such as 75 in French should, literally translated, mean sixty-fifteen (60 +15) and the number 99 translate to four-twenties-nineteen (4 x 20 + 19)! Numbers in French for us were just incomprehensible.

Then we had to face another challenge: the cold weather. It snowed during our six-week stay. We, of course, did not have the right clothes, let alone the right shoes. Slipping on that hard snow was not uncommon among us. Then we discovered gloves and we decided to buy some. We were not quite sure what their exact purpose was, but we noticed that they were popular. We already had coats from Paris, but we did not much take note of the boots. In our Namibian eyes, coats and gloves were just items of dress. You put them on and you kept them on! So, in the classroom, we would take off nothing. We occasionally took off the gloves because writing proved to be difficult. It took us time to take note that others always took off their coats and gloves as soon as they entered the classroom.

On one of the coldest days, it was my and Lydia's turn to do the shopping. We bravely walked to the supermarket and bought what was required. On our way back home, we took the full toll of a winter evening.

After rushing to drop off the food in the kitchen, we went straight to our room and put our half frozen fingers between the bed and the mattress. I cannot describe what we felt but it was a mixture of pain and itchiness. Although all this was a new and sometime exciting experience, there were days we wanted terribly to return to Zambia.

As is usually the case, our stay in Vichy was also filled with laughter. One of these occasions was caused by the reflex of one of our colleagues, Maria, who by accident stepped on the foot of a French lady in a supermarket. This can happen to anyone, one needs only to have the right reflex and to apologise immediately. That was also Maria's intention. She however, and most unfortunately so, mixed up the words. Between *'Excusez-moi'* and *'Merci'*, she no longer knew which one meant *'Pardon'*. So she thanked the lady for having allowed her to step on her foot. The other hilarious thing was the complaint of the only male colleague out of the nine of us. He repeatedly complained about the nice scented body lotion he had bought for himself. He so much liked the smell, but the lotion made his skin very dry. At first we did not pay much attention to that. After all, men normally do not apply so much lotion as women do. And since he chose the lotion and he found its scent nice, what else did he want? He however persistently expressed his disappointment in the nice scented lotion. To make him feel part of the group and for him not to feel completely ignored, one day we followed him to his room to see the lotion. He still went on speaking highly of his lotion as he searched for it in his cupboard. He emerged from it with a little plastic bottle, and when he put it on the table, some girls rolled on the floor with laughter. This poor man had been applying Cutex, the nail polish remover, on his skin. No wonder his skin felt dry.

As we went through all these various experiences and new discoveries, we had never forgotten who we were. Despite the distance and evident novelties around us, our thoughts often went back to our national mission, the liberation struggle. Yes, France was a nice place with a number of exciting things. Yet, we knew too well that back home, we had unfinished business which required constant input from all of us. During evenings and weekends, we often spent time in our rooms sharing our various experiences since we joined the liberation struggle. We tried to hear as much as possible about the happenings and developments. No matter where we were, we remained close to our struggle. This had become our *raison d'être*, an inexplicable source of inspiration and belonging. Whatever we were doing, wherever we were, the ultimate objective was clear in our minds: the independence of Namibia. At no point did we see this as negotiable. Our minds were set, and the urgency was intense. Some times more intense than at other times. In my case, this would be the right time. If only Namibia could get independence for me to return home and fill the vacuum left behind by my late mother two months earlier. Little did I know that it was still going to take another ten years.

⌣

As I battled with my thoughts I received an envelope from Germany. From whom could it be? I hurried to open the envelope and to my surprise, I had in my hand a letter signed by the highest authority of the Catholic Church in Namibia, Bishop Kopmann. As a Catholic, I knew who Bishop Kopmann was. He had confirmed us all. He could not possibly know me. I was just one of those thousands of children. I quickly went through the letter. I became overwhelmed with what was being suggested to me. He, or maybe someone else, found it absolutely necessary for me to return to Namibia. I could not have a better chance than that. Nor from any better place other than France. The itinerary was clearly spelled out. Somehow I would need to get to a certain place in Germany by train. From there I should go straight to some Catholic Church establishment. The name and details of the person I was supposed to meet were all there. This person would provide me with an air ticket and put me on a plane straight to Windhoek. I wouldn't need to worry. He, Bishop Kopmann in person, would be at the airport in Windhoek to receive me. And why did he want to go to such trouble? The explanation given was that in the absence of my mother, my siblings needed me back home.

I sat back and went through the letter several times. I could hardly believe what the letter just conveyed to me. How on earth could someone imagine that I could just pack up and return home? Returning home was a precious dream for all of us. But we all knew that it was not that simple. Neither was it, at that time, a foreseeable future. On the international level, the peace talks on the Namibian question were dormant. The UN talks on Namibia had collapsed. This was the time when we literally counted on nobody else, but on our own efforts. After all, this was our struggle. No matter what, we were the primary custodian of it and we were our own liberators. And we were all geared towards that as expressed in one of our revolutionary songs:

> "Many rivers full of blood to flow the Namibia's fight
> For real independence to come to Namibia
> We have suffered a lot and we're still prepared
> To suffer for our motherland
> We do fully know that we are fighting a just cause
> Thus victory is on our side"

As much as going back home was the yearning of every Namibian in exile, it could not happen at all costs. Independence was the prerequisite. And I couldn't be an exception. Even something as painful as losing a mother could not be a valid reason for abandoning the liberation struggle. As much as it could have been with every good intention, I was saddened by the thought of being lured into such a thing at a very vulnerable time of my life. I was still fighting within me to come to terms with the new reality of having no mother. The argument that I would be useful to my siblings back home did not make sense. One thing was certain, I would become an outcast and face total rejection from the community. In any case, it was going to be impossible to live at home, unless I could be at the side of the Bishop every minute. Anyway, whoever had this idea did not think further before putting it on paper. I confided in Lydia and she agreed with me that I should respond. Under no circumstances would I appreciate receiving such an offer again. Suffering and self-sacrifice was part of our life. This was meant for all of us without any exception. It could be losing a dear member of family back home, or having an entire family wiped out, or having a dear one languishing in detention. We knew of stories of PLAN fighters hiding under a bush for days with members of the SADF on their heels. Something which still inspires me is the story of PLAN fighters trying to outrun the South African soldiers. As a guerrilla military unit, they just managed to manoeuvre their way and climbed up a tree. These Boers, instead of continuing the chase, chose to rest under the same tree and opened their tins for a snack. This was the time to hold one's breath, and not to shiver. The other thing is: what if these Boers had decided to take a nap and lie on their backs? Certain things just make you cold down the spine. These were real challenges and sufferings. What was happening to me in comparison was bearable, although at that moment, I just felt empty.

I decided to write back and to put my views on paper. The Bishop never responded, but he did get the message. When we finally met in Windhoek after independence in 1996 at the celebration of the centenary of the Catholic Church in Namibia, I walked up to him and greeted him. He had no idea that I was that poor girl he wanted to help to come back home after the death of her mother. When I mentioned my name, he did recall the story. By then he was already retired and living in Germany.

Our six-week stay in France was drawing to an end. We looked forward to returning to Zambia. We had had enough of the cold and the struggle with the French language. As we were getting ready to leave, there was talk of a *grève* of the SNCF, the French National Railway Company. Since we did not know the word, we were not at all bothered. We went ahead packing and doing the final shopping. The word was being mentioned so often, including in the classroom. By odd chance, I got to understand that *grève* meant 'strike'. Those who were striking and for what reason, I did not get to understand. Just one day before our date of departure, it turned out that France was hit by a general railway strike. The notion of railway strikes did not really sink into our minds until the day we walked into the office which was responsible for providing us with our train tickets to Paris. No, they could not give us tickets. There would be no train to Paris for the entire week. And since there was only one flight from Paris to Lusaka a week, we could only leave a week later. This was unthinkable! Seven more full days of cold, and on top of that attend French classes for another week? No way! We were leaving as planned.

We left the office and a few minutes later we were back with a brilliant suggestion. Why not send us to Paris by bus? The French first looked at us with big eyes but after a few exchanges among themselves, without understanding what exactly they were saying, we could see that they were falling for our idea. They made a few phone calls and the announcement came: Yes, we would go to Paris by bus. There was no time to lose. We needed to be in Paris on time for our flight. Soon we were on our way, and since the speed of the bus was not comparable to that of the train, we had a glimpse of the landscape. I could remember hardly anything from the trip between Vichy and Paris. My heart was already in Africa. Of course I looked forward to sharing my experience in France with the others in Lusaka.

〜

Upon our arrival in Lusaka, Lydia and I were informed that our group had left two weeks earlier for Tanzania. We were to join them the next day. We could not lose out so much on our secondment period which was fixed at eight months. After a sleepless night trying to recount to friends events that spanned a period of six weeks, we were again on board a plane, this time to Dar es Salaam, Tanzania. The group had another two weeks there before proceeding to Nairobi, Kenya.

This was our third and final year at UNIN. During the third year, we were all required to go out and practise what we had learned during two years in the classroom. And this meant being sent out to work in the administration of a given institution, in most cases in other African countries. Many of us did not really know what to expect. After all, we had never put a foot in an office except on rare occasions when we were summoned to the offices of UNIN including the office of the Director to respond to specific questions. One had no time to look around and figure out what was happening in that room called the office. But of course we all looked forward to going out into the world of work. Our senior colleagues had done that in 1979 and their experiences were fascinating. I was most impressed by the stories of those who had gone to Ethiopia. But these were people who studied economics. No chance for me to go to Ethiopia, but my secondment was also going to be a life experience.

My group, consisting of the nine of us, was going to carry out a specific assignment in five African countries. We started off in Tanzania before proceeding to Kenya. After our two months in Kenya, we went on to Senegal for another two months. We then had a short stay in Mozambique before returning to Zambia for the rest of our secondment.

From the beginning, our assignment sounded very simple although I personally was not quite sure how to carry it out. 'We will see when we get there' was the attitude. SWAPO had planned an international conference on the Housing Policy of Namibia for the end of 1980. No one was certain when Namibia would attain its independence but policies had to be in place when that time came! The nine of us were sent out to those five countries to look at specific things in relation to housing. What exactly did these countries do to provide housing to their people right at the time they got independence? Where did they succeed, and where did things not work out, and why? And subsequently, what happened, and what measures did they take to remedy the situation? These sounded like straightforward questions. What we did not know though, was that this was a challenging mission. By the time we found out, we were right in the middle of it. The secondment of eight months had to be carried out to its logical conclusion. Otherwise, there would be no Diploma in Development Studies and Management. And with that, we were going to be part of the Public Service of independent Namibia. All these were big words which did not really speak to us. Yet, we wanted to be public servants one day in Namibia. And for our group, we would have made a contribution on the kinds of houses Namibians were going to get in an independent Namibia. All these were aspirations, but the secondment had to take place, and successfully for that matter.

Our stay in Tanzania was not eventful, especially for the two of us, the late comers. Besides some visits to some places and writing of short reports, I cannot recall much. Shortly after our arrival in Kenya, it became apparent that we were going to do serious work and have a taste of real challenges. But we also started learning a lot. We spent the first days of our two months' stay admiring the sky scrapers of Nairobi. We were going to spend most of our time in one of them. Here we had to confront a number of professors from the University of Nairobi. We first had an induction course on the history of Kenya and their liberation struggle, before listening at length to the many efforts after their independence. Our interest was in housing! What exactly did they do to solve the shortage of housing? There were no straightforward answers. We had to hear so many factors that influenced the way things happened. And on each of these things, we had to write an assignment. I did not understand the concept of an 'assignment' until I was in Kenya. And the professors prescribed a certain format for the assignments, what should be included and what should not, and in what order. I found some of the things unnecessary, but that was the rule of the assignment. It was not clear who set the rules, but our superiors back in Lusaka seemed to have been in agreement. So, we found ourselves having to do assignments in the required format.

For some reason, there were quite a few people involved in the programme. Upon our arrival, a highly sophisticated Kenyan gentleman appeared to be in charge of our programme in Kenya. While in Nairobi a Norwegian gentleman arrived and was introduced to us as our supervisor. The Norwegian supervisor was there to follow us literally everywhere. Then, we had professors. Despite being well supported by all these people, at one point, we had no money. We first talked about the matter among the nine of us before bringing it to the attention of our supervisors. The professors seemed not to have much to do with our pocket money. We finally decided to write to Lusaka. The money was simply not forthcoming. Yet the programme had to go on, including the assignments. Eventually, we got really frustrated with the situation and it was at this point that I realised how difficult it was to be in charge of human beings. A colleague who was slightly older than us was placed in charge of the group. I am not sure whether we elected him ourselves or whether he was assigned the task from Lusaka. Anyway, it didn't matter, he was in charge. We couldn't entirely rely on all these people who were around us. We were after all freedom fighters and must at all times have a structure. Poor Hinyangerwa Asheeke had to put up with our complaints and we sometimes blamed him for things which were not moving. If he was in charge, why could he not find a solution? He tried his best to explain why we were possibly not receiving money. But we were not interested in theories, we wanted money!

One day, when we were really pushed to the extreme, Asheeke tried again, 'You know, it could be that Mr Modise did not receive our letter, or maybe Mr Modise is not in Lusaka. Let's be patient. I am sure Mr Modise will respond.' Mr Modise was South African and he was head of our division at UNIN. He was the person directly responsible for our academic performance and naturally, he was the person we wrote to. But unfortunately he took too long to respond. After our colleague had tried his level best to explain why probably no response was forthcoming from Lusaka, instead of sympathising with this colleague in charge, we placed him in the same camp as Mr Modise. And when people become overwhelmed with frustration, it is quite possible that one fails to find words to argue one's case in a foreign language, in our case English. As soon as Asheeke had stopped advancing his explanation about the non response from Lusaka, I heard Mansweta saying, 'You are every day telling us about Modise, Modise this, Modise that, what Modise?' I am not sure if she made her point but I laughed about the intervention for some time, even way after our financial problem had been solved.

The assignments were quite challenging. Not only did we have to follow a specific format and structure, but each of us had to write on different topics. There was no trying to copy from the others. We had to prepare individual assignments. To make things worse, each of us had to work under the supervision of one of the professors. In other words, one had to spend time, one to one, discussing with these real academics topics that we knew little about. I am not sure if I always had something to tell my professor! I rather agreed with whatever he told me and would go and read up some of the material he advised me to. One day, at the end of our discussion, he suggested that I should phone him if there was anything I wasn't certain about. I heard myself responding in the affirmative. As I came closer to Lydia, who was standing nearby waiting for me, she burst into laughter. I seriously did not see what she was laughing at if I had not said anything to her yet. Then I heard Lydia saying, 'Did I hear you agreeing to phone the professor? How do you do that? Where do you find the phone to do so?' For the first time I realised that I had never touched a telephone in my entire life. Even if I had found one for argument's sake, what exactly should I do to phone someone? And did I have the phone number of the man?

After staying in Nairobi for two weeks or so, I was struck by the city. Once we had a vague idea of urban planning and such related matters, we were introduced to the informal settlements. I had seen similar set ups in Lusaka, but the day we were taken to the Mathare Valley in Nairobi, I could see the difference. The place was huge and looked like a gigantic mess. There was no way one could identify any kind of a system in this place. It was just a heap of things, and I wondered how people lived here. And it was stretched as far out as the human eye could see. Those teaching us had an explanation why things happened this way. Although in my eyes, I could not see what could be done to bring some kind of order, those in charge still had plans for this place. To our question whether there were similar places in Nairobi, the answer was yes, only that those were slightly smaller. For the first time I understood that running towns and providing housing were not easy undertakings. No wonder we were already thinking of having a housing policy, way before we got our independence.

We travelled through Kenya, spending a number of days in each town. We spent a lot of time in regional offices in charge of housing and in municipalities. In the evenings, back in the hotel, we sat together and tried to make sense of what we were told during the day. After all, this had to be reflected in our assignments and in the final report. Somewhere it was mentioned that at the end of the year there would be a conference on the housing policy for Namibia and we, as a group, needed to give a report at that gathering. It sounded like serious business, but we still had a number of months to go before getting there.

Our two months in Kenya were over and we were back at the airport in Nairobi for the next country: Senegal. We flew with Pan Am. After three months together, we had reached a stage where we could crack jokes and have a good laugh. As the plane went through clouds and we saw some lightning through the windows, we wondered what would happen if the lightning struck the plane. We had quite a number of theories, but one was that the plane could possibly fall out of the sky. And then? That was quite a challenging question, although I never thought that something as good as a plane could just fall down. That was way before I heard about plane crashes. That was going to come a few years later and when I got to hear of a plane crash and I thought back to when we went from country to country without the slightest understanding of such a possibility. But with Pan Am, this could only be a joke. After all, this was an American plane!

As soon as we had landed in Dakar, the French language hit us. As much as we had heard of French-speaking African countries before, I did not figure out that it would exclude all the other languages we knew. The airport routine was not difficult as one just had to repeat what the person in front of you did. Then we found ourselves in front of our Senegalese companion. We still had the Norwegian supervisor with us. With the appearance of the Senegalese companion, we understood that the Norwegian was the overall coordinator and for each country, we had a national coordinator. Our Senegalese coordinator was a tall and slender gentleman dressed literally in attire which we saw as a long dress. He greeted us warmly, shaking our hands in a hefty way. This was how he was going to greet us every morning during the two months in Senegal. We knew about shaking hands, but doing it that vigorously to someone one had been with the previous day was a bit unusual. But that's how things were done here and we went along with it. One good thing about this man was that he spoke English, in his specific style of course.

The next stop was our temporary home for the following two months. By now, we were used to temporary homes. Our hosts were an older French couple who spoke very little English, if any. The wife's voice was at least audible, the husband had no voice. He had a cut in his throat and had a device fitted in. We hardly heard what he said, but that did not really matter, hearing alone without understanding would not have helped much. We spent time just looking at the moving device as he attempted to speak to us and wondered how long he had been like this. In any case, our main contact with them was in relation to food. They cooked for us and as soon as we had eaten, we disappeared, only to come back for the next meal.

Nothing was really peculiar here, except for the outdoor life. It was not quite clear whether it was the limited space in the houses or the people generally liked being outside. One had an impression that most of the activities happened outside. There were chairs in front of houses and men in particular, sat in front of houses drinking tea from little cups. I am not quite sure where the women were and what they did. I even had an impression of having seen men washing their faces right in front of their houses.

It was also in Senegal that we came in close contact with Islam. The call to prayer from the mosque, especially in the morning, was already new to us, but when we came across people reciting their prayers on the street, we simply did not get it. We were not sure whether we should pursue our walk or stop and remain standing until the prayer was over. Neither did we know whether we should look or pretend as if nothing was happening. We simply had very little knowledge of what was unfolding in front of us, and it was difficult to ask questions. We made our assumptions about Islam and life went on. Of course we based things on Christianity which was not at all visible in the country. We learned that about three percent of Senegalese were Christians. All of a sudden, we had an interest to go to a certain place, not because of Christianity, but because we got to know that there were two Namibian pastors with their families who were not part of the Namibian exile community. We made the trip and met these two families from northern Namibia, with a mission to implant Christianity within a very Islamic country.

We stayed at the pastor's house. His name was Paulus Heita. I am not sure whether we had sent a message to announce our coming, but we were there for a weekend. For dinner we were pleasantly surprised that the pastor's wife, Meme Fiina, cooked the same food exactly the way we knew it back home. She had all the ingredients right there. What a delight! And this after exactly three years! As much as we had not known the family before, we spent a number of weekends with them during our two months stay. Was it really because we enjoyed staying with them, or simply because we enjoyed the food? It could as well be, we were not sure when next the opportunity would arise. After all, the two families were very kind to us. Their mission in Senegal on the other hand looked impossible. Senegal was a Muslim country wherever one looked. Their way of doing things was very different. Trying to introduce Christianity here in the 1980s really sounded like an impossible task. After independence, I met the two missionaries back in Namibia. I am not sure how much they managed in the end.

It was in Senegal that I realised that learning French was not only for France, but that there were many people on the African continent that use French as their official language or just for getting around, including for business purposes. What a complication, I first thought. The open market in Dakar was one of the places that really gave me this idea. As soon as these vendors realised that you did not speak Wolof, the lingua franca of Senegal, they immediately switched to French. They went on for a while until they realised that French was also not a perfect solution. We stood there, looked at them and smiled. In reality, Lydia and I understood a tiny bit, the others understood nothing. The two of us of course were prepared to assist with the translation but we too, had to make a tremendous effort to make sense out of the many things that were being said to us. The difficulty was that you had so many people around you. Coming from a sparsely populated country, that alone was confusing. These people were trying to sell you more or less the same thing, and certainly trying to tell you more or less the same thing as well. Instead of going slowly to allow us to process whatever they were explaining, they appeared to compete with one another to convince us. And then, there was the problem of accent and pronunciation! Yes, they were using the French words, but they said those words in a completely different manner than the French we had heard until then. As a result, we struggled so badly that sometimes we just gave up.

Nonetheless, and amazingly so, we enjoyed going back to the market. We found everything that happened there very interesting. But the most amazing of it all was that we did not need to buy items at the initial prices suggested by the seller. We were to determine our own price. From our observations of those who spoke the language you could even argue with the seller of the item as to why your price was the correct one. And customers ended up getting the prices they had proposed. So, we also went around, proposing prices using our hands, and most of the time, it worked. One of our colleagues, who really wanted to buy an item, but was frustrated by the seller who was difficult to convince, managed to put French words together which in the end sounded like a real French sentence. After what sounded like a heated debate, we heard him saying, *'Pourquoi tu combien?'* In reality, what he wanted to say was, *'Pourquoi ça coute si cher?'* He got the *Pourquoi* right. What he really wanted was to make the seller understand that his item was too expensive, but instead told him word by word: 'Why you how much?' These were words one heard so often at the market and what he really did was to combine and put them to real good use!

We travelled through Senegal, just as we did in Kenya. We picked up additional information on their efforts to solve housing problems. Obviously we picked up more French words. As it was the case in the other two countries, the two months were up and it was again time to move on. The next country was Mozambique, but to get there, we had to stop over in Lusaka for a day. For some reason, our stay in Mozambique was just for a week. By then, there was not much that was new to be learned; the housing problem was more or less the same on the African continent by then. After independence, rural populations moved to urban areas, but unfortunately faster than governments could provide accommodation for them. The end result was that people put up whatever structures they could afford, irrespective of the subsequent face of the urban areas.

Mozambique was no exception. The only exceptional memory from the one-week visit was the delicious seafood and my first contact with the Soviets enjoying their vodka. I had always imagined them as tough guys, but when I finally met them, I saw that they stood together, spoke their language, ate seafood and smoothed it down with vodka. More than that, I could not deduce much from observing them from a distance.

〜

Back in Lusaka, we had to wind up our work by comparing the experience of the past few months with the Zambian experience. Again, it was more or less the same thing. Soon it was time to present our findings at an international platform hosted at UNIN. Out of nine, Paulus Shilunga was selected to do the presentation. I do not know why he was chosen, nor did it bother me. I was only happy that the choice did not fall on me. Paulus did a great job. Speaking in front of these big and sophisticated academics was not simple. I do not know how much our input contributed to the Housing Policy of Namibia, but we shared the platform with those who produced the document, and that was the beginning of mingling and rubbing shoulders with intellectuals, although we hardly said anything.

As 1980 was coming to an end, we were getting ready for our graduation. It took place in January 1981 and the ceremony really moved me. It was the first time that as an individual, I felt a sense of accomplishment. My own name was called out and I moved up to the stage to receive my diploma. Although it happened to all of us, that fraction of a minute devoted to me alone in that big hall meant quite a lot. Besides speeches both from UNIN and SWAPO leaderships reminding the graduates of the responsibility lying ahead of us as future public servants of Namibia, our parents were represented at our graduation. Mr and Mrs Hoebeb had travelled all the way from home and were specifically there to represent our parents. Although their own son Michael was also among us as graduates, we were filled with joy to share his parents at our graduation, an event that propelled us into our next assignments.

Immediately after the graduation, the majority of our colleagues left for Luanda, except for Lydia, Elisette and me. By then, the SWAPO Headquarters had shifted from Lusaka to Luanda and every time we accomplished an assignment, we had to report to the Headquarters for further instruction. In the case of the three of us, it appeared that we were cleared already for the next assignment. We were to go for further studies to France, and this was not news to us by then. As soon as we had returned from Mozambique, the appropriate authority at UNIN engaged the three of us. First as a group, but when it became clear that we were a bit overwhelmed, it became a one on one discussion. The appropriate authority was none other than the late Mosé Tjitendero, the first Speaker of the National Assembly of the Republic of Namibia. He had the gentle manner to convince us.

↬

In April 1981, we were ready to return to France; this time for university studies. It really did not sound real. We were going to study in France, and in French, and at university level! Studying abroad among Namibians in exile was nothing extraordinary. Young Namibians left so often to various destinations for studies. People were constantly leaving for or arriving from the Soviet Union, the USA, Canada, the GDR, Nigeria, Cuba, Sierra Leone and many other countries. But until then, no one spoke of France. And here we were, getting ready to study in France.

The departure date arrived and we were on our way to the airport. The French Ambassador to Zambia was there, so was the Director of UNIN, Comrade Hage Geingob. He did not say much to us, he spoke most of the time with the French Ambassador. His presence though made us feel that he understood our anguish. When the time came for us to depart, he walked a bit with us, and as the aircraft closed, we were somehow certain that he stood there to make sure that we left.

Arriving in France this time was not eventful. We had been there just over a year ago and we knew what to expect. We returned to the CAVILAM language centre in Vichy and we settled in. The Namibian students who were there had left to various parts of France for further studies, and we would do the same after we had completed our language course. We went through the various levels of the French classes and I must say, we started enjoying learning French. In September the same year, we joined a group of Caribbean teachers of French who arrived there to study for a Diploma in Teaching French as a Foreign Language. Obviously, this was a course specifically for foreigners who taught French as Foreign Language. It was a combination of improving one's ability to speak French while at the same time, acquiring pedagogical skills to teach French. I wasn't sure at the time that we were in France to learn how to teach French, but it became clear that this was the agreement. It didn't matter either who was involved in the agreement, but as things stood at that time, I was on the verge of my career as a French teacher, but without the slightest clue as to whom I would teach French.

The course that served as the first step for my newly discovered career took place in two different towns. Half of the week we attended classes in Vichy, but the second half of the week we had to travel to Clermont-Ferrand. That meant taking a train to get there in the morning and to return to Vichy in the evening. The back and forth travelling was not hard, but the classes at the university were out of our reach. The first day, when we rushed from the train station straight into a lecture hall with hundreds of French students, it became a completely new world. As soon as we had settled in, a professor would walk in for French Literature. After a few lessons, I knew that French Literature was not for me. The book used, *En attendant Godot* by Samuel Beckett, was just inexplicable. But the professor and a handful of French students made sense out of each paragraph. I knew that we were supposed to have read the relevant parts before the class, but it did not help a single bit. I did not understand half of the vocabulary; I hardly understood the concept, and I obviously missed the meaning. This was not a one day or a one week business. I was to endure this for the entire academic year. I knew I was not alone in this, but these are times when one really feels personally challenged.

After months passed at a snail's pace, I managed to scrape through my exams. Today, I am in possession of that famous teaching diploma of the French language, only meant for foreigners who are teachers of French as a foreign language. A bit complicated, but that is my first French qualification.

After this hard and proper French academic year, we had again to return to the language centre to sharpen our French language skills. In September 1983, we were going to move to Clermont-Ferrand to study full time at the University Blaise Pascal. We already knew the town and the university set up. We needed only to adjust as full time residents and students. I was to remain here for the next three years. During those three years, besides studying, I did a few other things including getting married and having my first child born in the very same town.

5

Married just for a few months

Towards the end of 1980, I met someone I considered to be nice and responsible. And indeed he was. His name was Aaron Uazeua. By then, he was a second year student at UNIN where I was about to complete my studies. Early in 1981, as I waited to go to France, he left for Ethiopia for secondment. Our relationship was going to survive on letter writing until he was sent to Ljubljana, Yugoslavia, for further studies in 1982. Ljubljana was not next door to Vichy in France where I started off, but we were at least on the same continent. This was the time I discovered travelling in Europe and all that it involved.

After Aaron had visited me twice in Vichy, we agreed that it was my turn to go to Yugoslavia. When agreeing to such things, one normally does not foresee details linked to the undertakings of this nature. I knew that my going to Ljubljana would mean taking a flight from Lyon. Closer to the time, I also found out that I needed something called a visa. I had heard about visas before from the French teacher at UNIN. Every time we went to France, he spoke of the importance of obtaining a visa for each of us. The difference however was that before, someone else was responsible for obtaining visas for us. This time things were different; I wanted to go to Yugoslavia and I had to obtain my own visa. I eventually found out that a visa would be issued by an office of the country where I was going to, in this case, the Yugoslavian Consulate. How would I find the Consulate? I needed to go all the way to Lyon. And since I had no clue about the procedure, I traveled to Lyon and back to Vichy. A few days later, I took the train back to Lyon, this time to catch my flight. Were I smart enough, I would have just gone once. But smartness on such concepts was very remote then.

My first visit to Yugoslavia was straightforward. Aaron was at the airport in Zagreb when I landed, and all I did was follow him. A few months later, I decided to go back to Yugoslavia for Christmas. It was very cold and this time I wasn't alone. I went with another student, Aaron's friend Appolus. Since we were two, we didn't see the need for Aaron to travel from Ljubljana, just to pick us up in Zagreb. I was confident that after my first but only visit I would find my way.

The bus trip from Zagreb to Ljubljana was perfect. The final destination of the bus was the main bus station of Ljubljana. At the bus stop in Ljubljana, I had to find the bus to the campus where Aaron and the others were supposed to be living. Naïvely, I believed there was only one university campus, and I had been to this specific one before with Aaron. When the bus driver did not react when I mentioned that we were going to the university campus, I was not concerned as I was certain of recognising the bus stop closer to the campus once we got there. Pretty soon I was going to find out how very wrong I was. It was late and already dark. Since it was winter everything was buried under snow. Looking through the window didn't help as I could hardly see. And with a lot of snow, everything looked so different. But on top of that, it became very certain that the bus was going in a direction I had never been.

From our departure point, the bus was packed full of people and after a while, there were just the two of us. The driver looked at us through the rear view mirror, and said something to us. We came closer to him to explain that we didn't understand and that we wanted to go to the University campus. The man attempted again to explain what was about to happen, but there was no communication between him and us. We were not yet worried. Nothing could go wrong in the bus. Once he had gone to the final bus stop of his route, he would go back to the main bus station where we started off, and we would disembark and figure out what to do next. But this was not the plan of this bus driver. At one point he stopped to explain something to us and he tried to back up his explanation with energetic gestures. We looked at him and comforted ourselves that he would understand our dilemma when we got off at the main bus stop.

Next thing we found ourselves in a parked bus among so many other buses, of course also parked for the rest of the night. The driver got off and indicated to us to do the same. By the look of things, it was knocking off time for this man and he would return to town only the following day. Looking at the time we had spent on the bus, it was clear that we were completely out of town. And if this driver didn't understand English, how possible would it be to find someone in this place who could direct us to find our way back to town? The situation started to look serious.

We started walking without knowing in which direction to go. We just knew that we had to move. We desperately needed to get somewhere and find people to assist us to find our way back to town. We knew the language would be a challenge, but we were in a situation that required urgent assistance. We had no clue where we were, the weather was unbearable and if we were not going to find assistance in an hour or so, the cold would take its toll on us. We were going through soft snow that came up to above our ankles. We did not have suitable shoes, or warm and rain-proof clothes. I could feel my wet feet getting numb and my wet clothes stuck on my skin. We were really cold. As we walked on without knowing whether our path was leading anywhere, we noticed a faint light in the distance. We hurriedly struggled through the snow towards the light. As we came closer, we noticed that this was a small petrol station. If these people could just let us in somewhere to get out of this wet and cold weather, even just for five minutes! As soon as the light of the petrol station shone on us and the petrol attendants had taken a close look at us, they hurried into a little room and the whole place went motionless. We didn't despair immediately. We still walked up to the little room and knocked at the door. When there was no response, we knocked again. We had seen people going into this room, why were they not responding? After our second knock, one of them dared to barely push aside the curtain and peep at us. Then the curtain closed again and it was a total silence. If we had a car, we could have taken as much petrol as we wanted. These guys were not going to come out.

We had to give up and hopelessly moved on. When would we get help? And what if we didn't? The thought was just too scary, so we convinced ourselves that somewhere, someone would come to our rescue. After a while, we saw a group of people standing under the falling snow. They must have been waiting for something. There were quite a number of them and there was no room close by in which they could lock themselves. So, we decided to walk towards them and see if they could assist us to get transport back to town. From our conversation backed up with gestures, it turned out that they were waiting for a bus to Ljubljana. We had finally made it. We were no longer certain about how and when we were going to find the Namibian students. At this stage, we just wanted first to get back to Ljubljana's main bus station.

The bus came and as we finally sat in the bus, out of the rain, out of the cold and out of the dark, we tried to make sense out of what had happened to us since our arrival in Ljubljana some four hours ago. Certainly, we, in particular I, had made silly mistakes including getting on a bus without paying attention where exactly it was going. Appolus was obviously unhappy with me because this was his first time to Yugoslavia and I assured him that I knew the way. But this was not the time to criticise each other. But why had those people at the petrol station locked themselves in that little room? After a number of speculations, we concluded that we must have been far out in remote areas where these poor Yugoslavs had not seen black people before. We couldn't find another explanation.

Back in Ljubljana at the main bus station, we had to find our way to wherever the Namibian students were. The problem was that the last time I was here, Aaron and his colleagues were still doing a language course and resided at an International Centre where most foreign students stayed. It was a well-known place and one didn't really need to know the address. The Centre was close to a university campus to which we went on foot. I was convinced that we could just ask around and be directed to the place, and from there walk over to the campus. What I didn't know though, was that after completing their language course, the Namibians moved to a different University campus in a completely different part of town. What a nice way of finding out that there are after all so many different campuses in Ljubljana. Amazingly, I had not taken note of the exact address of the campus where Aaron had moved. He must certainly have given it to me, but addresses were not concepts we assimilated. We still believed in descriptions on how to get around.

At the bus stop, we started asking whether anyone knew Namibian students. Certainly, hardly anyone there had heard of a Namibian nationality. By then, it was about 02:00 in the morning. One kind man offered to accompany us to one of the campuses, but he made it clear to us that there were many of them. At the entrance of the first campus, we thanked him, and we took off in search of our compatriots. One of the students, whom we met on the ground floor of one of the residences, told us that at the entrance of each residence, there was a list of names of the students living there. Only then did we understand that there were many campuses and each of them consisted of several residences. We took time to go through the lists at the entrances of all these buildings, but no name sounded vaguely Namibian. Next, we decided to look for a name that sounded a bit African. We found one and decided to go up and knock at that door. We woke up the person and he turned out to be Cameroonian. After apologising and explaining what we had gone through since our arrival in the town, he took pity on us. He went with us to wake up another African who would probably know some Namibians. After having woken up a number of people, someone called a taxi to take us to the right campus and finally the right residence. Aaron had no words when he saw us. Meanwhile they had phoned France ten times to establish whether we had really left. He didn't want to remind me of how long he had stood at the station waiting for us. Instead, he warmed water for us to put our feet in to bring life back to them after what the cold weather had inflicted on them.

～

After this cursed winter visit, I was to return to Ljubljana during the 1983 summer holidays, this time to marry Aaron. I didn't give much thought to my getting married. At that time and at that age, and in my little way of thinking and perceiving things, that was the right thing to do. I was twenty-five years old and, back home, many girls married much younger than that.

Before embarking upon yet another trip to Yugoslavia, I paid a quick visit to my friend Nangula Kalomoh in Paris. I first met Nangula at Pendukeni's home in Lusaka in 1978. By then, her husband was the SWAPO representative to Senegal and Nangula and I cemented our friendship during my two month stay in Senegal in 1980. In early 1981, her husband was reassigned to open the SWAPO Office in Paris and since then, I had been a regular visitor in Paris.

This particular time, however, my quick visit, just a few days before my departure for Ljubljana, had a specific purpose: I went to borrow Nangula's wedding dress. I am sure today people find this unthinkable, but that was exactly why I went to Paris on that particular occasion. After trying on the dress and after Nangula's many hilarious comments about the fashion and the bad luck this might bring, I neatly packed everything I needed for my wedding. These were hard times. And I was a student, so was Aaron. Fashion was not an issue, and those days, the meaning of bad luck did not mean much. I had all that I needed for my wedding, including plastic flowers. The only two outstanding items were the ring and the shoes, and I would find them in Yugoslavia.

This time, my trip to Yugoslavia was uneventful. After landing in Zagreb, Aaron was there to pick me up. The wedding was going to be pretty soon after the 26th of August celebrations. I joined Aaron and his fellow students on their tour for the celebration of this day which was held high by all SWAPO cadres. This was the day, back in 1966, that SWAPO started the armed liberation struggle against the illegal occupation of Namibia by apartheid South Africa. The date was celebrated by all SWAPO members, irrespective of where we found ourselves. In August 1983, Namibians in Yugoslavia toured a number of towns to raise awareness about the Namibian plight. So, I simply went along.

There was not much to prepare for the wedding. We quickly found rings and shoes and I was ready to get married. Tate Billy Mwaningange, SWAPO representative to Yugoslavia, had to travel for more than 10 hours all the way from Belgrade by train to marry us in accordance with SWAPO laws. We could have married under the Yugoslav laws, but others had married under these laws in the camps both in Angola and Zambia and we were going to do exactly the same. The ceremony did not take long. Soon we were in a small room sharing some food and drinks and chatting with a few comrades who were around. No family members, no close friends. Pretty soon thereafter, Tate Mwaningange, the only person there I could claim I knew closely, shook my hand and took leave to return to Belgrade. I thanked him for having performed the rituals and we parted.

I did not feel any different compared to the previous day. Was this all that getting married was about? Step into a white dress, smile a bit and state 'I do' and one was really married? This seemed to be the case. I stayed in Ljubljana for another week or so after my wedding and it was time to return to France.

October 1983 was the start of my first year as a fully-fledged university student and I had to be there on time. Married or not, I still had studies to complete. Back in France and in Clermont-Ferrand, I reflected a bit on my new status. It didn't really have any effect on me. Maybe it did not have to! I took up my room on the 7th floor at Philippe Lebon Residence and student life started in all earnest. I was a second year student and there was work to be done. Although my French was good and I had captured what could be considered sufficient reasoning in the French system, I still had to work harder to obtain my *Diplôme Universitaire d'Etudes Generales* (DEUG) in June 1984. This is the very first qualification in the French university system before pursuing a *Licence* (the equivalent of the Bachelor's degree) and *Maîtrise* (Master's). Since this DEUG was the key to anything associated with success at university level, I started working right away. The continued support of a scholarship by the French Government for the following academic year also depended on my academic performance. SWAPO was interested only in knowing whether I had accomplished what I came to France for and not what I had achieved in addition to that. I would also not have been proud of myself to have excelled in extramural activities but not have academic qualifications to present.

Well, as I applied my mind to my studies, I also tried to get my marriage going. Disturbingly, Aaron responded only occasionally to my letters and as the time went by, a month could easily pass without hearing from him. Yet, post office services and telephone calls between France and Yugoslavia worked perfectly well. And he had phoned regularly in the past. What could be the matter? I couldn't really figure out a reasonable answer. I decided to concentrate on my studies and to sort out my marriage when the right time came. I was far away from home and I had a mission to accomplish. Getting worried about a husband who was so far away was only natural but seemingly there was nothing I could do about his sudden silence. If he decided not to phone, maybe he didn't have money. We were living under difficult circumstances. Things would certainly improve soon, I hoped. Others had husbands on the battlefield and they might not have had news for months. Yet they kept faith and hope. Nonetheless, Yugoslavia and the front were two different things. But I decided not to bother myself. There were more serious things to worry about!

I pressed on with my studies and did just well. That's why I was here! Marriage was a new phenomenon in my life and it did not have much meaning for me yet. Yes, in my culture, it is expected that young people get married at a certain age. I must admit I was satisfied with myself for having got married and looked forward to a harmonious and caring marriage. But since this was still something I was to experience, I did not attach so much importance to it.

I had friends and comrades who cared about me. I received news from my family in Namibia from time to time. Besides my mission to study as my humble contribution to the liberation struggle, I had my siblings back home whom I would hopefully give a helping hand to one day. This would be a golden opportunity to stand in for my dear late mother. And nothing else could give me so much sense of fulfilment. So, as much as marriage was important, I had quite a number of other callings to attend to. I gladly would have carried out all my callings but under no circumstances would I drop everything else simply because one was getting stagnant. I decided to fortify myself with the other callings that were as important. These were struggle days, and as cadres of a liberation movement, endurance was part of the struggle.

Five months after my wedding I received a substantial letter from Aaron. He had no money, and he wanted money from me to come and visit me in France. The letter reached me as I was about to leave for Paris for Easter holidays. I was quite pleased to hear that my husband, who had gone quiet for a while, was after all coming to see me. I cannot remember how much money I was supposed to send, but I vividly remember going to the Post Office in Paris to send the money in French Francs. It was not clear to me as to why the amount had to be in French Francs and not the equivalent in Yugoslav currency. It did not really matter that much and I just sent the money. After sending my French Francs, the date I was promised that Aaron would come, came and went. The episode disturbed me. Aaron asked me to send an exact amount of money in French Francs, which I did. Yet, not only did he not come for the promised visit, he did not bother to provide an explanation.

Women are people with hearts and I was going to be just that for a while. I tried to understand why I was requested for money for transport for a visit to France. And this after a lengthy period of silence. After the dispatch of the money, there was yet again complete silence. I became analytical and reasoned that, by nature, men are weak. Marrying a man and leaving him alone must have been too hard for him. Maybe I shouldn't have done that. But what was it that he didn't understand? We both were members of a liberation movement and we knew too well that the liberation of our country came above everything. There were no exceptions. I would go back to Yugoslavia and make him understand all this. I decided to be firm next time. But he was politically mature. What then could have gone wrong?

∽

By June 1984, I had my exams behind me. As soon as I knew that I had successfully completed my DEUG, I booked my ticket for Ljubljana. I would leave in early July and only return to France on 12 October. I was comfortably accepted in *Licence*, the third year. There was absolutely no rush to come back. I would only be back for registration a few days before the resumption of classes.

I had communicated timely to Aaron the date and time of my arrival at the Zagreb airport. The first worrying thing was that he never responded and when I arrived in Zagreb, Aaron was simply not there to meet me. And this was exactly nine months since we last saw each other. I was of course bothered that he was not there but since I had come this far, I could just as well get on the bus and get to Ljubljana by myself. By then, I knew my way to and within Ljubljana. I went straight to his room and knocked on the door. No answer, but the room was not locked. I put my luggage down and went to find out from other Namibians who were living close by. As soon as the first compatriot I met had set eyes on me, there was a distinctly surprised gaze. Why that surprised look, as if to mean that seeing me here in Ljubljana was the last thing he would have expected! Yet he had seen me here several times before, and he had even attended my wedding nine months ago.

We greeted and he mumbled some explanation why Aaron was not in his room at this time of the day. He advised that I should return to the room while he went to look for Aaron. I had no difficulty with the proposal and I returned to Aaron's room. After an hour or so, Aaron turned up. He wore a confused look and clearly, something was not right. I immediately started blaming myself. Why did I marry this poor man and leave him by himself? He was maybe not as strong as I first thought. What happened to him while I was gone? He somehow explained that he found himself in a difficult situation, but he also made it clear that there were a number of things he could not talk about at this stage. Although disappointed, I felt pity for him and I decided to give the situation some time. I was not in a hurry. I was after all here for close to three months. Within this time, we would certainly have sufficient time to talk things through.

After a few days, I was certain that Aaron was no longer the same person I had known. Although I could not point to anything specific, I sensed that something dramatic had happened. I was not even in Ljubljana for a week when Aaron spoke his mind. He went straight to the point. He did not think our marriage could continue. He wanted a divorce immediately. He kept it short and chose not to advance any reason. His pronouncement could not get through to me. Either I did not expect it, or this was the sort of thing I had been scared to hear for a while. At the pronouncement of the word divorce Aaron left, leaving me alone sitting there with a blank face.

What Aaron told me was devastating. I sat there by myself and tried to make sense of what I was going through. I literally could not process anything. But I was certain of one thing: Aaron stated his intention clearly. And the way he sounded, there was no room for changing his mind. I had to see how to deal with the issue, with myself and by myself. After I had overcome my shock, I pulled myself together, literally picking up pieces of myself, one by one, to become a whole self again. I picked up courage to return to the same compatriot I had seen the day of my arrival. He appeared to have expected me to come back. He had no words to console me. He told me that Aaron was going through a personal crisis. He was at pains to assure me that the cause of that personal crisis had absolutely nothing to do with me. He was perhaps right in his assumption but Aaron's personal crisis was affecting me directly. To put things mildly, I was right in a big mess. What would I do?

I went to see other Namibian friends, this time female comrades, two sisters whom I had known since secondary school days. One of them was studying in Ljubljana and the other one had come from Moscow to spend the summer holiday with her sister. Their advice was that in situations such as the one I found myself, one shouldn't rush into a decision. They insisted it would be prudent for me to take my time. They would be there for me and I could go and see them any time I felt it was necessary. It was a very kind offer, but I was still looking for a different explanation. The question of what I would do remained unanswered. And Aaron was not there to respond.

When he reappeared two days later, he had not changed his mind. He wanted a divorce as soon as possible and he wanted me to go back to France. This sounded final. As confused as I was, I knew that I had better find a way out of this situation. The same day, Aaron took me to the travel agency to have my air ticket changed so that I could leave on the next available flight. After having presented my case to the agency, I got a disappointing explanation. I had the cheapest students' air ticket which gave me only two options: either to get on the plane on the date indicated on the ticket, or to simply put the air ticket in the dustbin and purchase a new one. That infuriated Aaron and his position remained unchanged. He wanted only to see three things happening: immediate divorce, his ring and surname back, and my return to France the earliest I could. He disappeared again for a number of days.

This was certainly too much for me to bear. I was away from my usual base, France, I had no money to purchase another ticket, and I was simply at a loss. What had I done? What went wrong? How did Aaron change from the gentle person I had known for years to the cruel one I was now facing?

My tormented life for the next few months was set, and nothing was going to change the course. Aaron had left again and I was left alone. I turned to other Namibians, especially the two sisters, for meals and companionship. I spent most of my time with them and I confided so much in them. I also relied heavily on their support and advice. If only I knew how to get out of this mess! As I struggled to find a way out of the situation I suddenly felt funny, a feeling I had never known before. Getting sick would be the last thing I needed at this stage. After having described how I felt to the two sisters, all indications pointed to one sure thing: I could be pregnant. Bravo! I thought to myself. This on top of all troubles I was going through! The thought of a possible pregnancy did not disturb me as much as my terribly gloomy predicament of being rejected and abandoned while stuck in this place. Nothing prepared me for what I was going through all by myself. My thoughts wandered from one thing to the next and I considered everything, including committing suicide.

This crazy thought occurred to me often at night. I even knew how I was going to do it. Aaron's room was on the eighth floor and it was certain that if I let go, I wouldn't fail. After several nights wondering whether or not I should deliver myself from the agony, one night I just happened to think of my mother. Alone in the room, engulfed in the darkness in a foreign country, desperate for a solution which was impossible to find, I all of a sudden thought of my mother and of my feeling the day I received the news of her death. Could I subject my siblings to yet another sudden loss? My mother had no choice, but I did. No, I would not do it.

My two sisters and compatriots noticed my distress and tried their best to counsel me. By then, I was drinking, and even tried to smoke. Nothing was helping. I must have looked terrible and they spent as much time with me as possible. I could feel how gradually I was slipping into mental instability. I would walk to town without knowing why I needed to go there. When I happened to find myself in town one evening without knowing why I was there, I knew it was high time that I called myself to order. I went straight to catch a bus and returned to the campus. Back in the room, I sat down and this time I spoke to myself. Not in a whispering voice, but loud so that I could hear my own message to myself: 'I cannot afford to destroy myself because of another individual. Aaron was someone I have met away from home and he had really no obligation towards me. I have an obligation to myself, to the noble mission to liberate my country, and I have an obligation to my eight siblings some ten thousands of kilometres away from Yugoslavia. Why should I make Yugoslavia the place of my demise? I will pull myself together.'

Clearly, I would not be able to do this in Yugoslavia. I needed to find a way to return to France. At dawn, I got up and went straight to the compatriot I had contacted the day of my arrival in Ljubljana. I didn't want to keep him awake so early in the morning. I just wanted to ask him to do whatever he could to lend me money for my return to France. I undertook to send the money back to him as soon as I had reached France. He had no such money, and I understood that perfectly well. We agreed to rule out the flying back and to concentrate our efforts on getting money together for a train ticket. The means of transport was not an issue, as long as at the end of the journey I would return to France. He promised to consult his fellow Namibian students in Yugoslavia and see how much money they could collect for me. He advised that I should in the meantime obtain visas for the countries through which I would travel. This was already something, and I left feeling hopeful.

I did not really know how to find Aaron to tell him that I was finally organising myself to leave. If he happened to pop by and I wasn't in the room, he left a note saying: 'I was here.' When he finally turned up again, certainly to check whether I was still around, I told him that I was finally about to leave. I however needed his assistance to go to Zagreb to obtain some visas. He was quite pleased with this development and agreed to take me to Zagreb. I decided not to tell him my suspicions about my condition. This was my problem and everything else was postponed until after my return to France.

Aaron had suggested the date we were going to travel to Zagreb for my visas. The evening before our travel, he came around and appeared friendly. All of a sudden he wanted to know how I would manage once I got back to France. We no longer spoke of the divorce. We must have taken it as the obvious next thing to do. I personally was interested in nothing else, but to return to France. The rest could wait. To my dismay, Aaron informed me that for some reason, he could no longer accompany me to Zagreb the following day. He quickly added that I did not need to worry because he had arranged assistance with his friend, a Kenyan who lived in Zagreb. His friend would wait for me at the bus station in Zagreb, and would assist me to get to the Italian and Swiss Embassies. I did not insist on anything. It did not matter who assisted me to obtain those visas, as long as I got them.

As we were concluding discussion on my travel to Zagreb the following morning, another Namibian dropped in. When he heard that Aaron was unable to travel with me to Zagreb, he offered to take me. He expressed concern that I was going by myself to a town I did not know and I did not understand the language either. It was agreed there and then that he would come early the following day to accompany me to Zagreb. He and Aaron then left.

⌒

Early the following morning the two of us boarded the bus and three hours later, we were in Zagreb. We started with the Italian Embassy. I was assured that the visa could be issued in an hour's time. Instead of waiting in the Italian Embassy, we thought of going to the French Embassy to ascertain that with my student and resident cards, I wouldn't need a re-entry visa. One never knows! I had flown out of France and I was now entering by train. As I was desperate to leave Yugoslavia, I wanted to make one hundred percent sure that my journey back was not hindered by any careless omission from my side. We did not have the exact address of the French Embassy. We walked a bit in the direction the Italians had indicated, but we decided to stop to ask for directions. To my recollection, we stopped in front of a pharmacy. Right there, the unexpected happened and things moved really fast. I can remember a sharp pain on my forehead and small red stones and blood streaming down my face. Then my memory blanks out. The next thing I remember is being in an ambulance with my dress soaked with blood sticking to my skin. I remember screaming and a doctor trying to calm me down in a foreign language. I vaguely remember entering the hospital and a dose of some sleeping fluid must have been administered to me.

The next time I woke up I was under such bright lights and surrounded by many medical personnel. For the first time in my life, I felt vulnerable and could vividly feel my life slipping through my fingers. What had happened to me? Why, after so many precarious situations in the bush, was I now lying here in a faraway country about to die? I definitely needed to understand what had happened to me and what so many people were about to do to me. My eyes must have expressed panic and the team must have deemed it important to reassure me. But in which language would they reassure me? The first one spoke in their language and I demonstrated clearly that I didn't understand a thing. From my body language, they understood that they needed to respond to my question first before doing anything to me. What had happened and what were they doing to me? I first tried in English and clearly, no one understood. Next, I tried in French and again, no reaction from my medical team. Then I thought of repeating my question in my broken German and one of them reacted. Their story, the way I understood it, went like this: Somehow a huge stone landed on my forehead. I was very lucky that it landed where it did and not slightly to the left. I was also lucky because the X-rays did not reveal any crack of the skull. However, I had a deep cut on the forehead that necessitated eight stitches. The story was crystal clear and all the team expected from me was my calm cooperation. What else could I do? I was in trouble again and these people were only doing their job. Despite so many questions going through my mind, I decided to allow fate to decide. If I needed eight stitches, let it be so.

After the whole saga, the doctor explained that if he had had it his way, he would have kept me in the hospital in Zagreb. However, having heard the explanation of my companion, he gave me a recommendation letter addressed to the hospital in Ljubljana with the understanding that I would report to that hospital as soon as we got back. I thanked the doctor as I received the letter and I walked straight to my comrade. For a while, we walked quietly next to each other. I am sure that my appearance was also not conducive to conversation. My dress with dried blood all over it and my bandaged head must have been horrifying. The poor man could not reconcile the image of me in the morning with how I looked now. Even the Italians did not know what to say when I returned to pick up my passport.

We decided not to subject other people to my appearance. I was personally also terrified and wanted to get out of this town. But we decided to walk past the place of the incident just to ascertain that there was no construction activity happening. Maybe a builder had dropped a brick by accident. There was no sign of building activity. What happened then? The events of the day had worn me out and on the bus back to Ljubljana, I absent-mindedly gazed through the window without seeing anything. Once we had arrived in Ljubljana, my comrade suggested that we should immediately inform Aaron of what had happened. I had completely switched off and did not care what might happen to me next. Nothing worse was possible at this stage. He knew where to find Aaron and I simply walked behind him.

We stopped at a bar and he asked me to wait outside. I waited. He entered the place and soon thereafter, he emerged with Aaron. As soon as Aaron set eyes on me, he muttered something like, 'Such things can happen here.' Whatever it was, all that I wanted was to lie down and rest. The companion of the day took me to the students' residence. In the room, he tried to explain how important it was for me to rest and he advised that I should not lock the room. I did not look too well, and he would return the next morning to check on me. My system had completely given up and whatever was suggested to me was just fine. So, I fell asleep and woke up the following morning. I was still alive.

Early that morning, my comrade came. He reckoned my face was swollen and he advised that we go to the hospital. I did as I was told and pretty soon thereafter, we were in a waiting room at the hospital. The doctor examined the wound, said something in his language and I simply nodded. He must have noticed my indifference and he went to explain something to my comrade. They agreed and we left. We came back the next day, and it turned out it had to be every day. For the next few days I found myself walking to and back from the hospital. I do not know for how many days and I cannot recollect what exactly happened to me at the hospital. Time must have come to a standstill, and to a certain extent, so did my life. I however recall the day the doctor removed the stitches and declared that I did not need to come the following day. With that news, my mind clicked.

A few days earlier, Gerson Tjihenuna whom we called GT, the compatriot I had requested to collect money for my train ticket had informed me that he had enough money and the ticket could be purchased at any time. Straight from the hospital, I went to tell him that I was ready to go, there and then. My distress must have overwhelmed everybody and everybody was prepared to go out of their way to get me out of my misery. In no time I was informed that there was a train the same evening and if I was ready, I could travel the very same day. What was there to be done to get ready? I got my few personal items together and I was on my way to the train station. I did not have details of the train, but this did not really matter. What mattered was that I was finally leaving.

Almost every Namibian in town was there to see me off. This was a clear indication that from a distance, my comrades and compatriots observed me as I went through my agony but without knowing how to reach out to me. Now that the time had come for me to get out of this pathetic situation, they were all there to express their sympathy and care. A handshake, a stern look, a shy smile and a pat on the shoulder, each of these gestures carried a message of care and encouragement. Just before the departure of the train, Aaron rushed into the station on a bicycle. He managed to mutter a few words of goodbye, and the train pulled off.

Devoid of any feeling I left Ljubljana, a town where I suffered untold pain for four weeks. Yet, I was not bitter. I just wanted to get away. For endless hours, the train wound through a number of towns, stopping from time to time for passengers to get off and on. Except for getting up once or twice to go to the bathroom, I remained fixed in my seat. Nobody bothered me, not even the immigration officers as we went from one country to the next. It was a long journey; I might have slept occasionally, but my memory remains blank about this trip. Some time during the following morning, the train arrived in Paris. I immediately connected to go to Vichy.

As I stepped out of the train station, the hard reality hit me. I had left this town a month ago very excited to spend three summer months in Ljubljana. I was now arriving back, two months earlier than planned, after a full month of experiencing unbelievable hardship. All of a sudden a sensible question occurred to me: What will I do now? I had no answer and decided to get to my room first. There, I hoped to find some sort of answer.

Vichy was an obvious place to come back to for our holidays. Other foreign students including Namibians from various university towns were back here. I went to one of the hotels where I previously stayed to find a room. Having found a room I put down my bag but I remained very restless. I walked out to make a phone call. My friend Nangula answered the phone and she sounded very concerned. She advised that I should get back on the train and return to Paris. I do not know whether I did so the same day or only the following day, but I returned to Paris pretty soon.

I did not need to explain much. Nangula already knew all that had happened to me. She did not want me to bother about how she knew but rather to focus on regaining my well-being. In her eyes, I was not well and needed to recollect myself. We spent time speaking and when I mentioned to her the possibility of being pregnant, she lost no time in taking me to the doctor. The doctor confirmed my suspicion. Now, we had to figure out the way forward. I still had six weeks before I needed to return to my studies and Nangula was convinced that she was able to assist me in becoming psychologically fit and ready for my third year university studies. I put my trust in her and abandoned my whole being into her hands. She was, after all, a trained nurse by profession and she sounded convincing.

⸏

By the time I left Paris for Clermont-Ferrand in early October 1984, I was a healed person. My usual spirit had returned to me and I felt ready to continue my studies. Did I only feel this while in Paris next to Nangula or would I slip back into my pathetic hopeless situation once I was alone again? Maybe not; Nangula had repeated enough times to me that I had an additional responsibility, the child I was carrying. With renewed vigour, I returned to Clermont-Ferrand and took up my room on the 7th floor at Phillippe Lebon Residence. I knew that in my condition, I would not be allowed in the residence for too long. Taking up my room was only temporary. In two months, at the latest, I would have to be out. This didn't bother me at all. I settled in and registered, just like all the other students. The classes started and my student life was back to normal. I decided to shut the four weeks in Ljubljana out of my life. My responsibilities were back in my mind: my studies and my silent pledge to my eight siblings back home. I definitely had something to strive for and my mission was clear. Nothing could distract me!

I decided to confide in Monique, the French cleaning lady on my floor, about my condition. She was in her late forties and she showed me a motherly understanding. I was quite pleased with her reaction and I spent a lot of time speaking to her. I had unexpectedly found a perfect accomplice. I could sleep between classes and thirty minutes before the next class, she would gently knock on my door to warn me that it was again time to go for classes. A month later, I could hardly conceal my condition any longer. I managed another two months in the residence thanks to my accomplice. As usual, the office of the matron of the residence was on the ground floor and it would have been extremely difficult to pass by her office without her seeing me and I had to pass by at least four times a day. Monique offered to be a spy. Every time I needed to go out of the residence, she would quickly go down to check the whereabouts of Madame Primot, the matron, and she called me to rush out when it was safe to do so. If need be, the matron was just distracted while I was passing.

⤿

Time came however for me to move out. With the assistance of the Social Assistance Service of the university, I had found a one-bedroomed flat in the vicinity of the university. But the flat was unfurnished! Monique, a cleaner and with a butcher husband, was there to render me a helping hand in the time of real need. She found a way of providing me with all the basics: a bed, bedding, kitchen utensils, furniture and a television. On top of that she would pop by to check up on me. My friend Nangula phoned often and I could go to Paris any time I had a long weekend. Other Namibian friends, in particular Marina and Chief Kaulinge, phoned often from Berlin. We called him 'Chief' because his first name was Mandume, the first name of the last king of Uukwanyama, Mandume ya Ndemufayo. It is true that I was in trouble, but so many friends and comrades cared, and that was an absolute consolation for me. I still recall and cherish late Maxton Mutongolume's phone call from somewhere in Europe, just to say that he was aware of what was happening to me. Such gestures are simply special.

As much as I had this tremendous support and show of solidarity, deep inside my heart I was still concerned about my future as a young woman. I was hardly married, left the man I married a year ago in the most uncertain circumstances, was one month pregnant, and had total silence from him since then. What would I do? Would I get divorced? What did divorce entail anyway? If I did, what would I do next? What about the child I was carrying? And, and, and... The questions were just endless and I couldn't find an answer to a single one.

Amidst all this, sleep completely deserted me. As much as I felt tired in front of my black and white television, I was wide awake as soon as I got into bed. I saw myself helplessly getting into a situation where I went to bed by 23:00 and got up at 06:00 to get to classes, but without closing my eyes for a minute. And this was not for a day. It was for weeks and at least for more than three months. I was tired but I had to attend all my classes nonetheless. My doctor got worried and prescribed sleeping pills. He explicitly explained that taking sleeping pills in my condition was not at all advisable. In his own words, 'We have no choice.' The sleep was simply not forthcoming.

I decided not to burden my friends with this development. They had helped me enough. I had to go through this last bit by myself. During one of the visits to the clinic, the doctor repeated the examination over and over, and as he was murmuring to himself citing numbers, I could guess that there was a problem. When he finally put his instrument aside, he bluntly told me that the baby was no longer growing, and that was a real cause of concern. This was my first time, and I could not really grasp why the doctor was getting anxious. He decided that I should go for a medical check up every Monday. I had no problem with that. My faculty was not far from the hospital and every Monday, I would drop in on my way from classes. Again and again, the poor doctor explained to me how concerned he was because of a number of technical issues. I naïvely listened to him and once he was done, I took leave from him undertaking to see him again the following Monday.

Things were really not fine although, despite my sleeping trouble, I felt perfectly fine. It was April 1985 and the doctor had predicted that the baby would arrive at the end of May. We still had time. I was wrong! On Monday, 22 April, I stopped at the doctor as usual. To my surprise, the doctor's opinion was brutal and alarming, 'We can no longer continue this way. The time has come to act and this has to be today, not tomorrow.' As much as I looked forward to the arrival of a little companion, I had anticipated this only in a future perspective. I seriously didn't expect this to be thrown in my face that particular Monday. With what this doctor was telling me, the process had to happen that particular day and by the next day, there would be a baby. This was a huge development and change, and although I had already purchased some baby clothes, I wasn't at all prepared to have a baby the next day. This French doctor was not at all concerned about my view on his proposal. It was about lunchtime and by 17:00 latest I must be back at the hospital for admission. Next patient, please! He was done with me and he would see me later that afternoon after my admission.

I breathed hard and walked home to pack my bag. Before I started packing though, I called Nangula and another friend in Germany. They were both not alarmed and promised to call me once the baby was born. They both had gone through this and could only wish me well. I wanted to hear something else, although I didn't know exactly what. In the absence of the solidarity I was looking for, I packed my bag and walked back to the hospital. I didn't feel anything that suggested that I was going to have my baby in the coming few hours, but this was what the doctor had said. Back at the hospital, I settled comfortably in an individual room. The doctor came around and explained the procedures and before he left, he stated confidently that I would have the baby latest in the early hours of the following morning. That was not too far, I thought to myself, and lay there with eyes wide open waiting. I could not afford to sleep, I should not miss out on anything. In the middle of the night, I felt exactly the same way as when I had arrived at the hospital. Next thing I saw the staff going around serving breakfast. I still had no baby and there wasn't the slightest sign of a baby coming.

The next doctor on duty appeared to be perplexed that I was still lying there smiling. He again went through my file and left the room. When he returned some thirty minutes later, he had a different suggestion, and he was convinced this time it would work. I was moved to a different room full of different equipment. Two smiling nurses arrived and I was put on a drip. Besides the pain of the needle, the following two hours were very pleasant. The nurses were friendly and did not leave me alone for a minute. We chatted about Namibia and I happily answered all questions in every detail possible. Homesickness made one say so many things about the very same thing. And I was not in hurry, all indications pointed to one thing: I would be here for the rest of the day. So, why rush through my explanations. Little did I know that I was wrong! From one minute to another, my explanation came to a sudden halt. Whatever was happening, did not allow me to continue my conversation. The French I had accumulated over years deserted me and the only language in which I could make myself reasonably understood was Oshiwambo. The nurses did not show any surprise, they must have often experienced this sudden change in the manner and mode of communication. Over the next 10 hours, the kind French nurses were there to perform their job, and they did it to the letter. The process which started at 09:00 in the morning was still going on in the evening. At about 20:00, I had enough of all these machines and I pleaded to be allowed to go home. 'This is definitely not the time to go home', one responded. The response was very clear and I waited for whatever was to happen to me. It couldn't be worse than what I was going through already. At 21:30 exactly, my daughter was there. Did she really need to take this long? The doctor happily showed her to me, stating how pretty she was, the nice colour of her hair etc. I seriously thought that this was not the time to make all those compliments to a little baby girl who took all her time to come into this world.

After that kind of a night and day, altogether a total of 24 hours of wakefulness, I badly needed my sleep. I could see the baby the following day. She was here to stay. When I woke up the next morning, I was in the ward and was informed that I would stay seven full days in the hospital. The rule prescribed a full week's training in all matters related to young babies before going home. And that was not the end, social workers would drop in at home occasionally, unannounced for that matter, just to make sure that mothers were not in any away mishandling their own children. I considered it hyper supervision, but that was how things were going to be. Meanwhile I had all these many days to rest and to observe how the nurses bathed and fed my daughter, and occasionally, I had to demonstrate whether I had assimilated what was being passed on to me. I really made use of the seven days to catch up on my sleep. Being among so many other mothers and surrounded by so many professional workers reassured me so much that I slept most of the time. After all, I had months of sleepless nights behind me.

6

My life gains new meaning

I called my daughter Palenyondjila (Paleni for short), meaning 'pave the way (back home)'. Seven days later, I was back in my flat. The sudden difference in my life was amazing. The first development was that I was no longer alone. I had this little companion. Initially, I was scared of getting back into my habit of sleeplessness. Surprisingly, the seven nights at the hospital had just got me into the sleeping mood. My baby was also a reassuring phenomenon. Quietness and silence were no longer part of my flat. My life was all of sudden lively and meaningful. From there on, I got myself into a remarkable and enjoyable routine. Either I was feeding, bathing or simply busy with my daughter or I was cooking, eating, and then, whenever it was possible, I was studying as much as I could. I had my hands full. It was the best thing that could have happened to me. I had no time to be worried about anything.

Three weeks after the arrival of my daughter, it was time to go back to my classes. In just less than a month, I would write my final examinations. I took Paleni to Monique at my old residence whenever I had to go for classes. Other students also offered to babysit her whenever they were free. The offers were overwhelming and I felt blessed in so many ways. The sense of abandonment deserted me completely and I found myself enveloped in a wave of care and true solidarity. I experienced a real sense of contentment and a real release from a trap. The mere presence of my few weeks' old daughter suddenly gave me a real sense and pleasure of life. She was the only thing I had, and her being there with me constituted my new purpose in life. One thing was constantly on my mind, I was solely responsible for her existence and I quietly vowed to her to make her well-being one of my core purposes.

With such a vow, I was to forge ahead. My exams were just around the corner. I organised my life better and created a routine for my daughter. Early evenings she was sleeping and I plunged into my notes as long as I could hold out. During the days of exams, I carried my daughter to Monique, with my writing pad under my arm. Three or so hours later I was on my way back to collect her. Back home, we went through our daily routine which ended with more revision. After a few more exams, I was done with the third academic year and if all went well, I would receive my *Licence*, equivalent to a Bachelor's degree.

As soon as I had my exams behind me, I packed a few belongings and together with my daughter left on a train to Paris for the summer holidays. I was not sure how long I would stay in France, but I was ready to return to SWAPO. I was convinced that 1985 would be my final year. Why should I go beyond the BA? Surprisingly, the French Ministry of Foreign Affairs offered me a one-month advanced French language course at the Alliance Française in Paris. But this was not the only reason I was going to Paris. I was also going to spend time with Nangula. I had come to rely heavily on her and every time I had a few free days, the only natural thing for me was to go to her. I could not imagine myself doing otherwise. Why exactly was I to do a one month French course? The most important thing was that it was going to be in Paris and I would stay with Nangula.

⤸

Once in Paris, I started my French language course. Nangula looked after Paleni. A month later, I received my exam results. I had my *Licence* and the French Government offered another academic year bursary for *Maîtrise*. My goodness, did I really need a Master's? What would I do with all these papers? I did not even have a country to make use of these qualifications. Who on earth was going to look at these pieces of papers and offer me employment? I thought I had struggled enough to obtain a *Licence*, and now with a baby, it was really time to go back to the camps. The SWAPO Representative to France, Nangula's husband, had a different view. Independent Namibia would need a qualified work force. If the French Government was offering this kind of support to SWAPO, we should welcome it. What was it that I was going to do in the camps? There were thousands of others sitting there keenly waiting for these kinds of opportunities. We were to make use of the time and opportunities optimally. A year would be over fast and a Master's would definitely be better than a *Licence*. He and his wife were there to offer any support I would need. So, I must make use of the opportunity because so many others would come after me, and it was always good to show that we were serious and appreciative of the support offered to us as a liberation movement.

After such motivating, comradely but authoritative advice, I agreed to give it a try. It was not a question of agreeing; this was an obvious reaction expected from Party cadres. Ours was a life based on absolute discipline and orderly following of SWAPO Party orders. At the end of my three months' holiday in Paris, I packed up to return to Clermont-Ferrand. Nangula and her husband had shared with me and my daughter, whatever basic baby items they had for their son who was born during our stay. I returned to Clermont with all that I needed for my daughter, including a pram. What a relief for my student life!

My academic year started off well. The social workers at the university advised and assisted me to apply for financial support for my daughter. All of a sudden I could buy disposal nappies and other goodies for Paleni. I could even pay for the sort of baby daycare service offered by baby sitters at their private homes called *Nourrices*. Every morning I would drop my daughter at the *Nourrice* and pick her up later in the evening. To my delight, my student life became normal again. I could spend the whole day at the faculty, eat at the cafeteria and spend time in the library. All these without the slightest rush! The *Nourrice* was so kind and Paleni was an uncomplicated little one. She could really be with anybody.

The year passed very quickly. Soon we found ourselves bracing ourselves for the winter at the end of 1985. I would push Paleni in her pram through snow and one evening, after a very cold day, I noticed some swimming white mucous in her eyes. I panicked and there was nobody to advise. I completely forgot to phone Nangula. The obvious thing for me was to phone the doctor to inform him that my baby was suffering from some kind of terrible eye condition which I imagined could lead to blindness. The doctor seemed to have known a little about my imagination by then and did not sound alarmed when I called him late in the evening. He politely listened to me and after a lengthy explanation of why I was absolutely convinced that my daughter's vision was in the final stage of destruction, the doctor simply stated that this kind of minor eye infection was a usual occurrence during cold weather. It would clear in a day or two, he reassured me. With that, I took another close look at my daughter. She did not at all display any signs of suffering. She was as playful and loud as usual. I decided to wait till the following morning.

This was not the only day that I phoned the same doctor with some unusual story. One evening, when Paleni was just eight months old, I found her unusually loud in her baby language. I decided to call the doctor and informed him that my daughter could be mentally challenged and that I definitely needed an appointment to bring her in immediately. The doctor, without making me feel stupid, again reassured me. Should there have been the slightest doubt about the mental status of my daughter, they would have informed me accordingly by the time I was three months pregnant. What a statement! After those two incidents, I decided never to call the doctor. When Paleni one day playfully picked up one of my belts and turned it into a microphone during one of her singing episodes in her baby cot, I just looked on and hoped that nothing was seriously wrong. Without realising it, I was gradually getting out of the panicky phase of young motherhood.

Soon Paleni was a year old and I was about to write my exams. My life had completely turned around and I was a normal person again. My focus was on two things: my daughter and my studies. As a mother, my daughter became my natural occupation number one. My focus on my studies was naturally linked to my belonging to our liberation struggle and obviously to my wishful pledge to my siblings back home. Amazingly, other concerns got cut out of my life. I was just happy and content with what I had at that moment. Paleni was a real entertainer, and my days were filled with joy. This was an achievement for me.

Never did I want to look back until one day I received a phone call from Chief Kaulinge from Berlin. Obviously, when I heard his voice, I was very happy. This was not the first time he had phoned. He phoned me often to reassure and encourage me. But this time he phoned for a different reason. Someone else wanted to speak to me. I trusted Chief, so I curiously waited while he handed over the phone to the main caller.

'Hello, it's me. I'm in Berlin on my way to Angola. How is the child, and when are you coming to Angola?' I certainly knew the sound of Aaron's voice, but when I listened to him this time, my whole being was shielded from any emotion. I listened, and I heard his words, and I finally heard myself responding, 'What child?' He knew about my daughter? And it was only then that he was asking? That was way too late! He went through a long explanation of being aware of my daughter and that he was looking forward to seeing us back in Angola. That was a good assumption, but my heart was at a standstill. It was close to two years since I had left Ljubljana, emotionally dead and a month pregnant. I went through what it took to heal my soul and to bring my child into this world. Other people helped and supported me without fail until I finally got back on my feet. Two years later, my husband's only question was, 'How is the child, and when are you coming to Angola?' This was nothing else but a simplified way of looking at things.

After the unexpected phone call, I calmly continued my student life. I wrote my exams and in October 1986 I was ready finally to return to Africa. I did not quite have my Master's Degree yet. I had to rewrite one subject. For one subject, I would not spend a whole academic year in France. I would come back for a supplementary exam. It was high time that I went back. Although I had arrived in France from Zambia, SWAPO's Headquarters were in Luanda, Angola, and that was where all of us had to report. My ticket was booked accordingly.

⤳

I packed the belongings I had accumulated over a period of five years. My baby daughter as well! I hadn't been back to Angola since 1977, and that was where I was heading. I had no clue what to expect upon my arrival, but I happily gazed at the clouds racing by as I sat on the UTA flight bound for Luanda. My one and half year old daughter, when not sleeping, entertained me. I was taking her away from the only environment she knew to the unknown. My life had been on the move for the last nine

Left: At Canisianum in my favourite yellow Sunday dress in 1975. We looked our best on Sundays.

Below: Together with Agnes, affectionately known as Koipwata, also on a Sunday in 1975. Agnes was among hundreds of young Namibian people who were massacred during the Cassinga attack on 4 May 1978. May she rest in peace.

Right: My best and admired friend Marina, the girl who caringly carried my blanket on 20 April 1977 on our route into exile. She passed on in Windhoek in November 1995. May she rest in peace.

Below: My parents and my seven brothers in 1979, just before the death of my mother.

Above: My first wedding, to Aaron in Ljubljana, Slovenia (former Yugoslavia) in October 1983.

Left: With my first daughter Paleni in Clermont-Ferrand, France, in May 1985. A calm baby is a delight for a young student mother.

With Wilfried right at the beginning of everything.

Getting married to Wilfried in Windhoek in December 1990.

Above: My four daughters in 1992 – a busy, but enjoyable period of parenthood. (Left to right: Tuna, Pena, Peya and Paleni).

Left: My grandmother, Nambashu, holding her great grandchildren, my twin daughters Peya and Pena in August 1992.

Right: While pounding millet and carrying babies on my back were my daily activities at their ages, my daughters Paleni, Pena and Peya tried them out for a show.

Below: The Brock Clan in Brock Street in Windhoek in 2006.

My four daughters in 2016, seated in the same order as in the photo of them as babies in 1992. (Left to right: Tuna, Pena, Peya and Paleni).

Already 25 years married – celebration of our silver wedding anniversary in Windhoek in December 2015.

My sister and five brothers made it to the silver wedding anniversary. We all thought we should be standing for the photo, but Flori decided to be an exception.

With my daughters, Tuna and Peya in Dakar, Senegal, at the first celebration of Namibia's independence during my time as Ambassador.

years, and she being part of me, would have to manage. I was on my way back to our 'struggle life' and I had a little addition to the liberation struggle population. Others brought along little comrades from China, the USA, the Soviet Union, Ghana, Nigeria, Cuba, Finland, etc., and I was bringing a little comrade from France. Besides qualifications and skills, some of us brought reinforcements along.

Upon arrival in Luanda, I was immediately transferred to the Transit Camp, a camp established on the outskirts of Luanda. As the name indicated, it was purely a transit camp to accommodate those who were arriving back to or departing from Luanda. The camp also accommodated those who worked at the SWAPO Headquarters in Luanda. Here, I met friends whom I had not seen for a number of years. I particularly recall old colleagues from secondary school days whom I had not seen since 1977/78. Most of them were on their way from the GDR. Marina was one of them and she happily invited me to stay with her. Since her caring gesture of carrying the extra load of my blanket back in 1977 when we left Namibia, our friendship was unwavering. She had a spacious barracks room left behind by her husband who had just returned to Moscow. Thanks to Marina, who had arrived from Berlin a few months earlier than us, Paleni and I had proper accommodation on the first day of our arrival.

Through Marina, we easily integrated into the camp's life. I immediately found myself going to collect food, water and other basic items. After all, I had lived in camps before. Paleni also, amazingly, adapted to the camp life. She was not very keen on food, but I had brought some tinned and powdered food for the transition. When she wanted some yoghurt, I could quickly produce some powdered yoghurt. Then she discovered chicken, certainly the first live animals in her life, and she spent hours running after chickens. In Marina's neighbourhood, there was a little girl who was born in and arrived with her mother from Czechoslovakia. As Paleni played happily with this little girl, we adults played cards under a tree.

Camp life was pleasant until calamitous fate struck. The day started off with the usual happenings and before I joined others to play cards in the early afternoon, I decided to quickly go and visit my cousin on the other side of the camp. Paleni was happily playing and I asked Marina to keep an eye on her. I was hardly at my cousin's place when someone rushed in to ask me to go back as my daughter was experiencing some problem. In panic I rushed back and as I approached, I could see an agitated group of people but I couldn't see the one person I desperately needed to see, my daughter. As I struggled through this mob of people, I first took note of a distraught Marina, and then my daughter struggling to free herself from milk feeding. Her face was covered in milk, and she was desperate for consolation. What could have happened in the short time I had been gone?

I could not figure it out the same day, but a few days later, I made sense out of the whole thing. As soon as I was gone, Paleni spotted a cool drink can. She obviously could only recall what she knew in France and lost no time in consuming the contents of the can. What she saw as a cool drink, an adult saw as a perfect container for paraffin. Once the adult had satisfied the need to light the fire, the paraffin was left right there in reach of a child. And that child happened to be my daughter.

With such an occurrence, from one moment to the next, Paleni became seriously ill. She became progressively sick, to the extent that her life was in real danger. In the eyes of many, it was a matter of time. Out of despair, and a bit of confusion, I did whatever was possible. First, I immediately took her to the camp clinic. Marina came along. She felt responsible for the unfortunate occurrence. We were told to come back later. We didn't understand exactly why, but we returned a short while later. We were again asked to come later. By the time we returned to the clinic for the third time, Paleni had fever, was vomiting and had a running stomach. That was too much for her little body. We were told how serious her condition was. Such a condition warranted an injection every six hours. This was the reason why we were sent back twice. Injection needles needed some time to boil.

From a joyful, lively and energetic little girl, my daughter was reduced to a miserable, motionless and expressionless little being. She would sleep most of the time, even when she sat on her potty. Many people came around to see us and expressed their concern. Others advanced some advice but I did not know what to do with it. I helplessly sat by and looked at my child getting worse every day. Interest in anything else, including playing cards, deserted me. All I could do was to wait for the six hours to pass and to carry Paleni to the clinic for the next injection. This was going to be my routine for a good number of days.

As usual, help came, this time at a very critical moment, though I did not see it coming. It was triggered by a letter. My dearest struggle mother, Pendukeni, who was by then working at SWAPO Headquarters in Luanda and living in town, had received a letter written in French. She immediately thought of me and sent a certain Fiina, one of her colleagues who daily commuted between the office and the transit camp, to ask me for a translation. Fiina came around several times to the barracks where I stayed but was told every time that I was at the clinic with a daughter who was not well. Well and good, she would come back another time. Since no one understood French, it was unclear how urgent the letter was. They would attend to the matter whenever I could translate the letter.

One late afternoon, as Fiina was returning from her numerous unsuccessful visits to our barracks, she bumped into Marina and me returning from the clinic. When she took a look at the child in my arms, she muttered a few words of how sorry she was and she left us. There was no indication that she had been looking for me. Neither was I aware that her search for me had been ongoing for some time. Marina and I proceeded to our place to wait for the next six hours.

The following morning, as I sat there vacantly, I heard a car stopping right in front of the barracks. The cloth that served as a door to our part of the barracks was hurriedly pushed aside and a well dressed lady stood in the door. It was Pendukeni. She spoke very fast and it was clear that she was talking to me. In the process, she started picking up a few things and threw them in a bucket that was standing nearby. She took Paleni from my arms and she headed right back to the car. I literally had to run to catch up with her. Not much was said between the two of us in the car and in no time, we were in town. In such a rush, I can't remember if we stopped by the doctor or if she had secured the medication beforehand.

All I can remember is the two of us with Paleni sitting in a flat and Paleni taking medication. As Pendukeni was administering the medication, she was seriously unhappy with me because I had not thought of sending a message to her regarding the condition of my daughter. Was I aware that the combination of vomiting and diarrhoea was a fast killer of children? Was I not aware that she was in town? Well and good, I had seen her coming around to the transit camp, but I was not aware how far she was or how easy it might have been for me to get in touch with her. After all, under the circumstances, I must say, I no longer thought straight. The whole very unusual thing happened unexpectedly. I had become engulfed in a desperate situation and had concentrated on what was available and what I could do.

Pendukeni took charge of my daughter. Her flat was quite small and every night when the three of us retired to this one bedroom with one bed, she would sit at the edge of the bed, nursing Paleni before putting her to sleep. She would wake up, and put on the light to attend to her in the middle of the night. I would sometimes take note, but in most instances I would sleep through all this. I was exhausted. Improvement set in fast. Pendukeni concentrated first on stopping the vomiting. 'One thing at a time,' she said. The strategy seemed to be effective. After two days or so, Paleni stopped vomiting and we moved to the next phase. In less than a week, the Paleni I used to know emerged from the weary motionless bundle of being I had been carrying around. The environment she had known and the sight of a fridge could also have contributed to her speedy recovery. Pretty soon, Paleni was walking up to the fridge demanding yoghurt in French.

I had no words to thank Pendukeni. I guessed she did not want to hear any thank you from me. It all came naturally. Before I even came to think of returning to the camp, she announced her departure on a mission and expressed her hope that I would take good care of my daughter during her absence. She explained everything in relation to the flat and who to contact if need be. There was sufficient food for a month and she handed over to me a card for the purchase of perishables. The main thing was, she insisted, that I saw to it that Paleni was well fed and looked after.

⌒

As soon as Pendukeni was gone, I realised how scared I was to stay by myself in this flat. The flat was not on the ground floor, but I was very scared nonetheless. There were so many other people on the same floor, but no ways of communicating with them. So, we remained locked up in our flat, and only looked at our neighbours through the burglar door as they passed. Paleni happily played but also with anything. One time, she played with the flat keys and that was the last time I saw them. This was followed by an episode of our being locked up in the flat for two solid days. After the officials at SWAPO Office got tired of my many daily phone calls, someone came around to break open the lock. They brought a new lock and my only worry was how to explain to Pendukeni about the new key holder.

Paleni and I nonetheless had a wonderful time in the flat in Luanda. I played music throughout the day, and in the evening, I tried on Pendukeni's dresses. We often also got the driver to take us shopping. I obviously bought food stuff for Paleni as Pendukeni said I must but I also bought other things. By the time she returned, out of a significant amount of thousands on her shopping card, there was only the figure 3. I am not sure what currency the money was, but I felt embarrassed when I handed over that card with the figure 3. No explanation was demanded from me and our life went on. It never crossed my mind to think of going back to the Transit Camp and I just became part of those who lived in town.

As I conveniently continued my stay in Luanda, it also happened that I occasionally found myself around the SWAPO Headquarters. This was a place one naturally went to whenever the opportunity availed. One such day, I bumped into someone by the name of Nahas Angula. After a short explanation of why I was in Luanda and where I was before that, he invited me to his office. Seemingly my story was of interest to him. In no time I found out that my interlocutor was the SWAPO Secretary for Education. Based on my explanation, Nahas Angula suggested that I should go to Lusaka where I could continue to practise my French while SWAPO explored the possibility of my return to France to sit for my one outstanding examination. It would be a pity if one subject prevented me from obtaining my Master's Degree, he argued.

In March 1987, I again packed up to go to Lusaka. For some reason, Pendukeni was also on the same flight as Paleni and me. I still recall the flight because once we were on board, we were asked to disembark again as there was some technical problem. There were a number of Namibians on the flight, and as we were waiting for the technical problem to be attended to, some of my compatriots recounted their previous experiences on flights that had technical problems while in the air. The worst was late Simon Mzee Kaukungua's story of being onboard a flight which had to crash-land in a sandy field near an airport. Although I also joined in the laughter at all these hilarious stories, I only realised later onboard and in the air, that these stories had had a serious effect on me. Shortly after we had taken off, I left Paleni with Pendukeni and went to the bathroom. As soon as I was alone, I had a weird thought which made me rush out of the bathroom. Pendukeni was surprised to see me back but with eyes about to pop out. I explained to her that while in the bathroom, I imagined what I would do if I came out of the bathroom into an empty plane. Her immediate question was, 'What would have happened to all the passengers in such a short time while you were gone?' She found my thinking so weird that to date, she still laughs when she thinks about this story. What she did not know was that I am such an anxious person, that I get terrified just imagining myself in a silly situation. And this has nothing to do with my life in exile or the war situation.

My family back home knew about my extraordinary anxiety from when I was very young. I still remember my late mother's big eyes the day she realised how irrational I became when I had an anxiety attack. The first time that she took serious note of this was one morning on a normal school day. I happily left home for school and on my way I happened to have placed my hand around my neck. I did this as I was going through a bushy place which we as children referred to as a forest. There is absolutely nothing wrong with placing one's hand around one's neck, but the moment I felt my hand around my neck on this specific day, I was seized with a feeling that my neck felt much shorter than usual. That feeling, imagined as it certainly sounds, was enough to throw me into a panic. The only sensible thing I could think of doing in such a state was to climb up a tree. Why? To date, I have no explanation why I thought I would be safe with my short neck up in a tree. But the story refused to die as it was recounted by many other school children. Since I was wearing a red dress on that particular day, everyone who passed the same route to school could spot me up in the tree. A boy neighbour, Arnold, on his way to school called out to me and asked whether I was not going to school. I responded that I was unable to continue to school as my neck was shorter than usual. And with that I went back home. My explanation really worried my mother. I had other similar incidents and at one point, my poor mother decided to send me away to her elder sister for a while. Many years later, these panicky situations were still assailing me very far from home and in this case, up in the air.

↬

Lusaka was my hometown by now and I was very happy to be back. My friend Marina had also left Luanda earlier than I had to work on a SWAPO farm in the vicinity of Lusaka. Other friends and old colleagues were also around and my coming back to Lusaka was a real pleasure. I first stayed with a friend from school days, Bernadette, who was teaching at UNIN at the time. She studied in Czechoslovakia and she had completed her studies one year earlier than me.

I joined the French teacher to assist with French teaching although I wasn't yet officially in the employment of UNIN. Through my connection to teaching and speaking French, Paleni was admitted to the kindergarten section of the Lusaka French School. Her attendance was fully taken care of by the French Embassy.

In the middle of 1987, Paleni and I were allocated one of the Zambian Government flats that were assigned to UNIN staff members. What was explained to me was that since I was not yet working and therefore not earning money, another alternative to paying my rent was identified. The explanation was that Namibians who worked at UNIN contributed a percentage of their salaries to a certain fund, and those who were in charge of the administration of the fund deemed that the payment for my monthly rent met the requirements of the fund. Not only did the fund pay my rent, I was also paid a monthly allowance from it. The fund assured my shelter, my food and my clothing. What more could I require? I was not asked to apply for, neither was there talk of a loan. In return, I taught French and prepared for my exams in France. With such a perfect arrangement and a life well taken care of through pure solidarity, the year 1987 sped by and came to a close.

7

Arrival of a white comrade

By the time the year 1988 started, I had quite a full record. I had been in exile for ten years. I had travelled and lived in a number of countries and had experienced a fair share of cultural shock. I had faced a number of challenges but also a number of pleasant surprises. In short, I had lived and overcome every imaginable situation. I could claim to have experienced all possible challenges. What else could come up? I could not think of anything. Certainly, from now on, my life could only be plain sailing.

Truly so, I started the year 1988 on a positive note. I had no major concerns and my life seemed to move in the right direction. I had my own place and my daughter was in kindergarten. I was about to be offered a formal position as a French tutor at UNIN and things were getting clearer about my return to France to sit for my last exam. All these of course pointed to more responsibilities and more work. But these were normal developments which were perfectly in line with my expectations. Adding any new development would only overload my balanced life. Things could not have been better. 1988 was clearly going to be a challenge free year, something that had been elusive in my life for a while. At long last this was indeed within my grasp.

When I signed my first ever contract, I was not aware that another three compatriots were going to fall under the same category as me as tutors at UNIN. They of course were going to be tutors in something else and not French. Understandably we arrived at UNIN at different times. This could be the explanation why it took a bit of time until I bumped into them one by one. In any case I was not aware of them and my functioning was completely independent of who else was a tutor at UNIN. I therefore calmly started my official duties in a very familiar environment.

I set up my office in the same room that used to be my French classroom some ten years earlier. It was in this very room that a few others and I had spent endless hours twisting our tongues trying to get the French pronunciation as close to right as possible. Ten years later, I was sitting in the same room, preparing French lessons, and devising the best ways of lessening the torture of getting this unusual language likeable to Namibians. From experience, I knew too well how hard it was.

Now and then I would listen to the conversations of students as they walked past my office. The only window of the office opened towards the corridor that led to the dormitories of the students. I could clearly hear every word they said as they converged on this, the only passage, on their way to their rooms, classrooms, TV room or dining room. My office was really at the crossroads, and I knew it only too well as I too had passed there several times a day ten years ago. And we had done exactly the same, speaking about and laughing loudly at the same silly things. This did not disturb me at all, but at the same time I no longer understood the relevance of the conversations or the reasons for laughing quite that loud.

Not only was my office close to the students' dormitories, classrooms and their other facilities, but it was also isolated in relation to the offices of other teaching and support staff. The only office close to mine was the Office of the Registrar. That was indeed an important office, and that was precisely the reason why senior officials, including the Director, walked past my office. If not, I would not see any of them the whole day long. One fine morning in February 1988, I for some reason decided to step out of my office for a while. As I turned into the long corridor leading toward the main entrance of the Institute, I bumped into the Director, Comrade Hage Geingob. The fact that I was no longer a student, but a tutor, did not help me much. The Director was always an authority, not only academically and administratively at the Institute, but most importantly, he was a national leader. He was not there only for work related matters, but also, equally important, for Party related matters.

So seeing him in the corridor did not only make me feel guilty that I was not performing the duties entrusted to me, but also put my discipline as a Party cadre at stake as well. Why would I be walking around instead of being at my desk? But this particular time, encountering him struck me slightly differently. He was in the company of a young bearded white man. His colour did not strike me at all, but his height did. The Director was very tall, but the fact that his companion was taller than him was pretty unusual.

As I apologetically tried to pass them without disturbing their conversation, I uncomfortably noticed their slowing down. I had no choice but to slow down as well. As I smiled uneasily, I barely heard the Director introducing the visitor to me, 'This is Comrade...' I got stuck at the word 'comrade'. I did not get the visitor's surname. Nor did I hear the Director introducing me to him. None of that mattered because my mind was brought to a halt. Did I really hear the word 'comrade'? The Director, of all people, referring to this fellow as comrade! Why did he do that?

Comrade was a sacred word for us. So many white people had come here, but never did I hear the Director referring to any of them as a comrade. Yes, maybe once before and that was way back in 1978 when late Comrade Anton Lubowski came to Lusaka. But at that time I did not understand much about what was happening to us as Namibians and by then the word had not yet acquired this special significance in my mind. This time I definitely knew and perfectly understood our fate as Namibians. Although this was not an official position, we at the back of our minds knew that whites in Namibia were the reason for our struggle. Yes, it was a system, but the system was run by whites and at the same time this system gave privileges to whites only. And hence our plight! And here I was in front of one of my respected national leaders introducing me to a white comrade! Those days, when we spoke to each other, and referred to each other as comrades, we meant Namibians. Could this be the case? If things were all right for this white person back home, what was he doing here?

As soon as the Director and his comrade had taken leave of me, I dismissed the whole thing. It must have been a joke, I concluded. There was no white person in Namibia who with a right mind would take that huge step to come to Lusaka. We had heard of some young white Namibians who, in protest at being conscripted into the SADF would leave the country and go to Europe. But joining SWAPO in exile and coming to Lusaka was unheard of! The Director and his comrade went their way, and I went my way too. Out of sight, out of mind! For some reason, I never enquired whether others had also had the same unusual introduction to this new comrade. So, the incident died a natural death and life went on.

⌒

A month later however I was going to bump into the same comrade. A few days before this second encounter, I had been requested by Father Kaishara, old Father Heimerikx, the Catholic priest, to cook fish for him before he left for Europe for a few months. He was very fond of the Zambezi bream and I happily cooked it for him. But to make it more interesting, I always invited some friends, one of them being Bernadette.

As we knocked off one Friday late afternoon, I met Bernadette in the yard of UNIN, just in front of the Administration Block. We chatted a bit and I made use of the opportunity to invite her for lunch the following day with Father Kaishara. As I was right in the middle of my invitation, all of a sudden a shadow fell right between Bernadette and me. As we both looked up, here was the comrade of a few weeks ago. Was this fellow still here? Where had he been all this time? And how come I had not seen him since the very striking introduction? This time he was just coming from the Administration Block, specifically from the Finance Office. This was a clear indication that he somehow belonged here. Instead of going around and leaving through the usual exit, given his height, he decided to step over the short wall and stopped right next to us. We looked at him and all three of us said 'Hi' almost at the same time.

Instead of continuing on his way, the comrade remained standing as if he were part of our conversation. And I of course had to conclude my invitation to Bernadette. The lunch was the next day! And there were not many telephones in Lusaka those days. If I did not provide all the details to Bernadette right there and then, what then? I therefore had no choice but to complete my invitation in the presence of this smiling fellow.

Again, as fate would dictate, at the end of my invitation to Bernadette, I heard myself saying, this time addressing this comrade, and evidently surprisingly so, 'Would you also like to come?' The response followed immediately and it was, 'Yes.' Certainly, he did not know what the invitation was all about. But why did I do this? In this whole confusion, I had invited the unusual comrade. And Bernadette, who possessed a car, had immediately offered to pick him up. How would Father Kaishara react to the new addition on the invitation list? It was way too late now. We would have to find a way to explain the whole mishap to him.

Amazingly, Father Kaishara was not at all surprised that we had dared to invite an unknown person. He had already invited the same person to the Longhorn Restaurant. Longhorn was our favourite restaurant. So, how come he took this new comrade there without us?

Father Kaishara was someone we had known for a long time. His real name was Gerhard Heimerikx and he was a Dutch Catholic priest. He arrived at my local church at Okatana in 1952, long before I was born. He was the priest to whom my father had to explain why he was marrying his cousin. The same Father Kaishara married my parents and baptised me and a few of my siblings. By the time we could recall anything, he had moved to Otshikuku, another Catholic mission station in the northern part of Namibia. He however visited Okatana often, and I also saw him later in Anamulenge during my secondary school days.

Sometime in the early 1980s, Father Kaishara unknowingly upset the South African occupation army in Namibia. A gruesome massacre of an entire family took place at a village close to the Otshikuku Mission Station. There being no other administrative set up in the area, the neighbours of the murdered family went to report the killings to the mission station. Father Kaishara went to the scene to take note of the incident and to support the community in the wake of such a brutal occurrence, but he also took some photos. Immediately after the incident, the South African authorities were fast to point a finger at PLAN, the military wing of SWAPO. The story went around that the Otshikuku massacre was committed by SWAPO freedom fighters, whom the South African army referred to as terrorists.

Father Kaishara did not see anything wrong with sending photos of the massacre to Europe to portray the cruelty with which the entire family was wiped out. To his surprise and to the surprise of many, things developed pretty fast and the unexpected happened. The same photos appeared in some European publications shortly after they had been received. The South African apartheid regime was among the first to take note of the negative publicity and they wanted an immediate explanation of the origin of the photos. The villagers were fast to point out that cameras were not items to be found among their possessions and European publications would simply not mean anything to them. In no time, the trail led to Father Kaishara. He knew too well what the consequences of his deed would be. The South African administration was ruthless with individuals who did not condone its actions. Father Kaishara therefore lost no time getting out of Namibia while he could.

Things were not going to be easy for him. Living and working in Europe, after having been away for thirty years, was more than he could take. He approached the SWAPO leadership in exile and enquired whether he could join the clergy that worked among the exiled Namibians. This was granted and he came to Lusaka where he ministered to the Namibians in Zambia and Angola. This is how we bumped again into Father Kaishara in Lusaka.

How did he move from being Father Gerhard Heimerikx to Father Kaishara? This is indeed a long story. Most Catholic missionaries who worked in the north of Namibia were mainly Germans with a few Dutch like Father Kaishara. With time, each of them got an Oshiwambo name. Kaishara's full name was Kaishara ka Nangombe. Yes, the man even had a surname, but this was an exception. Others had names such as Kapunda (Father Nienhaus), Andili h'Eengongo (Father Duttmann), Tsheetekela (Father Knuff), Kafula (Father Houben), and many others.

Father Kaishara was however used to the specific routine of Catholic mission stations in Namibia. Initially, when we lived at Catholic mission stations, we did not understand why things had to happen at specific times. If they did not, the priest or the sister was extremely unhappy. For a very long time, we wondered about this urgency of almost everything. Although we fell into line with the rhythm, it was only much later that we understood that this urgency came mainly from the German trait of punctuality and a particular way of going through the day. When Father Kaishara came to Lusaka and shared a home with other Catholic priests including some Americans, this exact order and punctuality fell away, or at least it was no longer systematic. And having food cooked for and served to him, was no longer automatic. It was not unusual for each of the priests in the home to make a breakfast according to individual tastes. Having lived long enough at Catholic mission stations in Namibia where there were sufficient hands, I can just imagine the expression on Father Kaishara's face observing the preparation of individual breakfasts.

With such a set up, and of course, with nostalgia, we had a gentleman's agreement with Father Kaishara. He came to our respective homes for certain meals and when it was his turn, he took all of us to Longhorn Restaurant wherewe enjoyed what we later learned to be Indian food. Now we found out that he had gone to our favourite restaurant with this new comrade and this time without us. And he only revealed this to us when we apologetically informed him that we had taken the liberty to invite a new comrade, a certain Wilfried Brock. Clearly, he knew much more about the newcomer than we did.

The lunch was uneventful. We had eaten so many times with Father Kaishara. He enjoyed his fish, and he took leave from us for the following few months. Bernadette also wanted to leave and we expected her to give a lift to our new comrade. The comrade, however, was not in a hurry to leave. We found out that after an entire month in Lusaka, he was still living in a hotel and he was not in a hurry to return there. This was quite a sensible sentiment, as staying in a confined room of a hotel is quite challenging. If the comrade wanted to stay a bit longer, let him do so. Staying longer included dinner, but for him this was a nice break from the monotonous hotel food and the lonely four walls of the hotel room. It was only normal that one was considerate.

～

In the weeks that followed, the comrade visited regularly. He had no car, but our flat was in walking distance of his hotel. He came for dinner and stayed for a chat. By then I had a friend named Maggie staying with us. If we had to cook for the three of us, we could as well cook a little more to include a fourth person. In the Oshiwambo fashion of cooking, it was a matter of adding more water in the pot. If the comrade was tired of hotel food, he was welcome to share whatever meal we had. And why not chat to him for an hour or two before he returned to his hotel room? One day, when he would get to know other Namibian homes, he would also go there. For the time being, he only knew about our flat and that was why he came here. My daughter, who enjoyed chatting, enjoyed the company of the new friend. If he was not talking to my friend and me, he was entertained by Paleni. And the four of us did not see anything unusual about our newly acquired routine. And after having chatted to Wilfried a few times, we came to the realization that not all Namibian whites were bad people.

After an extended stay of about two months at the hotel, Wilfried was allocated a flat. What an achievement, I thought. The poor man would no longer need to walk that distance to and from our flat. He had a kitchen now and would prepare food in accordance with his taste. The hotel food was certainly monotonous and besides feeding yourself while gazing through the window, it was of course costly as well. When he again turned up at our flat shortly after he had moved into his new flat, we took it for granted that this was because he was still settling in. The process of acquiring pots and a few more kitchen items needed some time, especially when it comes to men. Allow him enough time and he would start eating at home. Although eating alone could also be a problem.

Unexpectedly, a solution presented itself. One colleague, Loide, who worked in the UNIN Library, had gone to Angola to get married. Upon her return to Lusaka, the rent of her flat had gone up drastically. There was no way she could afford it. Comradeship was an answer. She was advised to ask Comrade Wilfried Brock whether she could stay with him. After all, his flat had three bedrooms. Loide was quite courageous. She walked up to him and made her enquiry. Of course yes, she may occupy one of the two vacant rooms in the flat. With the moving in of Loide, Wilfried would now have company and would no longer need to eat alone.

The trend however continued. Could it be that Loide's cooking was unknown to the poor comrade? But he was not obliged to eat what Loide cooked. He could also cook whatever he wished to eat. Or was my cooking, with a French touch, so tasty? Well and good, culturally for me, food was there to be shared. And during the exile years, saving was not part of our vocabulary. After all, we went straight from secondary school into sharing with others. For what did we need to save? Everything was provided. For the few of us who happened to have a salary, it was for sharing with the others. Putting money aside did not really appeal to us. After all, we were not certain of what was going to happen the following day. The attitude was therefore: If I bought for three persons or for four, so what! So, let the poor guy come and eat with us. Maybe he felt comfortable with us, and therefore preferred to eat with us. He occasionally also brought Loide along.

Having Wilfried with us in the evenings became a natural thing. He ate with us, stayed longer for a chat, took his leave politely and walked home. The following day we would see him at UNIN and life went on. One day, as I walked around the UNIN yard, I met Wilfried in the company of a German girl. He introduced us to each other. Her name was Dagmar and she was at UNIN to do research for her studies. She was somehow involved with the SWAPO Office in Bonn. She had come to UNIN with the assistance of Tate Shoombe, the SWAPO Representative in West Germany at the time. She and Wilfried had met at the SWAPO Office in Bonn before. How nice! Besides Maggie and me, Wilfried had another friend, this Dagmar. And the fact that they spoke the same language would make it even easier for him to spend time with her instead of with us. Dagmar first stayed at the UNIN campus as students had vacation at the time of her arrival. When the students returned, Dagmar had to find another place. Meanwhile she got to know Loide through Wilfried and it was only natural that she moved in with the two of them. With that new development, there was really no reason why Wilfried would want to eat and chat with us.

Seemingly it is hard to get rid of old habits. Since his hotel days, Wilfried continued popping by. Maybe it was taking him a while to get used to spending time with these two new ladies. Settling in with new housemates always takes time. As things stood, Wilfried was with us more than with his new housemates. We all joked and laughed about it, and again we all got used to his ways. If it was really what he wanted, why not? My daughter Paleni was delighted to hop around and chat to Wilfried. She followed him around. The man was not at all troublesome, he was polite and correct. There was absolutely no reason to be mean to him. If he didn't mind walking back home in the dark, I wasn't going to make a big deal about cooking for one additional person.

It so happened that I got used to seeing Wilfried around to the extent that seeing him was no longer a particular occurrence. He was always there. Even at work, he chose to sit under the same tree where mainly we, the female colleagues, sat during our one hour lunch break. We lazily sat around under the only big tree in the UNIN yard and chatted and enjoyed laughing at whatever stories we told one another. I wonder how much sense Wilfried made of our stories, but he and a few other male colleagues continued to join us. I had no reason to check closely at what exactly Wilfried did under the tree. I saw him so often and I knew that he would pop by later in the evening and we would continue our usual chat about who he really was, what he thought of this and that, who I really was, where in Namibia I was from, what I had done since I had come into exile, etc. I however withheld the question on how he came to the idea of going into exile. I still found the thought very weird.

꙰

As time went by, some people started seeing things differently from the way I did. Maria was the first one to draw my attention to what she saw. Maria was the nurse at the UNIN clinic. But for me, she was not only the nurse, but also the wife of Makarius who was from a village neighbouring my own village in northern Namibia. During exile years, he was as good as a relative. He had left Namibia two years earlier than me and I had already met him in Cassinga. At that point, being slightly older than me, he felt that natural responsibility towards me far away from home. I still recall his kind gesture in giving me all the money he had and a coat as it was freezing cold, back in 1977, just before he left Cassinga for Luanda, on his way to the Soviet Union. When we met again in Lusaka ten years later, he felt the same responsibility towards me. He introduced me to his wife Maria and she too showed me that special care and interest.

Maria had observed something under the tree. One day, when she indicated that she urgently needed to speak to me, I casually followed her into the clinic. At that time, whenever I was summoned, I would quickly go through recent events just to ascertain that I was not in trouble. And that was exactly what I did between the tree and the clinic. As far as I could recall, I hadn't done anything wrong. So, I was certain that there was nothing to worry about. After having closed the door behind us, Maria faced me and her question was short and very direct, 'Are you completely blind? Can't you see how that man looks at you?' I looked at Maria, very perplexed. What man was she talking about? She smiled and asked how I could possibly not know which man she was talking about? There was only one. Why should I pretend I didn't know? When she mentioned his name, I could hardly believe what I was hearing. There were natural reasons why a sensible Namibian couldn't come to such a conclusion. Maria had obviously come to the wrong conclusion and there was only one thing to do: forget about it. Maria smiled, and we returned to the others under the tree.

The same evening, Wilfried came around as usual. We ate, chatted, and I walked him to the door as usual. He politely took leave and left. I closely observed him and I was more than ever convinced that Maria had got it all wrong. I was particularly happy later that evening when I visualized Maria's face earlier in the day in relation to Wilfried's correct behaviour. There couldn't be any doubt. Both Wilfried and I were from Namibia. That was the country where we were born and bred. Race was part of our upbringing and of our lives. Things were made clear and very obvious and we all had it fixed in our minds. Certain things were simply beyond bounds and there was no room to think about them. Once your brain has been drilled with something as particular as race was in our case, it becomes part of the mindset.

The notion of being white in Namibia during those years was really notorious. The superiority of Whites was inevitable. They were in charge and Blacks were at their service. This master and servant relationship was enforced not only by the system but had also been enforced by individual Whites for generations. In the end this type of relationship became a norm and it was pointless for a black person to complain about abuse by a white person. How do you complain about a white person and to whom do you complain? Whites could only be good those days. As a result, non-Whites grew up with this notion of Whites being bosses and it was compulsory to always respond to them by saying 'Ja baas', meaning 'Yes boss!' I guess that it was inadmissible to respond 'No Boss'. It always had to be yes. This special status of whiteness was automatically extended to their children. White children were simply *klein baas* (small boss). This kind of subjection could only lead to a deepened division between Whites and non-Whites.

As a child, I did not come so much in contact with white people other than the German Catholic missionaries. When the settlement known as Oshakati was established 4 km away from my village in the mid-sixties, we would occasionally see white people in cars but really from a distance. We did not have reason to go closer to their homes until my father had the brilliant idea to establish a proper garden. With the knowledge and experience from some of his contracts in urban areas, he planted tomatoes, onions, guava and papayas and since he really enjoyed his garden, his produce became exceptionally good. My mother saw the garden produce as an additional source of income and she started regularly selling home produced vegetables and fruits to Sister Gabriele at the Okatana Mission kitchen. Not long thereafter, and to expand her market, my mother had the wonderful idea of selling tomatoes in the white part of Oshakati. It was during one of her business expeditions that I experienced first-hand disregard of black people by white people.

As I walked next to my mother in the street with well-arranged houses on each side of the street, I observed white children playing in huge yards. After having stopped at several gates to show how appealing our tomatoes were, we came across a mother with her daughter walking along the same street. My mother lowered her basket from her head to show the tomatoes to this potential customer. As the mother was inspecting the tomatoes, the little girl grabbed a tomato and started walking away. Naturally, my mother expected the white mother to call her daughter to order. No, this was not going to be. What then? My mother protested while mother and daughter proceeded in the opposite direction. As the distance between us and them was increasing, my mother became anxious. Although linguistically we had no means of communicating with them, the mother of the little girl must have understood that my mother was not at all happy about the perceived donation. Instead of coming back to return the tomato, the little girl decided to roll the tomato back to us. And off they went. I was not marked by this first encounter of snatching one tomato. I would not have minded if the girl had eaten the tomato but the fact that she chose to throw it back to us was just something very new to me. In my culture, it is unheard of for a child to treat an adult in this manner. And the mother of the little girl saw absolutely nothing wrong with the behaviour of her daughter. I was to grow up to hear many unbelievable stories including from my own father of his experience from his various labour contracts.

As young black adults, we knew too well that Whites were there to mistreat, abuse and belittle us and our minds were set to quietly find a way to protect ourselves. When possible, the best was to stay out of their way. Later when I studied in France and lived in a university residence, I was surprised to discover that Whites were after all normal people. They eat, they drink and they go to the toilet. You would not get that image from the Namibian Whites. They appeared just to be too good for many things. They were served and worshipped. From a distance, they were literally semi-gods. It was with this mind frame that I perceived every white person from Namibia. A white person from Namibia could only be different from Whites from elsewhere. That we ate almost on a regular basis with this Wilfried was already overdoing it. But the poor man was in exile, alone among so many of us. Certainly he needed to have some connection to us. And he happened to have found that through us; Maggie, Paleni and me. Why not afford him the opportunity? After all he chose to be with us. We would never have dreamed to ask him to do so.

Of course, my chat with Maria began to work a bit on my nerves. What if there was the slightest truth in Maria's observation? No, it could not be. Even if there were a remote possibility, I had so many layers of protection around me. I was married, I was a mother of a three year old daughter, I was slightly older than Wilfried and most importantly, our different colours were an overriding factor. We had discussed enough over so many weeks and I had responded to all of Wilfried's questions. So he knew everything about me and there was no way he could think of anything close to Maria's observation. His interest could only have been to have contact with other Namibians for a chat, to eat, drink and laugh together. After all, we were comrades. Yes, I had a shift in mind regarding that in the meantime. We were made to understand that Wilfried found himself in the same boat as the rest of us. How possible and reasonable that was, was hard for me to understand. Our leadership seemed to be convinced, so we followed suit.

⌒

As much as I was confident that Maria's observation was completely out of order, I was somehow getting worried. I could not afford to have this suspicion circulating. Besides Maria, who else might have noticed something? To dispel this unrealistic suspicion, I started counting on this Dagmar. She spoke the same language and had so much in common with Wilfried. So I felt that she could have an influence on him. The first thing he needed to do was to start staying and eating at home. It was not safe for him to walk up and down in the darkness. I understood that it was difficult for him to get rid of old habits but at some point he needed to make his flat a home for himself and thereby avoid walking around in the darkness. We could go over during the weekends and the three of them could occasionally come to us. Dagmar listened to my arguments and nodded. We had hardly started trying out this arrangement when one evening Dagmar and Loide walked to our flat to request me to go over to their flat because Wilfried looked depressed. They went on to say that they had cooked and it would be nice if we could go over for dinner. The invitation for dinner was appealing. When we arrived at their flat, there seemed to be no problem with Wilfried. We had a nice meal and spent a pleasant evening. I did not find anything unusual with the episode until Dagmar walked into my office a few days later.

This was not the first time that Dagmar had popped by my office. But this time she immediately wanted to talk to me about something. Since we had spoken about so many different things in the past, I set aside whatever I was busy with and listened to her. 'It is about Wilfried,' she said. 'What about Wilfried?' I asked. In a rather direct manner, she explained that she had come to discuss Wilfried's feelings towards me as I seemingly did not understand. To my question as to how she found out or had come to such a conclusion, she told me without a trace of guilt on her face, that he had discussed it with her. This was simply too complicated for me. How would I deal with this? Here was someone, as kind and correct as you could get, but another person saying and seeing what he never portrayed or said directly to me. We had been friends for almost two months, we had seen each other often, sometimes on a daily basis, and nothing vaguely of that nature was ever said between the two of us. Yet others had observed and had heard what I could not imagine. What next?

Dagmar's visit to my office threw me into turmoil for a while. I immediately ruled out misunderstanding since the discussion between the two of them must have happened in their mother tongue. I did not manage to ask Dagmar to carry a massage back to Wilfried. She had clearly approached me as a friend and not as Wilfried's envoy. There was no doubt that in Dagmar's view I was missing the point. Well, I accepted her argument for the simple reason that as a foreigner who had never set foot in our country, she had no idea about the depth of the division between Whites and Blacks in Namibia. She had certainly read or heard about apartheid, but this was by far insufficient for her to fully grasp the issues. How could she possibly be aware of all racially discriminatory laws in existence in Namibia? She would not even have heard of the existence of a law which prohibited multi-racial relations. Although the law had been repealed by then, it was in force during my lifetime and I knew of people who had to leave Namibia because they had become entangled in multi-racial relationships. This was no fiction. I had hard evidence on the matter and under no circumstances would I complicate my life which for practical purposes was complicated enough.

Dagmar's talking to me was unexpected but revealing. At the same time I felt disappointed and worried. What would I do next time I saw Wilfried? Would I ask him? He was so kind and very correct, but was he aware of the speculations? Was he aware that Dagmar came to see me? If this was at all true, why had he not spoken to me himself?

One thing was certain, I needed to find a way out of this awkward situation. Clearly, I had to take a distance from Wilfried in order to protect myself from speculation. The difficulty however was how to start distancing myself from someone who had been in my circle for months and against whom I literally had no case, so to speak. What harm had he done to me? Could coming around, sitting around, sharing a meal and eventually taking leave be classified as an offense? No! And that was all the man had done.

The same evening after Dagmar's direct talk to me Wilfried came around as usual and he behaved exactly the same as he had for the last two months. My goodness, what was I supposed to do? And Wilfried continued coming around. Every time I saw him, he wore his usual smiling and innocent face. When it was again time to leave, he would politely take his leave until the next time.

This situation, as simple as it may sound, was beginning to wear me down. There was not much I could do about it. I abandoned my idea of asking Wilfried. What if he denied knowledge of anything? Or what if this were the opportunity he had been waiting for? Either way was not going to be easy for me. But somewhere at the back of my mind I knew he was not completely innocent. Could I then just start being mean to him for unintentionally having provoked speculation? Of course not; I would not be able to prove my point. But one thing was certain: his being around me would soon cause me some embarrassment. And I gradually started to feel the need to act. But what action could I take? The only thing I could do was to behave in such a way that would discourage Wilfried from coming around. I couldn't be directly mean to him but my new attitude was going to have an impact on him. All of a sudden I was quiet, sad and just not interested in anything. Why was I all of sudden this different? He had always known me as a smiling and welcoming person.

A period of serious misunderstanding ensued between the two of us. Wilfried tried by all means to understand what the matter was. I wouldn't allow him to pose the obvious question on his mind. As for me, my mind was made up on a number of points. Yes, Wilfried was a nice person but he was a man. And I had had my fair share not too long ago. Secondly, in Namibia, a relationship of this kind would have been unheard of. Why should we ignore this reality of our society back home simply because we were temporarily outside the country? Thirdly, in my mind, I was still married, and I had a daughter. Fourthly, I am just less than three years older than Wilfried. In my culture, all these things count and are obvious. Under normal circumstances, I would have been shielded by sufficient solid defences. Any sensible person would have understood my position. Agreeing with it was seemingly another matter.

Wilfried had talked to and had observed me long enough. He knew me better than I thought. He was going to persist against all odds. I was however also determined to stand my ground. I would not give in. My new attitude however did not deter Wilfried from being around me. It was not that I minded his being around, but I minded speculation about me. Wilfried all of a sudden became careful and did not really say much to me. He seemingly preferred to play a neutral game to wait and see. Clearly, to a certain extent our friendship had been affected.

The unavoidable was however bound to happen! As careful as one wishes to be, human error is always bound to happen. As he was leaving one evening, I was convinced that I had noticed a kind of sign in his eyes. Whatever it was, it confirmed what I did not want to believe. But was I certain that I saw what I thought I saw? Did I have facts at hand to prove and defend my observation? What if it was a cultural way of looking at people which I was only finally noticing then? The puzzle was getting more complicated. The real trouble was: the man never said anything to me thus far on which I could base my case and therefore provide a base on which to engage him. He continued to be friendly, helpful, caring, and anything else one can attribute to a good friend. With such a dilemma, how could I start stating my case? 'I no longer want to see you because you are too friendly, too kind, you are too much around me...'? As much as I wanted to do that, it simply did not sound right. In fact, it sounded weird.

As I was struggling to figure out my case against Wilfried, he continued coming around. As we sat, and ate and chatted, my mind was focussed on one and one thing only: I needed to state my case to Wilfried. But how would I start the discussion? How could I accuse him of something he never said? And how would I explain why I thought that he no longer could come by for a visit? Should he ask, 'What wrong did I do to you?' I seriously had no explanation. Yet, something inside me clearly pointed to a problem. But there was no way of putting a finger on it! I simply could not put it into words. On the other hand, there was this dilemma that had developed over a significant period of time. We knew each other so well, we worked together, we were seen together so often, and we were naturally invited to the same social functions. After all we went in groups and it was not really an issue of who arrived with whom. But certainly, in my mind, I was getting worried that assumptions were being made.

When an invitation came to go to the Director's house one evening, Wilfried naturally indicated that he would pick me up. This would be his first time at the Director's house and since I knew the way, it would be good if we could go together. Initially, I sincerely had no problem with going around with Wilfried as a friend, a colleague and as a comrade as we had done in the past. So without giving it serious thought I initially agreed to his proposal. But just a few hours before the agreed time, I thought about what was about to happen. How would the arrival of the two of us at the function be perceived? I immediately saw a problem. I had to get out of the arrangement of arriving with Wilfried at the Director's house. Under no circumstances did I want to confirm what many colleagues and comrades had started to suspect. Going up to the Director's house by myself would be challenging though. But I wanted to go. All of a sudden I had the idea of going with Bernadette who lived in the opposite direction of the venue. Given the precarious situation, I got into a taxi and travelled that many kilometres in the opposite direction, just to get into Bernadette's car to travel back again. Of course I did not explain to Bernadette why I chose to come all the way to her house by taxi, just to travel back with her again. When Wilfried came around to pick me up, no one really knew why I was no longer there. I was seen not long ago, but where exactly I went, no one could tell. Of course, Wilfried never turned up at the party and he didn't insist on an explanation from me.

⌒

Four months since his arrival in Lusaka, Wilfried was still spending a lot of time around me. He had not said anything to me and there was nothing for me to say no to. Everyone continued to see what I could not clearly see and what was not said between the two of us. Wilfried played his game pretty well. Despite my unpleasant behaviour, he found a way to silently make a point that he was not prepared to stop coming to see us. With astonishment and powerlessness, I watched every time he walked into our flat and behaved as usual. And when it was time for him to go, he would politely say goodbye and leave. The following day he would be back. He just acted as if there was no issue at all. By then I could clearly see that he was up to something. I knew too that this something involved me and that was why he persistently came around to ensure that his plan would not have the slightest possibility of failure. He did his homework and calculations in such a smart way that I could not even figure out the exact moment when things changed. Then he deployed his best tactic, his charm. With that, in his view, he had given me all the necessary indications. All that remained for him to do then was to sit back and wait for me to make up my mind. For the first time in my life, I realised how cultural and personal differences can be invidious.

I was in a fix. In my eyes at that particular time in my life, getting involved with a man was already a major undertaking in itself. And to this I was to add two other stand-alone aspects, each of them with its specific challenges. Firstly, Wilfried was a man and white and secondly, he was a white person from Namibia. How was I supposed to deal with all this? And what would the others think of me? Was I not about to betray my own race? But could I throw this pertinent and genuine concern in Wilfried's face in a direct and honest manner? The list of questions popping up in my mind was endless and answers thereto were not forthcoming. The few friends and comrades to whom I tried to turn, showed very little sympathy, if any. In their eyes, yes, Wilfried was white and Namibian, but he was different. I could not find any indication of an answer in this over-simplified opinion. This was certainly my issue and I had to deal with it.

While I was blinded by his colour, Wilfried was forging ahead with his conviction. Despite my utter hostility towards him, he continued to portray kindness, and a caring helpful attitude. Looking back today, I see he was always close by and as soon as he realised that I was becoming desperate and impossible, he would gently and quietly fade away. At the slightest realisation that I had sufficient breathing space, he was back again. In fact while I was tormenting myself about the best strategy to make Wilfried realise wordlessly that a relationship, just in case that was what he had in mind, was unrealistic, he was simply fortifying his presence around me. He was always a few steps ahead of me and I found no opportunity to contradict him. After all he never said anything, he was simply there.

Was he aware that I had a serious issue with his skin colour? Seemingly not! Even if he did, for him it was a non-issue. Seriously speaking, how could I win a war against someone who did not believe in my war? Either you overrun the enemy on day one or you endlessly keep on building your case against him. Either way is challenging. Whatever I did with so many well considered tactics, Wilfried successfully undermined me. In the end I found myself in a situation where Wilfried and I were good friends, comrades and companions. But would I then be able to take the next step which many thought was a minor affair? This would require me to decisively make up my mind. Being in the company of Wilfried together with others did not require any making up of minds. We were always in groups; this was our life-style in exile and Wilfried happened just to be among those who were in my group. But I knew by now that his motive of being in the group had changed and this definitely required me to make up my mind.

Well, what else could I do? Wilfried was always there. As much as I was convinced that a relationship between the two of us was unimaginable, Wilfried's charm, smartness and patience were just inexhaustible. By July I had completely stopped seeing a problem in Wilfried's presence. When he organised a party to celebrate his birthday at the end of the same month, I happily danced with him. I was of course embracing Wilfried, but alas, I was very far from freeing myself from my self-inflicted trap. My usual issues were still there and were going to persist for a while despite my perceived efforts. For months to come I was going to be in a very challenging state of mind with my daily thoughts shifting from, 'It's ok, why not?' And the next minute, 'I was right, I cannot be doing this.'

Poor Wilfried did not know exactly what I was up to. He could not get it when I suggested a very discrete relationship. It was not part of what he knew and he would not at all adhere to that. Although he showed some kind of sympathy, he was not keen on secrets. I knew that I had caused him a hard time already but I still expected him to be understanding. The trouble was that I did not explain much to him. In any case it was hard to explain. What else? All the ingredients for a stormy beginning were there.

Our relationship moved on for two months despite my unrealistic expectations which popped up often between the two of us. Wilfried once again resorted to his patience. I knew that I was overdoing it but I did not know what else to do.

To my rescue, it was time to leave for France for a month to re-sit my outstanding exam. As usual, I packed and took my daughter along. Wilfried offered to look after Paleni but I did not find the arrangement right. Although my one month stay in France was really to complete my Master's, I also made use of the time to review my position toward Wilfried. Should I really keep him hanging? Could I make up my mind one way or the other? Besides his colour, what did I actually find wrong with him? Yes, I had had a terrible experience with a relationship, but was it right to take this out on him? And why should every relationship go wrong?

After pondering a number of questions, to which I evidently did not have fully satisfactory answers, I decided to write to Wilfried. I did not really know what to say to him, but I did write. Yes, I wanted to a certain extent to apologise for my behaviour, but I also wanted him to understand my case. I, however, found it difficult to state what my case was despite the fact that I was convinced that I had one. In the end, I narrowed my case down to his casual dressing code. T-shirts and flip flops at work were not quite acceptable. I meant well, but was that enough reason to write a letter? I nonetheless felt better once the letter was gone.

The day of my arrival back in Lusaka was a Monday morning. As I descended from the UTA flight, there was Wilfried dressed in a decent blue, yellow, gray and white striped shirt with matching gray pants. And of course, he wore proper shoes and socks. I had never seen him this decently dressed in all the time I had known him. He later told me that he had arrived the same morning from Harare where he had gone shopping. My letter had an effect but I felt I had been a bit harsh with him to have compelled him to go to Zimbabwe for shopping over a weekend. He had done so, and he did not seem to be unhappy about it.

Back in the flat from the airport, I found visitors. My cousin's wife Maggie had travelled all the way from Luanda, Angola, to bring her daughter to stay with me. She was sickly in Luanda, and the parents wanted to see whether the Zambian weather was any better. My niece Nelao was just over two years old. Of course, I was happy to see them, but I was far from being ready to explain to my cousin's wife who this

Wilfried was. Those who were staying with me were used to seeing him around, but I thought I should say something to my cousin's wife. This was not easy and I decided not to explain anything. She could guess and go and relay the information further in Luanda. I had already gone through hard times, and I had made up my mind at least not to go back to feeling guilty.

~

Towards the end of 1988 I was confident enough to ask Wilfried to switch flats with me. Dagmar had long returned to Germany and Loide had just left to the United Kingdom for further studies. Wilfried was therefore alone in a three bedroomed flat while I shared a one bedroomed flat with Maggie and the two children. Surely he did not need such a huge place for himself. I was right because Wilfried did not hesitate for a moment to switch flats. In no time Maggie, the two girls and I were settling into the spacious flat.

The switch of flats worked perfectly well until a few weeks later when Wilfried suggested he move back into his old flat. In his eyes, there was absolutely no reason why I should object to his moving in with us. The other reason was that break-ins to cars in the open yard at his new flat, my former flat, had increased, and his car was all of a sudden at risk. My own initiative of switching flats became a point of contention and of course a trigger for yet another challenge for me. Unless I returned to my one bedroomed flat, I was going to be in the wrong, whatever justification I could advance as to why Wilfried might not return to his flat.

When I explained to Wilfried why he could not move back to his flat, he opted not to contradict me on this point. He however had to find a different solution to the parking problem. One thing he refused to do was to park his car outside for the night. He therefore opted to park his car in his old garage at his old flat. From day one, the arrangement was just weird. In the morning, Wilfried would walk from his new flat to his old flat. He would then drive Paleni and Nelao to school and we proceeded to work. At lunch time he would pick up the girls from school to take them home while I was sitting and chatting under the tree. In the afternoon, Maggie and I would drive back with him to his flat which was by now our flat. He would then park his car and walk home. The following day was another day. I knew that this was not right but I did not know what else to do. And I knew too what was on everyone else's mind. I made the poor man move out of his flat with a garage to move to my flat without any parking arrangement. As a result, for the security of his car, he had to spend a considerable time going on foot between the two flats, not only to get his car and park it but also to drive my daughter and my niece to and from school as well as Maggie and myself to and from work. I could feel how many friends and comrades found the arrangement a bit unusual. I became the evil one again.

Obviously, the switch of flats was not a good idea and as I tried to sort out things with Wilfried, I was getting into the next phase of confusion. Wilfried was gently asking to come back to his old flat and I was adamant that he was not considerate enough. He seemed to have forgotten that I preferred a not too obvious relationship. My reminder did not appear to have rung a bell. He simply could not see any problem with the two of us living together. I, on the other hand, could only see it as a huge problem and had to figure out how to discourage Wilfried from pursuing his idea. All the tricks I used never worked nor deterred him. I was the one who had to do something which somehow meant that he was, after all, right again.

At this point in my life, I decided to deal with my various areas of concern related to Wilfried. Without any discussion, Wilfried appeared to be prepared to allow me space and time. At least that was my assumption. I don't think that he knew exactly what the matter was with me, but I am convinced that he knew I needed to sort out myself. Silently, he was going to allow me as much time as I needed. Obviously, I did not know his exact position at that time. Neither did it really matter much to me.

I decided gradually to do a bit of work on my own person. To unpack and free my heart of some of the pain, unwind some of the protective layers I had heaped on myself, and slightly close my eyes to what others might think. What a hard process! I knew too well that in the eyes of my close friends, I had no case. There was no point in turning to them for support. Yet I knew better than anyone else about my pain and the subsequent devised protective blocks I had built around myself. I knew too that I had vowed to myself never to allow such pain to reach out to me ever again! Was I then not about to deceive myself? I seriously hesitated. On the other hand, I was also aware of the usual saying: life must go on. Yet, as much as I believed in that, was this a solid base to rely on? No, I needed to carefully watch my every step. Wilfried was gentle, kind and caring, but...

The following weeks were going to be hard. I was locked up in a battle with myself. I could change my view or my position from one minute to the next. If need be, I would also lock myself away somewhere and refuse to give any response or explanation. Wilfried would come around, take the girls to school and back, and also Maggie and me to work and back. Maggie and Loide (but another Loide), our closest friends, were going to be disappointed with me. Events were never predictable until they had happened. They both enjoyed outings outside Lusaka, and were utterly disappointed if I got into one of those moods and decided not to go along. The end result was always that the entire trip got cancelled.

Wilfried was going to prevail against all odds. I was completely beyond myself. My moods were unpredictable, even for myself. It was just hard for me to win the battle within myself. And unfortunately, it was going to be a long one. Wilfried patiently stood by and waited for me to sort myself out. He knew precisely when to get out of my way. Only once did he try to enquire as to what exactly was the matter with me, and how long I would continue with this indifferent attitude. I recall that we were in the kitchen when he put that question to me. I looked at him and the first thing I noticed was the contrasting colours around him. He wore a red shirt, had a touch of red in his eyes surrounding his blue iris. Although he always wore a kind and smiling face, it was not the case this time. For the very first time ever since I had got to know him, his look expressed a real sadness. I had no answer to his query. I knew that at that stage I simply did not know what I wanted. And as such, whatever he was expecting from me, which was seemingly simple and straightforward in his blue eyes, was seriously too difficult for me. I did not find words to put all this to him in a clear manner. I must have stubbornly said something vague in defense of my attitude. Wilfried must have taken that for an answer and on that note, returned to his flat.

Amazingly, we got along, but barely. And I, in my total confusion, was not at all concerned. Whatever the end result was going to be, either way was fine. Difficult situations are just such that one cannot help things. Yet, one day, when we were invited to a function, Wilfried asked me to go along. Again, I happened to have said yes, and this time I did go along. Why? I don't think I had an answer at that time. I just happened to have done so. But I wished that we should not make it obvious that we were together and by no means should we confirm what people clearly saw. Nothing was going to make me happier than if Wilfried had kept his distance, and I specifically asked him to do so. And that is exactly the opposite of what he did. I quietly observed him and knew exactly what I was going to tell him later in the car. Unfortunately for me, we were not going to be alone in the car on our way back. A friend, Frieda Williams, wanted a lift.

As soon as we were in the car, Frieda went quiet. In my mind, she was sleeping. This was my chance to make Wilfried understand that under the circumstances, I would highly appreciate it if he did not make things obvious in public. Wilfried couldn't get it. I went on for a while, despite his calm composure. Finally, I insisted to be dropped off first, before Frieda. Wilfried was taken aback by my unexpected outburst. Where did he go wrong? He kept close to me at the party and that was all. Well, that was the trouble.

The following day, as I was busy at my desk, my office door was abruptly pushed open and my dear mother Pendukeni was standing in front of me. With a broad smile, she wanted to know if I had time to go for lunch at the restaurant of my choice. I never said no to an invitation to a restaurant in those days, and when I was offered a choice, there was only one place: the Makumbi restaurant at the Lusaka Continental Hotel. I grabbed my bag and followed Pendukeni to her car. The car was not locked and there was someone in the passenger seat. This was none other than Frieda. Well and good, Frieda and Pendukeni were friends. I got to know Frieda through Pendukeni. If she was also invited, why not? I greeted Frieda and off we went.

It was not difficult to find a table and in no time, I was picking out my favourite food from the buffet. I just loved buffet at Makumbi! In fact, it was a new discovery for me. Choosing food at my liberty, and again and again at my discretion, things could not be better. With my plate generously filled, I settled at our table. Pendukeni chose to sit right opposite me. Just before I started enjoying my favourite meal, I heard her clearing her throat. As I looked up my eyes met a stern look. I knew she could get serious, but this was the first time that I had seen her act this serious towards me. She indicated that she wanted to speak to me. Oh dear, what had I done this time?

Frieda sat there very innocently. From her look, I could not see anything that could possibly indicate any connection to what Pendukeni was about to say to me. I cannot recall any introduction to the topic but from the long speech I got from Pendukeni, I gathered that she did not agree with my attitude toward Wilfried simply because of his skin colour. Did I have any suggestion on how he could change it? She went further to say that the time had come for me to be crystal clear with the man. Was it 'yes' or 'no'? In her opinion, keeping this man in further suspense was out of the question. Should I continue with my current flagrant attitude she would speak to Wilfried. In fact, her intention was to confront the two of us and to tell me exactly what she was telling me in the presence of Wilfried. She decided against her initial intention just so as not to cause me embarrassment. The bottom line in her view was that I had no right to abuse the poor man. I needed to free him from the suspense. And then she dropped the bombshell: 'After all, you are not the most beautiful girl that I know.'

At hearing that, I pulled myself together. You know the attentive reaction one gets from a sudden fright? That was exactly my instinctual reaction. Pendukeni did not smile. Neither did her look indicate that she was expecting a reaction from me. I was there to listen attentively. She made it clear that she was speaking to me, of course firstly as a mother figure, but also as a SWAPO leader. What did this guy think of her standing by and seeing him being literally abused by someone so close to her? I was not sure whether that was really Wilfried's feeling, but my opinion was not being solicited. Frieda concentrated on her food and acted as if she did not hear what was being said to me. Did she really not have anything to do with this? Was her being with Pendukeni on this particular day just pure coincidence? I did not care to find out. I left my nice food untouched, but amazingly, I did not feel upset towards Pendukeni. Was it because I had always had respect towards her motherly approach to me, or was it because she was right?

Not much was said to me in the car and I was dropped off at UNIN. I had the afternoon to myself before I had to face Wilfried when he dropped us off after work. One thing was certain, he would not find out about my lunch appointment with Pendukeni. I would keep this to myself for a while. As soon as I was alone, I started figuring out what I was going to do. Pendukeni was clear. The time had come for me to make a decision. She was not the first one to offer advice, but she had said it so eloquently and in firm terms. Could all close friends including Pendukeni really undermine me? Or was it I who was simply impossible? If the latter was true, when on earth was I going to deal with it? The hard part of the story was that I had to deal with it there in Lusaka, not only right next to Wilfried, but also right in front of those who all along had long thought I had been irrational and unreasonable. I did not want them to be right! Would that mean I had been wrong all this time?

Although I desperately needed to save face, I also knew that this time I needed support. Could I turn to Wilfried for that much-needed support? Then, it would be an overwhelming victory for him! No, I could not acknowledge clear cut defeat. I must hold onto something that could represent bargaining power. But could I still afford to continue being irrational? What if Pendukeni got to hear about it? Seriously speaking, how could I suddenly be so nice to the man after having been unreasonable towards him for so long despite his kindness and caring attitude? What explanation would I have as to why I had on numerous occasions locked him out, including out of his own old flat? What was it that led to these unnecessary outbursts without any provocation? It was hard to hope that he would not raise some of these issues once the dust had settled.

Be that as it may, I was simply going to be nice. I had close to six months to sort out issues with myself, but I had not managed. So many other people had noticed my wicked ways and had caringly spoken to me. None of them seemed to have approved of my behaviour, as much as I thought I had a valid reason. The final relieving occurrence was an unexpected visit of Chief Kaulinge, Pendukeni's first husband. He lived in Angola, and I did not have much contact with him since he had left Berlin for Luanda. He turned up unannounced late one evening and wanted to speak to me. Although I was happy to see him after such a long time, I found it difficult to guess why he had come for a visit at this late hour of the day.

Chief Kaulinge is a quiet but very gentle person. As soon as we were alone, he wanted to know what was happening in my life since our last telephonic conversation before he had passed the phone to Aaron back in mid 1986. This was just before he left Berlin for Luanda. I knew that he was aware that my 'marriage' to Aaron was as good as non-existent. I took pains to explain to him that I had, in the meantime, met someone else and I spoke at length about the man's many great qualities before I came to the last sentence, 'But he is white.' I took a long breath, sat back and waited for Chief's reaction to such an unexpected pronouncement. Calmly, Chief leaned forward, gently touched the back of my hand, and with fatherly care, pronounced these four words: 'With all my blessings.' I cannot remember what else he said after that, but those four words were tremendously soothing. Here were two people who, simply because I had lived with them and had looked after their son back in the late 1970s, had taken genuine interest in the rest of my life.

Whatever was pressing my heart was finally gone. My assumptions about a number of things on my peculiar relationship appeared to be invalid to so many of those who cared for me, including those who had watched over me from a distance. And Chief Kaulinge was one of them. His caring gesture meant so much to me, and had moved me to such an extent that for the very first time that particular year, I felt cleansed from my self-inflicted guilt. Did it really mean there was absolutely nothing wrong with my relationship with Wilfried? Did others, in particular those who mattered to me, really find it normal? It sounded genuine, especially because Chief Kaulinge had made the special effort to visit me at this hour of the day, specifically to reassure me of his approval. For the first time in many months I made peace with myself. This was the beginning of trying to pretend that all had been fine after all. As much as it was not going to be an easy shift, I was determined to give it a serious try.

⤺

The issue was not that I did not love Wilfried. I did, and had done so for quite a while already. The problem was that I had embroiled myself in immense confusion about a number of things. Although it sounds very simple today, at that time I saw myself getting into a complex situation. I was getting involved, not only with a man after my utterly unbearable experience a few years earlier, but with a white man who was from Namibia. These are three distinct challenges which in my eyes required individual consideration. Firstly, I might not have reacted the same way if I had not emerged from the kind of relationship I had known. Secondly, I might have reacted differently if Wilfried was a white man from a different country. As much as I admired his kindness and caring attitude, I could not find a convincing explanation about what he would do with his Namibian whiteness. Would he just throw it out of the window? How could he if he came from a community which capitalized so much on this whiteness, to the extent that it became a decisive element of their identity? Of course I could not clearly articulate this inner disbelief, neither to Wilfried nor to anyone else. Instead I kept it to myself and moaned about other minor issues such as age difference and my marital status. No wonder no one understood or supported me.

After a drawn-out and exhaustive torment, it was high time that I gave myself a break. Eight anxious months had been long, very long. Wilfried was white and from Namibia and he would remain that way. It was time to wait and see how things would evolve. In situations as this, predictability is hard to come by. Besides Wilfried himself, I knew no one who was closely related to him. Although an elder brother by the name Christof had come from Bulawayo to Lusaka for a short visit, this was far too insignificant to guess anything about their world back home. There was not much I could do about it. If Wilfried was prepared to gamble with his colour, I could also attempt to gamble with my life and leave my future to guess work.

At long last I was at peace with myself. Wilfried was there and we had both finally laid down arms. The flat issue had long been resolved too as Wilfried moved in with us into the three bedroomed flat. Wilfried held onto the key of his flat, my initial flat, just in case. He from time to time offered it to those who were temporarily homeless. His brother Christof stayed there when he came for a visit. I also recall my two old school mates who were on the way from their studies in Bulgaria staying there for a good number of weeks.

It was perhaps better for both of us that at that particular moment of our lives we had our hearts and minds cleared. Otherwise we, as Namibians, were going to miss out on something as important in our lives which was on the verge of happening: the independence of our country. Of course no Namibian who was right in his mind at that time would have missed out on this historic moment. It was only good that the two of us did not have to drag heavy hearts into such a jovial period. Whatever unfinished business there was, we could put it aside and allow ourselves time to partake fully in events surrounding the independence of our motherland.

8

Namibia gains independence

As we moved into 1989, all of a sudden the talk of Namibia's independence picked up and it became a real possibility among many in exile including myself. I just happen to be one of those who don't follow logic and I am often among those who 'click' very late. And this happened to me also with the approaching of the Namibian independence. Many of my colleagues pretended afterwards that they saw it coming all along and were 100% sure that this time it really was happening. In my case, I only realised somewhere in March, three months before the first group returned home. Was it because we were close to independence so many times before, and unexpected turns of events changed the course of events? Or was it because I didn't really understand how world politics worked? I don't know. It was probably both. Be that as it may, we were at the verge of gaining independence, and as unrealistic as it might have sounded to many of us, we were about to return home. All of a sudden, our lives were fully preoccupied with our return home: the repatriation, the forms, the vaccinations, who should leave when and why, etc. You can imagine the wild and imaginative thoughts that went through our minds! Would it be safe to return home? Where would we stay? Would we be able to go to our respective homes? How would we keep in touch with each other? Could we just be on our own within our families? I could not imagine how all this would work out. It was a question of waiting and seeing.

Things started moving very fast. Very soon people started talking about the first group to return home. This group was going to be composed of the main figures of the SWAPO leadership, to be led by Hage Geingob. Hage Geingob, in his capacity as Director of UNIN, and above all as senior leader of SWAPO in Lusaka, kept us informed about new developments. He saw to it that meetings were organised both at UNIN and outside, including at his house.

After so many years of waiting and unbelievably slow progress, things moved surprisingly fast. In fact, things moved so fast that many of us started doubting the practical reality of it. While some of us were doubting, the first group leaving for home were getting organised for the trip. Could this really be? That people were returning home? And that home was really Namibia? The story was just too good to believe. No, it could not be, it was again one of those bad dreams from which one takes so long to wake up.

We had spent days and nights, doing nothing else but thinking and dreaming about this Namibia! And as time went on, we had imagined what our families were possibly doing. What pain we went through, as we gradually glided into the determination to sacrifice for our motherland, even though unreachable for the longest time. *One day, but only one day, we would prevail.* At times that *one day* appeared to be within our reach. But there were also times, when that *one day* was quite remote. There were even times when that one day could be possible only in the lives of our children or even that of our children's children. But our background and our experience had sharpened our determination for high sacrifices for that *one day*, even if that *one day* would come way beyond our generation. What kept us going was that this *one day* would happen!

↬

Early in 1989, this *one day* was about to happen. We sat there, in one of the UNIN meeting rooms listening to Hage Geingob explaining the events leading to this possible independence of our country, and the high likelihood of our return to Namibia in the following few months. I looked at the man, and could hardly believe that this was happening in my lifetime. I had literally yearned for this day, had shed tears and cried myself to sleep so many nights before reaching the state of acceptance of the hard reality of our situation as a struggling people. Once that state was reached, we had our minds geared to travelling that challenging route towards our independence. And here I was, about to witness an extraordinary occurrence. And this Hage Geingob was very serious about our return to Namibia. He himself was going to lead the first delegation back to Namibia. It sounded like a joke, but at the same time, the man was serious.

A few days later, we were invited to Hage Geingob's house. There we got to know a bit more about the first group to return home. Unbelievably, a date was set for their departure. So was the itinerary: part of the group would depart from Lusaka and have a stopover in Luanda to pick up the rest of the group. We had even received a special invitation: those who wanted to see the first group leaving in style should go to the Lusaka airport on such a day and at such a time! Hage himself looked brave, composed and confident to lead the first SWAPO delegation back home. After having been in exile since the early 1960s, there he was telling us in a casual manner about leading the first group back to Namibia. We were of course very impressed and amazed. But a few years later, Hage opened up and shared a bit with us about how he felt as a human being in such a trying moment. This was a national mission. And he was to carry out this specific mission for the SWAPO leadership. With SWAPO teaching and discipline, an assignment for the just cause had to be carried out. And Hage Geingob had to do just that!

We observed as the first group prepared to leave. Things went so fast that I lost track. All of a sudden, for the first time, Wilfried spoke about his family. It really never occurred to me to figure out the kind of family he was from and since he never said anything about them, I also didn't ask any questions. I really would not have known what to ask about. I only knew him, and nothing about the society he was from. Now that things were moving and there was talk of going back home, Wilfried started wondering what the reaction of his family would be. Since I had no clue, I let him attend to his concerns. Wilfried was of course far from asking for my solidarity in relation to his family, but he was clearly looking for a solid commitment from my side. Was I ready to give that? I was not sure, but I did not indicate a clear 'no' either.

In the meantime, the UN was hard at work repatriating Namibians back home. Repatriation forms were completed on a daily basis, vaccines had been administered and busses ferried hundreds of Namibians to airports on a daily basis. The repatriation was really happening! Hage Geingob and his team had long landed in Windhoek and many other people had returned to Namibia. There were no major difficulties reported. Wilfried and I had been to Harare for a weekend. He needed my commitment and I finally gave it. Well, something had to be said between the two of us before we embarked on this sacred mission of returning home.

Our own repatriation was coming closer. It was going to be on a particular day in August 1989. I was going to be on the same flight with a number of colleagues from UNIN and the Extension Unit, a UN project that was created for the purpose of producing teaching material for the SWAPO schools.

We assembled at Mr Joseph Ithana's house, the UNIN Registrar, from where we were to be taken to the airport. We impatiently waited for transport. I was with Paleni who was four years old by then. She had no clue about the happenings, so she was not really bothered whether we left Lusaka that day or not at all. She happily played around with other children and that day was just a day like any other day for them. We adults grew impatient and when we were informed that we were only leaving the following day, we decided to camp in the sitting room of the house where we were until the next day. Was this out of protest? Or was it simply out of laziness, knowing that the next day we would leave anyway! The positive side of it was that we spent so much time speculating how things would be upon our arrival in Windhoek. We were not that concerned about the security. So many others had been repatriated since June. We were among the last ones to leave for home.

Meanwhile, Wilfried had left by car. He repatriated himself back home. For some reason, he knew that he needed his car back home and his only way home was to forfeit his repatriation air ticket and to repatriate himself. We did not agree where to meet in Windhoek. I knew nothing about Windhoek. I had never been there and there was absolutely no point in giving me an appointment anywhere in that town. I would have never found the place.

The following day, 7 August 1989, was going to be the definite date of our return home. I don't recall much about the events before our departure, but I remember the discussions on board the plane. Those who knew Windhoek spoke about specific places and people they would like to visit immediately after their arrival. The rest of us listened and constantly checked our watches to establish how close we were to the arrival time. When the plane started its descent, silence fell onboard. Those with window seats started searching for whatever landmarks they could recognise. I personally wondered whether there was anything to see at all. I would see whatever was there to be seen once on the ground.

꿈

As we disembarked, I looked around. Besides the few buildings of the airport, there was really nothing to catch the eye. Is this Windhoek, the capital, we have been referring to whenever we spoke about home? The dry season rendered the place gray. Well, this was apparently home. We got into the few buses that were waiting for us and were on our way to Windhoek proper, the others explained. Since I had never been there before, nothing really meant much to me. We drove through town and were taken straight to the Centre at Döbra. I had heard about Döbra before. I knew so many people who had studied there, but this would be my first time at this famous Catholic place. As we came over a hill, we saw a massive place with tents spreading out until just in front of the Catholic church in the background. We were just arriving from a life in exile where we had lived in tents, to take up our new lives in our motherland, but again, starting off in tents. I do not know why I didn't expect to see tents, but living in a tent in your own country seemed a bit weird.

Anyway, everyone without exception had to go through the Repatriation Centre. After queuing up for registration and receiving some basic items, a mattress, a cooking pot, a bucket to draw water and plates, we were shown to our tents. Here and there, one bumped into a friend or a study comrade and the hugging and quick chatting started. These were people with whom one had crossed paths, either in a camp, in Lusaka or on one of the trips or journeys. We moved around so much that we kept on running into each other. And here we were, finally back home, meeting in the Centre which, for practical purposes, was similar to a camp, just the way we had known for years. There were so many of us and one knew almost half the population of the camp.

I was hardly in my tent when I decided to go back to the reception area. There I bumped into Father Bernhard Nordkamp, a Catholic priest who worked in Okatana for a short while in the late sixties. I could not really remember him from that time but he had been Vicar-General of the Catholic Church in Namibia for a long time and we all knew his name. He had also visited Father Kaishara in Lusaka the previous year and we had had time to chat. After exchanging greetings, he enquired whether I would be interested to stay at a Catholic mission where he was staying, at St. Boniface in Pionierspark. The name did not mean anything to me, but Catholic missions are all the same. Once you have lived in one, you can live in any of the others. I also knew from corresponding with Father Houben that he was staying at the same place. So, I happily accepted the offer and off I went to collect my daughter and my luggage.

I was indeed happy to see Father Houben again. We spoke a lot about Okatana and the number of changes, the involvement and the contribution of the Namibian churches in the struggle for liberation of the country and subsequently in the repatriation process. Father Houben spoke at length of his experience in his efforts to assist Namibians in custody starting with the captives from Cassinga back in 1978. I was quite amazed at his creativity in handing over a bible to the South African Army authorities destined for an imprisoned person. If the bible was not returned, that confirmed the presence of the imprisoned person. This is how a number of aspects came to the fore, to allow appreciation of the efforts and challenges of those who were back at home.

⬿

From Pionierspark, I phoned my sister to announce my arrival in Namibia. Surprisingly, we did not have much to tell each other. After very stiff greetings and telling her of my return home, I had nothing else to tell her. She also expressed her happiness that I was finally back and the hope to see me soon, but more than that was simply not possible. For the first time, I had a vague sense of the possible challenge of communication between my siblings and me. Twelve years had been a long time!

A few days later we thanked Father Houben and his colleagues at Pionierspark for having hosted us for these very first days in Windhoek. It was again time to move on and gradually find my way back home. How and when exactly I was going to do that, I wasn't sure at all. All of a sudden there was an uncertainty and reluctance to take the steps towards home. In Windhoek, one knew where the others were.We were still returnees who relied heavily on one another.

From Pionierspark I moved to Khomasdal where Pendukeni and her family were allocated a house. Pendukeni, whom I first met as a student at UNIN, was by now part of the SWAPO leadership. After her studies at UNIN, she became Secretary-General of SWAPO's Women's Council and member of the Central Committee. These are the two positions she held at the time we returned to Namibia. After a customary phone call, I naturally moved in. Wilfried was in any case already there. He was part of those who were assigned specific tasks at the SWAPO Directorate of Elections, an office created specifically to prepare for SWAPO's participation in the UN supervised elections that would lead Namibia to independence. Hage Geingob was entrusted with the task of heading the office as SWAPO Director of Elections. As usual, many of us did not quite understand what was happening. After the overwhelming phase of the sudden, moving but unbelievable repatriation to Namibia, it was now time to understand practically what was going to happen to us.

First of all, we were now living in these individual houses and no longer in a community environment where the other comrades were just a few steps away. Secondly, the South African apartheid government machinery, including its military presence, was overwhelming and caused a constant sense of insecurity among some of us. The name of the South African Administrator in Namibia, Louis Pienaar, and exactly what he said about the process leading to Namibian independence was often mentioned on the news. In the city centre, we were confronted by the real Namibian population with all its shades and we started wondering how welcome we were here. And, lastly, there were these fellows with blue berets who belonged to the United Nations Transitional Assistance Group (UNTAG), the name given to the UN contingent that was sent to Namibia to ensure the smooth transition and to supervise the very first genuine elections in Namibia. The UNTAG consisted of a civilian administrative component but also a military component with real international flavour. They were under the leadership of Mr Martti Ahtisaari, a Finnish diplomat at the time, who was given the challenging task of being the Special Envoy of the UN Secretary-General to Namibia. As a Finnish national, Namibians placed confidence in him in this rather precarious situation. We were assured that members of the SADF who remained in the country were confined to the two bases at Oshivelo and at Grootfontein. SWAPO PLAN members on the other hand were confined to bases in Angola, very far from the Namibian border. But another worrying factor was another armed group that was an integral part of the SADF, officially known as SWATF (South West African Territorial Force), and another police unit commonly known as Koevoet among the black population. This was a notorious armed group consisting of Namibians, mainly Blacks, who really terrorised Namibians. In the eyes of the UN, these were Namibians and not South Africans, and could simply go home. Although demobilised by then, former SWATF and Koevoet members constituted a real threat in the eyes of many of us.

We developed a habit of just going to stand around the Office of the SWAPO Directorate of Elections. After having lived in communities in exile, not being in touch with others became a problem. Hanging around the SWAPO Directorate gave us a chance of seeing those who were working there who were mainly from exile, and other returnees who came to stand around just like us. Secondly, in exile, we were well surrounded and guided and this sense of guidance and belonging all of a sudden fell away, leaving us in a vacuum. Seeing others and chatting with them re-assured us of our togetherness although from a distance. There was no camp to go back to. And of course the element of insecurity was there and we spent time telling each other what we had seen and observed. The experience of the others and their views were very important as we struggled to find our feet on the ground in this new but harsh environment.

⁓

After a few days in Khomasdal, it was again time to think about going home. After an intense yearning while in exile to return to our families,

I was surprisingly taking my time to go home. After 12 years away, I was about to return home and face my family: my father, my sister and my seven brothers. They would certainly look different by now. My father would have grown older, my sister who was just a teenager when I left was now a mother of two and my older brothers were real men by now. My youngest brother whom I had never seen was by then already 12 years old. These were all new people to me. Twelve years had turned my family members into complete strangers and I had to learn to know them again. Did they have a similar concern regarding me?

As I was trying to figure out how to get home and confront my family, something else was bothering me and it was important for me to find a reasonable explanation for it before embarking on my way home. Two years earlier, my third brother Romanus, whom we called Roma, had gone into exile. When I heard about it while in Lusaka, I tried to find out from people who knew us from home, whether they knew where Roma was. I did not manage to find out. This was a war situation and people were on the move all the time. Young men came out of Namibia, had a number of months of military training and returned to the front. I took it for granted that that was what must have happened to Roma and that he would turn up one day. But things had changed now. People had returned to Namibia and I still did not know the whereabouts of Roma. My father would definitely want me to tell him where Roma was. Could I just say that I did not know? But I was returning from the same exile, how could I give such an answer? Could I then say that he was still coming? But how certain was I about this? I did not want to think the worst, but this could as well have been the case. We were waging a war of liberation and many compatriots laid down their precious lives.

As I was struggling to find an explanation which would stop my father from asking me too many questions about Roma, a security guard walked into the house to announce that I had a visitor waiting outside. A visitor for me? It could only be one of the many comrades from exile, I thought to myself. Who else could trace me to Khomasdal after only these few days in Windhoek? I rushed out and there stood a young boy with a face similar to my daughter's. There was no doubt that this was someone related to me. Could this be one of my brothers? But what was he doing in Windhoek, and how did he know that I was in Khomasdal, and in this specific house? I greeted the boy and enquired who he was. This was Linus, my fifth brother. He was at St Joseph's Secondary School at Döbra and he and other learners had spent long hours at the fence of the Repatriation Centre at Döbra observing the new arrivals with the hope of identifying a sister, a brother, an uncle, an aunt, returning from exile. When he had not identified me among the many returnees after standing at the fence every single day since the establishment of the Centre, he managed through other contacts to find out that I had indeed arrived at Döbra, but had gone again. Similarly, he managed to trace me to Khomasdal. After all, this was his second year at Döbra and he knew Windhoek a bit.

Here I was, in front of my little brother who had made all that effort to find me, yet I did not know what to talk to him about. Linus, who was five when I left, was not even in school at the time. Now, here he was, already a secondary school learner. We spoke a bit about home and about his school. When I mentioned to him that I was about to leave for home, his spontaneous response was, 'That's good. Father will be happy. Roma passed through Döbra a month ago and he's already at home.' My search for an explanation was over and I could go home without fear of being subjected to queries about my little brother, the only one to have been in exile with me.

~

It was now time seriously to figure out how I would get home. For the last few years, my life had been about figuring out solutions to challenges, one after another. The pattern had been, as soon as I had figured out how to go about a challenge, the next challenge would automatically present itself. Naturally I would start all over to figure out how to tackle the new challenge which could drag on for a few months. Ideally, I avoided having to deal with parallel challenges, preferring one at a time.

It is hard to imagine going to one's home becoming a challenge, particularly in our case when this had been our natural dream over so many years. This was going to be my second time on this road between Windhoek and my home, 750 km away. The first time was in 1976 at the age of 17 when I undertook a trip to Windhoek to get my first pair of eyeglasses. That was the closest place to consult an optometrist at the time. But I was in an ambulance and had not the faintest interest in returning to Windhoek one day. I knew no one and had really no business there. Here I was now, 13 years later, trying to figure out how to travel the very same route to get to my home, where I had not been for 12 years. Would I find a bus? Would I run into someone coming from the same area as me and we could find our way back home together? Or would I simply run into another person with a car and get a lift back home?

Questioning yourself on a matter you have far too little information about can lead to a nonsensical situation. I did not know Windhoek to be able to get to the part of town where I could enquire about transport. Neither had I any idea of the direction nor of signs along the way to enable me to know that I was indeed on the right way. I knew absolutely nothing and I would only be able to recognise anything once I was at the village bordering mine. Beyond that I would not be sure of anything. But I needed to go home and I needed to find a way.

As I was devising my various plans of finding other returnees from the same area as me to link up with them to wrestle our way home, Wilfried's plan had been ready for days. He knew for sure that he would soon hear me saying that I wanted to go home. Although he had never travelled that route before, he had looked it up on a map and apparently knew where to go. After all, there were not so many roads in Namibia. In fact, according to him, there were only four main roads out of Windhoek: one to the south, one to the east, one to the north and north-east and the fourth one to the coast (the west). In our case, we would take the one to the north and north-east and since there are clear road signs, nothing could go wrong. We could go any time whenever Paleni and I were ready to travel. It would be good though if it could be closer to a weekend so that the travelling would not interfere too much with his work at the SWAPO Directorate of Elections.

⌒

Wilfried had not changed one bit since I had come to know him. He took things in such a simple way and looked at them purely and solely from his point of view. I looked at him saying all this to me in a most natural manner, as if this was the normal thing to do, and everyone would just understand and take it exactly in the same simple manner as he did. From his look and tone, he expected nothing other than appreciation of and agreement with his proposal. I was again in a dilemma: if I disagreed with Wilfried, did I really have a solid plan of how to get home? No. But could I just turn up with this man at my sister's house and later at home and tell everyone, 'This is Wilfried'?

Again, the next challenge was right in front of me. I had hard facts at hand. Unless I found someone from the same area who could travel home with me, it would be a bit of a struggle to find my way home. Wilfried had made every effort and had diarised his travelling with us up north. Could I just shrug my shoulders and stubbornly stick to an impossible mission? No, I already had a bad record behind me and there was no going back. It would not be fair this time. But at the same time I knew that I had better have a good explanation by the time I got home. I could not just pretend to have run into a white man who was so kind as to drive me and my daughter all the way from Windhoek to my village! In any case, any other sensible explanation would be ridiculous in the Namibia of those days. I was never short of ideas and I would find one and see whether Wilfried would buy it. I really hoped to count on him this time. This was not the time for unrealistic ideas. This was the crucial moment of meeting my family after a lengthy absence, which was already a challenge on its own.

By the time we started off from Windhoek, Wilfried was well informed of my idea. We would pose, not as strangers, but as acquaintances of some kind. And since Wilfried was on his way to somewhere in the north, he gave us a lift up to the house of my sister in Ongwediva. After dropping us off, he would go on his way. He was to spend the night at the hotel in the vicinity and would proceed to his destination the following morning. Wilfried did not contradict me in any way in this story throughout the journey. Instead of commenting much on my well thought out plan, he pointed out a number of things he knew about along the way including the names of towns we passed through. In each town and settlement we passed, we took note of enthusiastic Namibians getting ready and eagerly waiting for the very first elections in their lives. We also took note of colourful political party flags displayed at houses and businesses along the road. As our yellow car sped by, enthusiastic people showed the SWAPO power salute. They did not need to know who was in the car, a SWAPO supporter or not, it did not matter. It was the spirit of the time. They must have been surprised to see a white arm emerging from the car responding to their power salute.

The spirit of the people all along the way was overwhelming. Compared to the cautious and careful population I had known 12 years ago, here were Namibians on the move towards their independence. The elections were still about two months away, with independence itself much later. But people were on the move towards the overdue liberation of their country. The members of UNTAG were visible everywhere. And their presence must have given the people so much confidence to display their happiness and determination to march forward. The further north we drove, the more people we passed, and of course the more we saw flags of the SWAPO Party, and power salutes. It was a moving experience. I had not known my people this way. They had always displayed their determination, but in concealed ways. For the first time I saw them saying it loud and clear and moving all in the same direction. It was encouraging. Yet, I still had my reservations about the environment of my home village. Would everyone be happy to see the returnees? I was not sure.

⤶

After six hours of driving through an ever changing landscape, from mountainous to bushy areas, we finally came to an area which resembled home although not quite yet. There were fewer trees, more homesteads but less neatly constructed. Every now and then we would drive past cuca shops along each side of the road. Their ever increasing number and the many people hanging around them was certainly a novelty for me. As a child, it was rare to see a cuca shop and adults went there only occasionally. It would now appear that some people if not many of them, literally lived in these colourful little buildings. Before I had left 12 years ago, cuca shops were drinking places for adults and absolutely not for children and above all, no one slept there. As we progressed, I wondered whether my village still had its trees and its neatly built homesteads.

Just after sunset, we were parking outside my sister's house in Ongwediva. Based on her directions provided over the phone, Wilfried drove straight to the right house. We didn't stop once to ask for directions. As I opened the door of the car, I took note of the surroundings. Everything was new for me. Yet this town was only about 4 km away from my village. I later realised that, as children, we had passed through this area between Omayanga and our first homestead. Since we passed through here on foot, home shouldn't be far. But all that surrounded me hadn't existed 12 years ago. That is why I could not orient myself in this place.

As we got out of the car, a young lady who was chatting to her neighbours rushed to greet us. I carefully watched her. Although a number of her features including her voice indicated she was my sister, I could not fully recognise in her my sister of 12 years ago. Although my sister had always been loud, this one was slightly louder. Being a spontaneous and daring person, she approached me in a well-rehearsed yet natural and courageous manner. I deployed a wait and see attitude. This woman threw her arms around my neck and embraced me in a welcoming manner. Without realising what I was doing, I also embraced her and responded to her greetings. This was indeed my sister Rita! She took our luggage and invited us in. Wilfried didn't react when his bag was carried into the house instead of being left in the car. Once inside and under the light, I tried to observe how much of my little sister I could make out in this full-grown woman. Not really that much. She spoke fast and suggested a number of things without giving us much chance to respond. Clearly, this was her home and we were her guests. She went ahead to serve us drinks and food. She didn't look alarmed by the presence of the white man. Although I introduced Wilfried to her, she didn't react the normal way of 'Glad to meet you'. Wilfried, instead of being a visitor, if not a stranger, comfortably settled into his chair and was also just naturally going with the flow. During supper, he spontaneously responded to Rita's easy talk and laughed along.

Soon after supper though, I disrupted their conversation and asked my sister to no longer delay the departure of this poor man, who had kindly given me a lift from Windhoek. I explained that he had a booking at a nearby hotel and it was getting late. He might not be able to check in if it got too late. Wilfried did not react to my utterance. Yet, he had a room booked at Continental Number One. He knew about it and he had agreed to the arrangement. But why was he no longer willing to play the game? Instead of seeing him taking leave and thanking my sister, I heard my sister telling him, 'Wilfried, we know who you are, please take your bag and follow me'. As my sister led the way, she took my luggage along and I watched at them disappearing into a room. They returned and resumed their chatting. I am not quite sure how much chatting I did. I was perplexed. How could Wilfried agree to a strategy and arrive here to be the accomplice of someone whom he did not know? All he knew was that she was supposed to be my sister.

Later, when we were alone in the room and I asked him why he unexpectedly changed his mind about the arrangement. He responded, 'Rita asked me to stay, and she is right'. I had no answer to that response. I did not care what my sister asked. The two of us had an agreement all the way from Windhoek. How could we possibly arrive here and fall for something suggested by someone we hardly knew. I knew she was my sister, but I was still to discover who she really was. But my dear Wilfried was just too happy to be invited to overnight here. We were in a new environment. And this was my territory. I knew my people and I knew that they would need preparation before knowing the reality about Wilfried and me. We could not subject them right away to this unusual reality. I repeated my disappointment several times to Wilfried, but he ignored me. In his view, it was high time that I accepted realities.

Well and good, this was not the time to pick a fight. The following morning, I was going to be taken home. Wilfried would leave early in the morning for Windhoek. I was indeed grateful as I wanted to do this last bit by myself. My return home was not going to be easy. Yes, I had longed for it, but now as I was about to do it, I knew it was going to be hard. Besides, there was another hard reality: my father, who would have in the meantime turned into an old man, and my siblings who would have been transformed from my little brothers into unknown young adults. My father and my siblings would be different from how I normally knew them. But my mother would simply not be there and I had never known home without her.

In the darkness of my sister's house, I tried to recall my last time with my mother. It was back in April 1977, the last day of my Easter holidays at home. I had to quickly finish pounding *omahangu* before getting ready to travel back to school the same day. My mother had also been busy the whole day and before it got too late, she had to take the cattle to be dipped. My father was in Walvis Bay on contract and my brothers were not yet old enough for such a household activity. There was no one else to do it but my mother. Before she left, she came around to take leave from me. She quickly explained that she had to go and she asked me to hurry up so that I could also leave to find a lift back to school. She impressed on me that Anamulenge was far away and I should avoid travelling in the darkness. She also quickly reminded me of all the household activities to be performed next time I would be back for holidays. I fully agreed with her and responded to everything she said to me with a 'Yes, Mother.' And off went my mother, and that was the last time I saw her. Never again in my life would I have the opportunity to say, 'Yes mother'. And here I was about to go home. Unlike my father who had to be away so often for extended periods, my mother was always there whenever we went home. This time, she would not be there. I knew for the last ten years that I no longer had a mother. But this was from a distance. And I managed quite well. Now, in less than 10 hours I would face that hard reality in its pureness.

Going home after such a long time and not finding my mother was already overwhelming. But it was not only her absence that would be hard. There was of course nothing more gratifying for me than to sit with my mother and tell her all I had gone through since I had left home. I knew I could do so with my father, but it is just not the same. I also knew too well that traditionally, when one had been away for a long time, one was always given a special welcome home. One is served a special meal before embarking on a long journey, and upon returning home after a long time. Coming home from exile was both unique and special. Being served such a welcoming meal from one's mother is such a unique experience. This was also the time that mothers would pass on whatever traditional attire and jewellery daughters might have lost on the twisting routes of exile or have simply missed out on because they were gone. For me, there was not to be any of this. As I lay in bed having all these thoughts going through my mind, I was overcome with intense pain. Facing home without my mother became unbearable. I thought

I was brave, but this time I was not at all. Starting with a quiet sob, I found myself crying like a child for a while. Wilfried tried to comfort me, but I was inconsolable.

The crying did me some good. The morning came and Wilfried said goodbye and started his lonely journey back to Windhoek. I was ready to go home. My aunt, my father's sister, arrived at Rita's house early in the morning to accompany me home. Everyone seemed to understand that this would be a difficult experience for me and everyone was ready to offer support. Rita and our first brother Noro (short for Norbert), came with me. After a 10 minute drive I could clearly identify our homestead. It did not stand at the same spot where I had left it but I knew this was home. The landscape had changed slightly. There were fewer trees and less grass as expected for the month of August. The usual sight of cattle grazing was no longer prominent as cattle had been moved elsewhere due to the dry season. Fields were barren but still dotted with big fruit trees: marula trees, wild fig trees and many others which gave my home area its usual natural characteristics. These trees provided abundant fruit, each at their appropriate time. They too provided cool shade during hot summer months. As children, we spent so much time under these trees, not only to enjoy fruit but also for our various games. One of the things we enjoyed under these trees were innovative swings made of palm leaves. How many times did we not fall those days? Either because we tied the swing on too thin a branch and fell with the entire structure or we did not double the knots and the swings broke. The landing on soft sand saved us from major injuries.

But the small bushes where we played hide and seek were no longer there. Numerous homesteads in the neighbourhood were therefore in full view through these big trees which stood high. I was surprised to see a considerable number of new homesteads. There were newcomers and the village had grown. During my childhood, it was always the same homesteads and the same people. This was no longer the case. Some fields had become smaller to accommodate the newcomers. With time I would meet them. I first needed to meet my family.

My father had invited two of my mother's best friends to come and greet me. My mother's younger sister also came. I knew that all this was well meant and done for me to feel at home again. Then I was introduced to my father's new wife. I knew about this, but being home and seeing it for myself was a different story. I managed the situation as best as I could. My father had pleaded with me not to cry. I understood. For them, it was over and done with, but not for me. Then came my youngest brother, Ruben, who was born just a month after my departure in May 1977. This was our first meeting. From a distance, he stretched out his hand to greet me. I shook his hand and looked at his empty gaze. I did not know what to think. Then came Martin, my second youngest brother. He was only two back in 1977. Even though I had known him as a baby, I had the same feeling as with Ruben. Generally, it was the same with most of my siblings. Were these the same people I had been longing to see? It was hard to reconcile what I had been feeling during the many years away from home and the reality at hand. As for my father, I could see much of my old father in him. He was slightly older but he was the same father I had known for years. He asked how I was but besides that, he did not know what else to ask me. Nor did I know what to tell him.

After I spent two days at home, I wanted to go to my sister. I also really wanted to see my grandmother. She was the only remaining person who was closely linked to my mother but she was no longer living in our village. Due to her advanced age, she had left Omayanga to live with her oldest daughter a number of kilometres away. I would again need my brother Noro, the only one with a car in the family, to find time to take me to my grandmother. Since Noro worked, visiting my grandmother could only happen over a weekend.

Meanwhile, I was advised to go to my mother's grave. Of course, I wanted to see her final resting place, but again I needed time to get ready for it. Seeing her grave would offer some finality to the situation. I desperately took as much time as I could, but one Sunday after the church service, it had to happen. A few relatives came with me. There, on a fading cross, stood my mother's name and the date of her death. A better proof of her demise could not be possible. It was time for me to make peace with my loss. To start closing my wound, a month later, I put a tombstone on the grave of my mother, to mark the tenth anniversary of her death.

From the cemetery on that particular Sunday, we got in the car and went straight to my grandmother. Although she was old and blind by then, her mind was as clear as always. She spoke at length about a number of things including the death of my mother. She also told me how she, after receiving news of my marriage in 1983, went several times a day to her sleeping hut, pulled the blanket over her head and ululated. In the Oshiwambo culture, a wedding is filled with ululating. Not only on the actual wedding day but at least during the three weeks that precede the wedding itself. My poor grandmother knew too well that I would not be aware of her ululating wherever I was. She nonetheless could not miss the occasion of ululating, though only symbolically, for a granddaughter getting married in an unknown land. She did not want to be subjected to any questioning, neither from the curious neighbours nor from the South African authorities, on how on earth she had received information on my wedding. It had to be between her and me and she was glad that I was finally back in time for her to tell me the story. I was indeed moved. She lived another five years and I visited her every time I went home.

⤿

I was going to spend the first month at home between Rita's house and Omayanga. As one got to know the people in the surrounding area, one also got to understand better the political dimensions among the people. This was not only true for the north, but for the entire country a few months before the UN supervised elections. These were the very first elections in a country that was just emerging from 23 years of war. Although the majority of the people fought for the liberation of the country, there were those who were drawn into the war but on the side of the South African occupation army. Those who were fighting for independence were bitter about those who were assisting the occupation army. But those who fought on the wrong side were bitter too because of the propaganda that sustained them as part of the occupying force in Namibia. Now that both the PLAN combatants and the SADF were confined to bases in Angola and Namibia respectively, we were to a certain extent left on our own under UNTAG.

The most challenging phenomenon was the former members of South West African Territorial Force (SWATF) and the military units of the Police, nicknamed Koevoet, who were back at their homes and were now mingling with the civilians. Koevoet had inflicted untold suffering including death among the black Namibian population during the war. Since they were part of the apartheid military machinery, they had stayed in army barracks and they only appeared among the population when there was need to terrorise them. And here they were now, back just like everybody else. Although their fire arms were not visible, they certainly knew where they were. And to terrorise people did not always require guns. Uncertainty, mistrust and suspicion were automatically unavoidable. To make things worse, we were not at all sure what UNTAG could do should trouble of any kind break out. All this for a nation that had known daily terror for more than 20 years!

We were going to spend those days observing each other carefully, speculating why this or that individual said something or made a certain gesture in a particular manner. This was also the campaign time and supporters were attending their political parties' rallies. People went around wearing their party colours and all this openly displayed loyalty to specific political parties added to the tension. In addition, there were reports of violence now and then. Something that really caught my attention was an incident where a young boy was shot in the head with an arrow. The thought of an arrow stuck in someone's head was just unimaginable.

Amidst all this, I was going to be a bit of a nuisance to my sister whom I hardly knew. The house next door to hers belonged to a former Koevoet guy who had occupied a senior position in this trigger-happy squad. Although he never showed me any adverse sign, I repeatedly told my sister how insecure I felt. When I aired my view one day to my sister that I did not find it normal that she casually spoke to the same man over the fence, she responded that culturally, neighbours greeted each other. Well, she was right, but under the circumstances, this was not a normal neighbour. My sister was not at all interested in such arguments. When I again remarked at another time that I did not feel safe in the presence of some of the people who came to see her, my sister suggested that if I did not trust her, I could as well move to another place where I would feel safe. Having been on the move constantly for the last 12 years, I was ready to move at any time. When an elder cousin passed by the same evening, I grabbed a few things and left with her. What I however underestimated was the distance between my sister's house and the cousin's village. As I walked behind her in the darkness, I again started wondering about my safety. Now that I had already left, there was no way of going back to my sister. At least not the same evening! I needed to stay away for some days to make my point.

Out of hospitality, my cousin slaughtered a goat. The meat was enjoyable the first day. When I again ate the same meat two days later in a homestead without cooling facilities, my stomach protested, and really severely. What did I do next? I again packed up and returned to my sister. As I appeared in the door, she could clearly see through her nurse's eyes that I was sick. Without making me feel that it was after all my own fault, she suggested that we go to the hospital. At the hospital we hardly said much to each other as I followed her through the long corridors from one service point to the next. She was aware that I was unhappy with her, and she decided to avoid confrontation. As she moved through her own territory, I could also clearly see that she wanted to make a point that in the condition in which I was, I was after all dependent on her. In the end, I was sorted out, and we took a while to discuss the matter. We knew that we needed to first rediscover and get to know each other again and this was only the beginning. I would also make similar discoveries with some of my brothers.

⤳

As I was struggling to come to terms with my family and the general situation at home and in the surroundings, I simultaneously had to attend to the last bit of my unfinished business: tell my father about Wilfried. When I told my older siblings about Wilfried, they didn't have much to say. But they didn't appear surprised either. The challenge was that I didn't know them that well to deduce an informed conclusion from their close to indifferent responses. But it didn't bother me that much, I was after all older than them and I was only informing them. It was a different matter with my father from whom I would have preferred to obtain clear approval. I knew that it wouldn't be easy for him. This was after all a rural community. It was not only about my father, but the entire community. Coming up with something which could be deemed outside the standard practice of the community was always difficult to present and of course to justify. I knew this too well as I was no newcomer to the village. I was born and bred there. I deemed to know the norms and here I was about to present an unusual story to my father and through him, to my entire community. Could my 12 year absence be an excuse? Certainly not, everyone would dismiss that right away.

I was however under time pressure. I had been home for three weeks and I had not yet managed to say one word about Wilfried to my father. Day after day I remained in a planning phase. The appropriate words and the right opportunity were hard to find. When would be the right opportunity? I gradually fell into the routine of going to bed every day just to rehearse yet again how I would present the story to him, fine tuning it every time in such a way to make it as sensible and comprehensible as possible to him. But every time I had an opportunity to engage my father on the matter, I surprisingly found myself speaking about other things, anything but Wilfried! And as I went to bed every single night, I was too aware that another opportunity had been lost. And to my horror, all of a sudden, I hardly had much time left to tell my father who Wilfried was. I also knew about Wilfried's wish to meet my father next time he came around. That next time was now in two days!

Our time in Namibia was limited. We both had to return to Lusaka for a year after the elections to finish up our respective jobs at UNIN, and we wanted to make use of our three months stay in Namibia to break this unusual news to our respective families. I wasn't sure how Wilfried was faring with his own family. But all the same, I had to deal with my own father. But here I was, two days before the arrival of Wilfried, and in the three weeks I had been home I had as yet not found the appropriate time or words to tell my father about him. My father might have heard rumours, but for certain matters, parents cannot rely, let alone act, on rumours.

No, I could not afford that. This was my father, my only living parent, and there was no one else but me to officially break the news to him. Culture expected nothing less from me than that. I just had to be brave and do the right thing. At this late hour, I decided to turn to my siblings for support. When I considered them, one by one, my choice fell on Roma, the only one to have been in exile like me. Although much younger, we had a few things in common and he was possibly in the right position to understand and advise me.

The same afternoon I asked Roma to walk with me from home to our sister in Ongwediva. It is a long walk and we would have at least two hours to discuss my complex situation. I made sure I started the discussion as soon as we stepped out of the house. There was no time to get carried away by other stories. Roma carefully listened to my explanation of the delicate situation. He did not interrupt me even once as I went through my story. Towards the end of it, I expressed my fear of presenting this whole thing awkwardly to my father and therefore running the risk of not meeting his approval. Throughout my talking, Roma did not appear alarmed. When he was certain that I was done with my explanation, his response was quite simple and somehow convincing. He literally sketched out the manner in which I should approach the matter in some kind of a road map, and it went like this, 'You tell father about your life in exile including your marriage in 1983. Explain well that this marriage did not last long and the happenings thereafter. You then met another man who is kind, caring and so forth. Provide a heap of good qualities about Wilfried to give father a good picture about the man! After you have sufficiently but carefully enumerated all the goodness of the man, conclude your presentation with the sentence, "But the man in question is white".' Roma emphasised that I should avoid going beyond this concluding sentence. He sounded certain that if I presented the issue according to his road map, my father would understand. We agreed that I would see my father the following day. A day later would be too late in any case.

The following morning, I got up and went straight home. It was time to face my father. By now I knew the whole story by heart, sentence by sentence, exactly the way Roma suggested it to me. As soon as I arrived home, I indicated to my father that I wanted to speak to him. I followed my father to the special hut where he received visitors. He must have sensed that I had something private to discuss with him and he chose a place where we would not be disturbed. As I followed him I knew that this time I had no choice but to drop the bombshell. As soon as we sat down, I was ready to talk. I did not want any small talk before getting to the real topic. My poor father must just cope. All that I was looking for was his understanding.

As I went through my story, my father was quiet, just making 'Mmm' sighs here and there, an indication that he was at least following my utterance. I knew very well that this was far from being a sign of understanding and approval. I bravely and steadily went through my rehearsed story and when I finally arrived at the end of it, I calmly dropped the bomb, 'But this Wilfried is white." My father reacted immediately as soon as I had stopped speaking. His first word to me was, 'Tsheeri', meaning 'my first born'. This was reassuring. In the worst case of him not being in agreement, my father was not going to scold me for what I had just told him. On that score, I comfortably waited for whatever was going to follow. I expected a lengthy discussion, but to my pleasant surprise, my father said only two short sentences, 'I have heard you, and I do understand. My only wish is that you get married in church.' Was this all? I had tormented myself for all these weeks just for my father to say these two little sentences, approving what I was almost convinced he would oppose? This was indeed awesome and I was grateful to him.

That was of course the first thing I told Wilfried upon his arrival. Although he was not as surprised as I was, he immediately indicated that although he was Lutheran, we would marry in the Catholic church. This would certainly appease the old man. Wilfried could finally come home with me to meet my father. Although he had to communicate to my father through a translator, he was glad to be able to come to my home. As for me, I was so relieved that my long battle was finally over. I was not sure how far Wilfried was with his but these kinds of battles are fought on the motto, 'Every man for himself and God for us all!'

⌒

A few days after our return to Windhoek from the north, I had to travel to Lusaka for two weeks. I was part of the delegation led by the then SWAPO Secretary for Education, Nahas Angula, to the International Conference on Teacher Education for Namibia at UNIN. I had decided to stay a week longer to settle in Paleni whom I took along for her school year starting in September 1989. The process of being born as an independent nation could not stop us from attending to other equally important aspects of life. Life had to go on. Children had to continue to go to school. Nothing could wait. Since we were still based at UNIN in Lusaka, I had asked a friend, Emilia, who could not be repatriated as she was pregnant, to look after Paleni until our return to Lusaka after the elections. As it was customary among the exiles to depend on each other, this was perfectly in order.

The two weeks were over and it was time to return to Windhoek. It sounded funny when one sat in Lusaka and announced to the others that you were going to Windhoek. I felt exactly the same way when I said goodbye to Emilia. This was something which we had been deprived of for a very long time all the years we had been there. But this time I could just say so and off I was to the airport. Upon my return Wilfried had evidently not made much headway with his family. He did not say that to me, but I could simply feel it. I knew this from my own experience. Since this was his issue, I gladly stayed out of it.

As Wilfried was struggling with figuring out how to start the process of telling his parents about me, I was savouring a challenge free period of my life. I had not known a tranquil time for a while. I was at long last able to sleep without any concern. This was however to be a short lived experience. Clearly, I had not as yet turned a page to start enjoying a casual life without major worries. As usual, something had to crop up. From one moment to the next, I all of a sudden felt unwell. But I could not figure out what the matter was with me. This time I do not need to tell you a long story. You know what was happening to me? I was pregnant. My goodness, could this not have waited for a while? I seemed not to come to the end of challenging and surprising times.

Wilfried found absolutely nothing wrong with the new development. Such things do happen, he casually reminded me. Of course I knew that, but in our case, it was wrong timing. Wilfried was perfectly fine with the situation and to a certain extent he seemed to find it a blessing in disguise. I was going to be nervous about the situation for a few months. Red lights were again flicking right in front of me, but all this in the presence of a smiling Wilfried.

The following day we went to town first thing after we got up. We walked into the first jewellery shop we came across and bought a ring. We returned home, went into our room and we were engaged. Even Pendukeni and Joe, our hosts at the time, were not part of the engagement ceremony. This was not an easy time for me, and Wilfried thought that this was the way to ease my anxiety. There were bigger things to get anxious about, he repeated to me. I was not at all convinced. For me, this new impasse would do nothing else but complicate matters further. We seemed to do nothing else those days than complicate our own lives. Wilfried appeared not to be worried at all. At the same time, he displayed confidence in his ability to come right with his family. Who was I to doubt him? These were his people and he would deal with and manage them. I clearly understood, and rightly so, that this had nothing to do with me. The pregnancy, however, had everything to do with me.

In early November 1989, the UN supervised elections took place as scheduled. Wilfried and I were among the first voters on the first day of elections. We stood in long queues waiting for our turn to vote for the very first time in our lives. Two days later I was on my flight back to Lusaka. UNIN had to resume to see the last and final group of students through to their graduation. My daughter was also eagerly waiting for me in Lusaka. Wilfried did not take long to arrive back by road. He did not say much on his progress with his parents and the rest of the family. Well, I had something else to deal with. My physical appearance would soon start to betray me, and that was more than enough to preoccupy me for a while. I'd better deal with my own challenge and leave Wilfried to deal with his.

Very soon, it became apparent that Wilfried had fallen into exactly the same trap as I had before. He too chose the easy way out. Like me, he started by chickening out of telling his parents and kept on postponing it to the next time. And what did he do when the next opportunity presented itself? Postpone again! I know it sounds straightforward to tell parents about a relationship, but in our case, biting the bullet was too hard. Hence all these constant postponements until one was at the verge of running out of time. If you thought I managed to pick up the courage to inform my father about Wilfried only at the very last moment, Wilfried did not even manage anything close to that. Every time he thought he saw an opportunity coming his way, the courage just deserted him or something unexpectedly cropped up. Days just sped by without waiting for him to regain his courage. He missed even the last possible opportunity. Next thing he was in Lusaka and had to rely on something else.

The occurrence of the UN supervised elections alone did not allay the anxiety among Namibians. The results still had to be announced and the date of independence subsequently had to be set. The South African Administrator-General was still in charge, and the SADF was still in the country, although confined to bases. The UNTAG forces were very visible, but the question at the back of our minds persisted: Would this UN be able to control the situation, should violence break out? What if one group decided not to accept the outcome of the elections? Mind you, this was the very first time that Namibians were voting, in the real sense of the word. And what we had known thus far over years as a nation was mistrust, confrontation and violence. Obviously, many people had their doubts. Pendukeni was no exception. She decided to entrust her eighteen month old baby daughter, Pendu, to us to take along to Lusaka. To make things easy for us, she had organised her niece Endunge to come along to look after little Pendu.

Endunge had been nowhere else other than her rural set up in the north. This was her very first time away from home. As we were sitting on the balcony of our flat in Lusaka one afternoon, she asked me, in a very natural way, whether the black men who were moving up and down in the nearby road were Owambo men who came to *uutshimba* (labour contracts). Although her question caught me by surprise, her assessment was not different from mine 12 years ago. First of all, in our eyes in those days, any black person should be an Owambo and secondly, a black man moving around town must be a contract labourer. This was our understanding of our world as children and it followed us into our adulthood and beyond our national borders. Little did we know that the contract labour system was devised by the South African apartheid system for us black Namibians for a specific reason: to manage us in such a way that our existence was to provide cheap labour to the white economy and households.

The election results were announced on 14 November 1989, a few days following the elections. This was the climax of anxiety especially among us, the so-called returnees. Except for those who were good at analysis and were certain of SWAPO's victory no matter what, many of us were still tormenting ourselves with many 'what ifs'. To prolong our anguish and for reasons known only to the announcers of the results,

results were progressively announced from the smaller towns towards the bigger towns and strongholds of SWAPO. For a good number of hours, other political parties but not SWAPO were progressively seeing their percentages of votes climbing. A single hour in such moments can be painfully long. Calling each other and speculating in this case was not helpful. But as the saying goes, every challenging situation has a happy ending. In our intense anguish, our happy ending was in the making. As the results from bigger towns were being announced, the possibility of finding one's way back into exile faded away and Namibians entered the jovial mood leading to independence. SWAPO had convincingly won the elections and preparations were underway to pave the country's way to the hard won independence! The national constitution was being drafted and 21 March 1990 was set as the day of the independence celebration. Clearly, this time independence was happening and there was no more turning back. Endunge and Pendu could return home.

↜

By this time everything seemed to move smoothly in the right direction. It was joy everywhere among us Namibians in Lusaka. It was not really about the fact that we would be returning home for good but just the simple thought that we could return home without any hindrance and at any time of our choice. We had been deprived of this natural way of life for so long, hence the endless joy. But at the same time, and this was specific to me alone, I was aware of my being a problem. Till then, I never imagined that as a person I would be a real problem to anyone. Suddenly, I had become one. Wilfried's parents were increasingly concerned about their son's position in relation to me. They had not yet met me, but they knew about my skin colour. It is easy to reverse roles, isn't? It was now my turn to have my colour become problematic. Would the problem go away naturally if it was ignored? It was initially hoped so.

Very soon, it became evident that Wilfried was forging ahead with his conviction but there was no sign that the problem was going away. Undoubtedly, the persisting problem became a serious concern, if not a family crisis. It was high time to deploy all mechanisms to contain the problem before it was too late. It was not only about the family, it was also about the neighbours and indeed the entire society. What would the others think and say? Was this not one of my concerns right at the beginning?

As is usually the case, we mothers are the first ones to be concerned about our children. My future mother-in-law hoped to have all her children at home during Christmas of 1989. Including Wilfried of course! There was no way out, Wilfried had to go. He knew what was likely to be discussed and he imagined that after a thorough and convincing discussion, he would have an opportunity to announce the good news of a grandchild that was on the way.

Upon his arrival at home, the sadness of his mother was evident. How could he do that to her? Could he reconsider? This was clearly not the right time to announce a grandchild on the way. Even the small moment he managed to have alone with his mother was far from being the long awaited opportunity to break the news to her. What then? Could he just leave it hanging with the hope that things would sort themselves out on their own one day? No, his parents had to know. If he could not tell them himself, then someone else should intercede. Wilfried decided to turn to his two elder brothers, Max and Chris. Max had already conveyed my existence to the parents a year earlier and Chris had met me when he visited us in Lusaka from Bulawayo, also a year earlier. Although they both knew about me, the additional information of a baby on the way necessitated a bit of thinking. At this stage, it could not just be thrown in the faces of the parents. The family still needed to have some sort of Christmas. And the two brothers would see how to pick up the issue with the parents, preferably when Wilfried was out of the house and back in Lusaka.

This was not a small issue. It required real team work and the third brother had to be drawn in. After Christmas, Max drove his little brother to the airport in Windhoek. On the way, they had a serious chat and under the circumstances, Wilfried had to place his full trust in his brothers. The first thing was to devise a strategy on how to communicate this rather delicate issue to the parents. For the family, the point of no return had been reached. On one hand, there was Wilfried, the youngest son who was convinced that there was absolutely nothing wrong with what he was subjecting his poor parents to. On the other hand he had parents who had been hoping to quietly get out of the situation without hurting their dear son but at the same time without having their neighbours and fellow society members raising eyebrows. But alas, this was simply not to be, and Wilfried's brothers had no choice but to find a way of carefully presenting the hard reality to their parents, in particular their mother.

The whole thing was close to an impossible mission. People had to take time off for our sake. Meanwhile we were just sitting in Lusaka, not fully aware of the stress the others were going through. The planning had to happen while having a drink away from home. The focus was to find the best possible way of putting the case of their little brother to the parents. At the same time, there was need to have damage control mechanisms readily available, just in case. Clearly the task of assisting their little brother with his unusually complex situation was pretty challenging, especially in his absence. Did they really have sufficient arguments for the case?

The Brock family dinners were always followed by a sip of wine and a relaxed chat in the comfort of the sitting room. This specific evening was going to be a bit different though. After some throat clearing, someone had to break the ice. It was first a question of explaining to the parents that Wilfried was old enough to be allowed to take decisions over his own life. It was also important to suggest to the parents that if Wilfried reckoned that he would find happiness with a black woman, he should perhaps be allowed to do so. After all, it was further argued, the parents should realise that there was not much to be done as a baby was on the way. That was certainly a bit too much in one go.

Today, when I think back as a mother, I can feel what went through the mind of my dear mother-in-law. All mothers want the best for their children. And that best can only be associated with what one is familiar with. Anything else is suspicious, if not mistrusted. By then, none of her neighbours or acquaintances had a black in-law. The only black people known to her were the gardener and the cleaning lady, and of course some of the workers at the family business, Woermann Brock. And here she was, confronted with a story of her beloved son in a serious relationship with a black woman. Not only was the relationship serious, but a grandchild was on the way. The irreversible fate she was worried about had indeed happened. And maybe, the culture would not allow much room to manoeuvre a way out.

Having dropped the heavy bombshell, it was now time to manage the situation. Arguments such as 'You do not know who this Trudie is. All you know is that she is black, maybe she is a good person after all,' to, 'Look, Wilfried is not asking to bring this Trudie here, she can only come if you are in agreement,' were advanced. I am sure such arguments were not helpful at that time. For the parents, this came unexpectedly, it was extreme and it had not happened to any of their friends, neighbours and acquaintances. Why should it have happened to them?

Wilfried was of course informed of the reaction of the parents and the efforts to reassure them. The parents however were not convinced. It was just one of the difficult times of parenthood. Children remain children and they are not always considerate of their parents. A silence was to settle between Wilfried and his parents. At that point, I had become used to seeing Wilfried enjoying reading regular yellow letters from his mother. All of a sudden, there were no more yellow letters. Even the phone calls which Wilfried enjoyed after having a phone installed, stopped. The silence was total. Wilfried did not show any sign of concern, but I was certain that this was hard for him, especially now that I knew the closeness of his family. He however portrayed his preparedness to stand his ground. If the parents were not prepared to accept his choice, he would not be able to help them, he repeated several times.

I was not sure whether I was in agreement with my future husband. Right at the beginning of our relationship, was my position not closer to that of my future mother-in-law? I think it was. Meanwhile, two full months passed without any communication. Wilfried had to rely on second hand information from home. He put up a brave face and seemed to manage the new situation. If his conviction would cause him to be cut off from the family, he was prepared for the eventuality. Clearly he was going to count on me, not only for support, but for full solidarity. Do you know what that meant in reality? Well, that the two of us would go it all the way alone. How possible that was, I was not sure. However, I still felt a bit responsible for the sudden development. Would I be able to assume the responsibility over the new development? I too belonged to a family, something I greatly valued. How could I possibly agree with Wilfried to cut the most natural link one had for the sake of our relationship? That would be the last resort. And by grace, that would not be.

One day, at the end of February 1990, mail was delivered to Wilfried. A yellow letter was among the mail. We were both excited and I was glad that at long last, a yellow letter had finally arrived for poor Wilfried. It did not really matter what its content was, the essential was that there was communication between Wilfried and his mother and, of course, with his family. At no time since I had known him was he cut off from his dear family before they had been confronted by our relationship. At long last, things seemed to normalise again.

On a closer look, we realised that the letter was not addressed to Wilfried, but to me. My goodness, this was a letter from Wilfried's mother to me! The letter was not long and it was written in German. Luckily enough, I had learned German at secondary school in Anamulenge, and I tried to sharpen it in my third and fourth years at the University of Clermont-Ferrand during my studies in France. In the first paragraph, my future mother-in-law explained that she and I had an interest in the same man, but of course for different reasons. And for that reason, she went on, it was in the interest of the two of us to put our differences and misunderstandings behind us. In the concluding paragraph, she informed me that they wholeheartedly welcomed us in the family and that from then on, Paleni and I should call them *Vati* and *Mutti*. Lastly, she pointed out that it was important for her to draw my attention to the fact that they as a family speak German, and they obviously would continue doing so.

I did not know what to think. Having followed a bit of the discussions, I had been fully convinced that I would never get to know Wilfried's parents. I knew what they thought and felt about me. I did not blame them. I understood and did not expect anything different. I was born and bred in the same country. That was simply how things were those days. In fact, at that time, I thought that it would be the simplest for both them and for me not to get to know each other. I was also very clear in my mind that under no circumstances would I allow my skin colour to be called into question.

But here I was now, confronted with a challenging situation. Wilfried's parents, whom I believed would never accept me and whom I obviously thought I would never meet, were welcoming me into their family. And by the way, the last sentence of the letter read, 'We would like to meet you in Swakopmund next time you come to Namibia'.

To put it in simple terms, I never expected such a letter. But the fact of the matter was the ball was now in my court. It was now my turn to adjust to the new situation. Could I do so under the circumstances? I had my serious doubts. We were now at the end of February and the Independence Celebration of Namibia was scheduled for 21 March 1990. By then, I would be seven months pregnant and my doctor had advised against travelling. I went to great length to explain how important it was for me to travel back home for the occasion. The doctor wanted to wash his hands of me and asked me to sign a document. I did. It was important for me to witness what had kept me outside my motherland for my 12 youthful years. This by no means meant not caring about the child I was carrying. I simply was convinced that if I had endured 12 long years, I would also manage the one week trip. But was I ready to meet Wilfried's parents? In a town I had never been to? For those who knew the town and its details, this could possibly be fine. The answer from me as a complete foreigner to the town was a 'no'.

Wilfried was understanding. I did not have to meet his parents if I was not ready for it. He would explain all this to them. After all, this was an unexpected development for which I needed time to adjust. Given my condition, it might take even longer. I was happy for the support. I seriously needed time to prepare myself. I knew my country and its people too well. And Namibia was just about to gain independence. One thing at a time, please!

$\backsim$

I, together with Paleni, joined my colleagues from UNIN on a flight to Windhoek for the independence celebration. The ambiance was just right. Meanwhile, Wilfried had yet again left Lusaka by car to Windhoek. We would need the car back home. Back in Windhoek, we headed to the north to visit my father and the rest of my family. My father had no comment on my physical condition. I was relieved. After a few days' visit, we returned to Windhoek for the independence celebration.

Wilfried absolutely wanted to be at the Independence Stadium for the occasion. His elder brother Chris had also travelled from Bulawayo and they would meet up at the stadium. I had to be satisfied with the live broadcast on TV at home. I must say, I experienced everything from a comfortable position.

After the independence celebration, Wilfried went home briefly. Paleni and I flew back to Lusaka and Wilfried joined us shortly thereafter. Life went on as usual, but I had the pending visit to Wilfried's parents on my mind. Whenever that would be, remained a big question mark. Meanwhile, the focus of the three of us was on the arrival of the addition to our family. The doctor had predicted 28 May 1990 as the due date. We all got ready for 28 May. This date came and went, and nothing happened. The month of May came to an end and the three of us looked at each other without any explanation. Babies take their time and we were convinced that this was exactly what was happening to us. The month of June started and we waited. One of these days, this baby would show up. And it did!

Early Saturday morning, 2 June, things started moving. We had arranged with Mrs Ncube, the wife of a Zimbabwean colleague at UNIN, who was a nurse, to assist at the hospital. We picked her up early in the morning hours and we made our way to the Lusaka University Teaching Hospital. I was soon transferred to a common delivery ward. Wilfried was not quite amused with the arrangement as he hoped to be next to me in the delivery room. In life, there are always surprises, and this was going to be one of them for him. As for me, this was not the time to think about details. I had one and only one thing on my mind and that was to bring this child into the world. I held on to Mrs Ncube, and she attended to me to the best of her ability. I did not realise that from time to time she went outside. And you know why? To reassure Wilfried that all was fine! I was not even aware that he was outside the delivery room all this time.

By 12:30 my daughter was there. I looked on as the nurse walked out with my baby without knowing what was happening. Later I learned that the nurse went out to show the baby to Wilfried. That was perfect with me. I needed to rest. We named her Tunehafo, meaning 'we have joy'. After some days, Wilfried told me that the baby was born on his mother's sixtieth birthday. First, nothing really clicked. My child was born on 2 June 1990. So what! Meanwhile, the reality was that exactly on the same day, my future mother-in-law had turned 60. Was this pure coincidence? Sure, but thinking of the trouble my mother-in-law went through to accept our relationship, this was amazing, especially that the doctor predicted a different date. My future mother-in-law was certainly as surprised as we were.

I had three months' maternity leave and I thought this would be time to rediscover my family. My preoccupation was to recover and get ready to return to my father and my siblings during a lengthy and calm time. The possibility of discovering my future in-laws, at least to start off with my future parents-in-law, was not yet in sight. I preferred to wait as long as it could take. I had just too many things on my plate and I really wished to do one thing at a time, preferably the complicated ones last.

Wilfried had agreed that the children and I spend July and August with my family up north. He would travel with us to assist with the two kids and see us up to our destination. He would return to pick us up at the end of August when he would attend the wedding of his brother Chris in Swakopmund. This was a perfect arrangement. We boarded our flight in Lusaka bound for Windhoek. Once on board, we were requested to be patient for a while. There was nothing unusual about waiting for a while, and our children were as calm as one could hope for. After a while, we could take off. As soon as we had taken off, Paleni, being a lively child, wandered off to the front of the plane. Behind a curtain, I could vaguely see her being picked up and settled on the lap of a man in a suit. I wasn't concerned, nothing serious could happen on board, and after all, this was someone in business class. A while later, the curtain flicked open and Paleni marched back into economy class holding the hand of none other than Sam Nujoma. He had been the President of Namibia for about three months. His smile was amazing and the whole economy class started waving and he waved back. He was surprised to see Wilfried, 'Comrade Brock!' President Nujoma explained that Paleni had convinced him to come and say hello to her parents. And that's why he came. He couldn't figure out who I was, but he clearly knew who this comrade Brock was. It was obvious that it makes things easier when you are just one among so many others. Of course, thanks to Paleni we now understood why we had to be patient for a bit in Lusaka.

⌒

Back in Windhoek, we went straight home to Pendukeni and Joe. We did not have much time; Wilfried had exactly one week's leave and he had to see us safely to the north before returning to Lusaka. There was one flight a week and he had to be on board the next one, the following Wednesday. My future parents-in-law were aware of our coming to Namibia. They were also aware that we wouldn't go to Swakopmund this time. In their eyes, this time, things were different. They understood that I wasn't ready to go to Swakopmund, but they definitely wanted to see their grandchild. If I wasn't ready to go to them, they would come to Windhoek. I had no further argument to advance, and Wilfried told me that his parents would be coming. And this would be within one or two days. I didn't know what to think, but I was reassured by the fact that they were coming to where I was, and I was not going to their home.

As soon as they were in Windhoek, I was confronted with the question of whether I would prefer to meet them at a house of a family member in Klein Windhoek or at a restaurant in town. With my little knowledge of Windhoek I was not sure where Klein Windhoek was. I was however convinced that if they were there, this would not be the place where black people would be. I definitely preferred the restaurant, the no man's land. I do not know why, but an arrangement was made that we went to Klein Windhoek for a short while before going to the restaurant, apparently for an aperitif. That's a bit about cultural diversity. Well and good, postponement was not going to be forever. I knew this too well and at one point, I knew I was going to make some compromises. I braced myself and went along to Klein Windhoek. I cannot remember much of the encounter, except that I was tense. I knew exactly what my future parents-in-law thought of me and this was going to impact our relationship, at least for the first few years.

At the restaurant, I kept to myself and except for occasional smiles, I gave very short answers. I did not know what to expect and I needed some time to get to know Wilfried's parents and of course the society he was from. They were so different and I knew that I had to take all the precautions that it required. For the time being, I preferred that they spoke to their son and I would sit by as an onlooker. When my future mother-in-law asked if she could hold her granddaughter, I politely handed over the crying child to her. When she failed to calm her down, she offered to go to a pharmacy next door to buy a dummy. Sure, she could. Gradually, and with the assistance of the dummy, we could have a quiet evening. At the end of the meal, my future father-in-law paid the bill, carefully counting the money from the little plastic bank bag, and not from a wallet! There are always these little things that get stuck in one's mind and from my first encounter with Wilfired's parents, this was one of them. I got used to seeing more plastic bags later.

The following morning, Wilfried wanted to take the baby and spend some time with his parents and some relatives around Windhoek. Sure, why not! There was absolutely no reason to be worried. The child was going to the father's family including the grandparents. They are equally related to her and should after all have equal access. Somewhere later in the day Wilfried returned with my daughter. I cannot remember details, but there was a query from his parents as to how we were going to travel to the north. Our initial arrangement was to travel by bus. Wilfried's parents however did not think this would be a good idea. What if they gave us their car for the trip? But then how would they travel back to Swakopmund? The response was that they would find a lift. Well, if they felt that they could manage to return to Swakopmund by lift, we would accept the offer.

I found the offer amazing. Especially that my future parents-in-law were going to find a lift back to Swakopmund. In my mind, they were literally going to hitchhike. And this for our sake? It was hard to believe. The next day, we had the car and we were on our way to the north. Wilfried no longer had much time left in Namibia. He would drop us and get on the way to return his parents' car to Swakopmund before heading to Windhoek to catch his flight back to Lusaka. We said goodbye to him and I looked forward to spending quality time with my family. I badly needed to get to know them again.

9

Taming my elephant

Wilfried phoned to say that he had arrived in Swakopmund and that he would hitchhike to Windhoek to catch his return flight to Lusaka the next day. We would see him in two months' time when he would come back to pick us up. The following day, the day Wilfried was supposed to be on his flight to Lusaka, he phoned again. Instead of being on the flight, he was still in Swakopmund. The explanation was that he failed to get a lift from Swakopmund to Windhoek and as we were speaking, he had missed his flight. Since there was only one flight a week, the next opportunity for him to travel to Lusaka would be in a week's time. With such an unfortunate situation, Wilfried explained, he would rather come to wait with us in the north. Well, why not, we would be happy to see him for another week. We agreed that he would come the following day. And the next day, Wilfried turned up. Of course in his parents' car!

We were so happy to see Wilfried. It would have been two full months before he came back to pick us up. After a few days in the north, Wilfried started speaking as if he was no longer part of the arrangement of my two months' stay in Namibia. The way in which he approached the issue was just unbelievable. He had given thought to our lengthy stay in Namibia and that he was no longer sure whether this was after all a good idea. Wilfried did not smile, he was very serious. I thought to myself, 'Where is this coming from?' Wilfried expected nothing other than sympathy. Well, I understood, but what about my time with my family? That could wait, he explained. After all, we would have only three months in Zambia before coming back home for good. Then I would have as much time with my family. But as things stood now, he underlined, it would be a pity if he missed out on the early development of his daughter. Wilfried had put up a serious case and the pleading was intense. Three months were not too much compared to 12 years I had stayed away from home and my family. If this would allow Wilfried to benefit from witnessing the development of his daughter during her early age, why not?

But there was something else. He was now in the north with the parents' car, and he needed to get it back to Swakopmund before we proceeded to Windhoek. And the natural way was for us to drive it down to Swakopmund, which of course would bring us closer to Windhoek. I looked at my dear future husband and I could clearly see the trap. I had this pending issue of visiting his parents and the plan seemed to be fully in place. Had he discussed it with them? Wilfried appeared genuine, at least his look conveyed that message, and I decided to give him the benefit of the doubt.

I would postpone my long overdue stay with my family. Wilfried was advancing two arguments. He had changed his mind about my long stay in Namibia and was pleading for us to return immediately to Lusaka with him. Secondly, there was the need to return his parents' car to Swakopmund. This was not the time to argue. The two of us had gone through a lot and we seemed to have quietly vowed to be supportive of each other. For obligation's sake, and as Wilfried had explained to me, we would go to Swakopmund for one night and then catch a train to Windhoek the following day to be on our flight back to Lusaka the same day. I decided to rely on my people's saying, *shokukweni kashi dhigu shapo owesh' umbatwetekwa*, meaning, 'whatever you freely decide to embark upon, you will always manage it'. In other words, it is never hard to bear the consequences of one's own decision. Being with Wilfried was my own choice and I must manage whatever comes with it.

I braced myself for Swakopmund. I was fully aware that this was my future husband's family and as such, my future in-laws. In my culture we say, *swala ezimo*, literally translated, 'the in-laws are equal to relatives'. I had the intention to comply with my people's saying, but not at all costs. I was ready to reach out to whoever was reaching out to me. But I must admit that I was cautious. I knew the general view held about me and I was not at all surprised. I expected it and was prepared for it. But

I held on to one thing, and that was that as much as I understood the reasoning and the reasons of such reasoning, we had just turned a page as a country and there was no going back. Antagonistic views about one another were certainly present and were going to accompany us for a while as a nation, but as long as they were held silently.

It was in this frame of mind that I arrived in Swakopmund. I vividly remember the event bringing together a number of family members and friends of the family to greet us. I am sure this was well meant, but my mind was stuck on my defence. I could observe a jovial conversation filled with laughter, but to date, I am unable to recall what was said at that specific occasion. It was not a language issue. I just happened to be there without really being there. Although not physically demanding, this overwhelming state of affairs can be exhausting. I was literally tired from simply sitting there for an hour or so, literally doing nothing but moving my eyes from one person to the next and inappropriately occasionally smiling. I had not done more than that. Yet, I was exhausted and needed my rest for the next full day before leaving for Windhoek in the evening.

↬

Well, I had met my future parents-in-law, but one thing was certain, we had a long way to go before we started getting along. We had absolutely nothing in common and any future relationship had to be started from scratch. That would, yet again, be a future challenge. I was by now used to life's challenges, and always seemed to have managed. I was not too sure about this one though. I would see when the right time came. For now we were on our way back to Lusaka for another three months. In the comfort of the environment I had known for years, I would certainly be able to figure out something for my new challenge.

After a full three months away from work, I resumed duties. Three months went by fast and soon we were speaking about going back home, this time for good. In October 1990, UNIN would come to a close and we would all return home. This would mean going back to settle down and fend for ourselves. I was not quite sure how this would work out but everything clearly pointed to the fact that SWAPO camps and Education and Health Centres had ceased to exist. Common kitchens and other handouts we had got used to would be things of the past. Others who were back home had already started 'independent lives'. So, it was time that we went to join the club.

My only challenge was what to do with my brother Roma who had joined us in Lusaka early in the year. After two years in exile, Roma could no longer return to school in Namibia. He was 23, had no qualification and needed to attend some courses to fill the gap. We therefore enrolled him at Evelyn Hone College in Lusaka for some basic courses including Mathematics and English. His English was so poor that he needed some serious catching up. I still remember how he went to buy milk every morning with a little red and white cooling bag. He had learned how to ask for one or two litres of milk and he knew the exact prices. One day however, on his way back home, he bumped into a Zambian classmate who stopped to greet him. As they chatted the colleague wanted to know where Roma was coming from so early in the morning. By then, Roma had not yet mastered the past tense in English. So he struggled with his response and he ended up responding, 'I was to buy milk.' He was however aware that his response was not quite proper English and that was the first thing he told us when he got back home. Evidently, Roma needed to be in Lusaka till the end of the year to complete his academic studies. We had no choice but to pay the rent of our flat for an additional two months.

∽

As we were doing all these many things, Wilfried and I were also discussing our wedding. We had no date in mind, but it would ideally be as soon as we got back home. We had no house, we literally had nothing, but we knew we were going to get married pretty soon. At the same time, as we were discussing the marriage plans, I still had a question mark hanging over my head. In my mind, I was still married because I never got a divorce. By the time I thought of applying for the divorce from the SWAPO Legal Department in early 1989, the response came stating that I was too late with my application as all documents were packed and the containers were on their way to Namibia. I was advised to wait until the new system was in place in independent Namibia. How long that would take, there was no clear answer.

I had to find a solution before I seriously got into the issue of getting married again. But where would I go? How would I start the process? The term divorce itself was somehow intimidating for me. In my village, the only place associated with marriage was the church. Being Catholic, I knew too well that one does not return there to ask for a divorce. The other thing was that I also knew too well that my marriage had not been anywhere close to a church. So, it was pointless to think about the church. As the days went by I decided to pick up the phone to call an old colleague who was knowledgeable in legal matters, and who was back in Windhoek by then. After a number of calls made amazingly early in the morning to ensure that I caught up with him before he went to work, he advised me to go and see a prominent lawyer in Windhoek next time I came home.

The next time I went home was for my rather short maternity leave. Although I had so much to do in such a short time, I couldn't afford to leave Windhoek without clearing my mind in relation to my marital status. I was a bit hesitant though as seeing a lawyer implies serious discussions. Besides the law lecturers that I had observed from a distance at UNIN during my studies in the late seventies, I had never in my life been in contact with a lawyer. And here I was about to see a prominent lawyer for that matter, just on my own and to discuss a huge personal problem. What would his reaction be? I nonetheless picked up the courage and I went to see the lawyer I was referred to. I do not even think I had an appointment when I walked into the man's office. He happened to be there and accepted receiving me. After having heard my story, the man calmly told me that under the law in force in Namibia at that time, I was not legally married.

Initially, I could not follow his argument. In fact, I was worried about what he was telling me. In simple words, the lawyer was telling me that I went through the trouble to get married, yet I was not married? And all this for the last seven years? This was incredible. After having experienced my usual drama, the lawyer asked me to re-explain the procedures followed when I supposedly got married in Yugoslavia in 1983. After my second attempt, the lawyer explained that if I were married under the Yugoslav law, I would have been legally married. He further explained that my marriage under SWAPO laws would only be legal once the new Namibian Parliament had pronounced itself on the matter. If he were me, he advised, he would get married before the Parliament made its pronouncement. My new marriage, he concluded, which would be legal under the legal system in force in Namibia at that time, would automatically cancel the first one which had been till then, after all, not legal. With that, I walked out of the lawyer's office with a clear mind. I explained all of it to Wilfried and his look seemed to say, 'I told you so!' Fine, in any case, the matter was clear, at least to me. We could therefore go ahead with our wedding preparations.

～

In October 1990, we packed up and finally returned home. My future mother-in-law had found a small flat for us to rent. That was quite helpful as we had somewhere to sleep the day of arrival in Windhoek. We started organising ourselves to set up a household. We managed to put Paleni in a pre-school for the rest of the year. Wilfried started talking of getting a loan to buy a house. What was this concept of a loan? I had no clue. Yet I went along every time to the SWABOU building where I would sit next to Wilfried listening to him advancing arguments why we needed so much money and how long it would take for us to pay it back and so many other things. Every time we walked out of this famous SWABOU building, Wilfried still had to do this or that for the loan. I would then walk to the building that housed the former SWAPO Directorate of Elections with the hope of bumping into colleagues from exile for a chat. By then, there were a number of Ministries around the area and obviously, there was no shortage of other returnees moving around and we could stop to speak about the good old days.

Setting up a household involves a lot of shopping. We got into the habit of going to one big supermarket in what would be renamed Independence Avenue for our shopping. I did not ask Wilfried why we always went to the same supermarket, but as is always the case with any routine, I followed him and after paying, we walked out again. The following day we would come back to the same place. At one point I noticed that Wilfried did not pay with money, but that he signed a piece of paper after showing a card. I thought to myself that this was unusual but since this was the time I was discovering town life in Namibia and I was overwhelmed with so many things, I chose not to ask why he all of a sudden did not need to pay with money. Asking questions to which you do not quite grasp the explanations can also be perplexing. Better to observe first and only ask when one deems to have sufficient understanding of the observations.

A few days later, Wilfried took me upstairs the same supermarket. There, I was handed a card and I was asked to sign the back of it. The man behind the desk neatly placed the card in a plastic cover and handed it over to me. He then had a quick chat with Wilfried in German and we left again. Clearly, Wilfried knew him. When we walked out of the supermarket, I wanted to know what the card was for. For buying in this shop, instead of paying every day with cash, we would buy on credit and we would pay only at the end of the month, Wilfried explained. What kind of a system was that, I wondered. At that point, Wilfried asked me to look up at the writing on the building that housed the supermarket. There stood 'Woermann Brock'. He explained that the supermarket had something to do with his family, and that was why his surname was part of the name of the supermarket. Later that evening, Wilfried spoke a bit about his family in relation to the supermarket and the family's history in Namibia. For the first time, I got to know a bit about him beyond his life in exile.

∽

The end of the year was approaching and we still wanted to marry the same year. So we picked 15 December as a perfect day. Only we quickly had to find a house. In fact all returnees were now looking for houses. It was exciting but a bit time consuming too. For the first time I was going to have a house and therefore a real home. After some paper work and visits to a number of houses all over Windhoek, we settled for a three bedroomed house in Hochland Park.

The wedding day was approaching. The ceremony was going to be at the St Mary's Cathedral and the reception at the Thüringerhof Hotel, the place where we had dinner with Wilfried's parents a few months earlier. A number of invitations were still going out. The guest list was limited to 100 persons. Two friends were still not invited because I was not sure how to contact them. These were none other than Nangula and Embassy (Tuliameni Kalomoh), the same people I spent time in Dakar in 1980 and who were in Paris between 1981 and 1986. When they left Paris in 1985, Embassy was to open the SWAPO Embassy in New Delhi in India. Were they back in the country? I had no information.

On 10 December, we went to the Old Location Cemetery for the commemoration of the 1959 uprising and subsequent massacre. As we stood around the grave, I lifted up my head and whom did I see among the crowd on the other side of the grave? Nangula! I was relieved to see her. It was not too late to invite them. As soon as the official part was over, I walked over to greet her. We had not met since their departure from Paris in 1986. I pulled her aside and informed her immediately about the wedding. She looked at me as if she could not hear what I was telling her. I could understand why she was not following. The four years since our last meeting were long and so much had happened in the meantime. I promised that I would explain everything when we had the time. For the time being I only wanted her to know that I was getting married in five days' time and that she and her husband were invited and must please be there. Seeing that I was getting agitated, she reassured me that they would come, but she wanted at least to know whom I was marrying. I pointed at Wilfried who was a distance away. She looked in the direction I was pointing, but she insisted that she could not see the person I was pointing at. When I made it clear that I was indeed pointing at Wilfried, her reaction was, 'Oh Tshiwa, shono otshilumbu,' to make it clear to me that I was pointing at a white person.

That was exactly what I needed from a close friend five days before I married the man! 'Yes, he's white,' I replied, before adding that I had known what she had just observed for more than two years by then. Worried about upsetting me, and noticing my despair for her approval and support, she murmured something that sounded like she was fine with the situation and that she would come to the wedding. 'Thanks,' I replied. As we were just concluding, Pendukeni approached and noticing our agitation, she asked what the matter was. Nangula attempted to explain that I was about to marry a white man, and wanted to establish whether Pendukeni was aware of it. Of course she was, she replied and wanted to know what was wrong with it. Nangula, although perplexed, stated that she was perfectly fine with everything. She would absolutely come to the wedding, she repeated. Clearly seeing what was going through her mind, the two of us agreed to talk about it after the wedding. I knew the story by heart and I would tell it to her as such, including what Pendukeni's role was in the whole thing.

‿

The five days went by fast and 15 December 1990 arrived. Father Franz Houben had agreed to celebrate our wedding. Pendukeni and Joe had agreed to let us use their white Mercedes Benz. Wilfried's parents, his three brothers and a sister were in Windhoek for the wedding, as were other relatives and friends including the then mayor of Swakopmund. As for my family, my father, my sister, two brothers and two aunts travelled all the way from the north to Windhoek. I was quite pleased to be surrounded by those who came to represent the family. Then, and most importantly, I had my family from exile.

I had my attire ready, exactly the way I knew it from home. Besides the dress, I had the white plastic hair band with hanging white pearls (certainly fake), a white pearl necklace and mixed white and purple flower bouquet. Everything really looked pretty and fitted well together until my mother-in-law to be walked into our house. There was no discussion and from one minute to the next, my dressing code changed. She walked in with a bucket she called *Eimer*. Guess what was in the *Eimer*? There were flowers, pretty roses, but real ones! When she sorted them out they were my hair band, hand bouquet and a bunch for the car. As soon as she had placed the first two flowers in my hands, she energetically walked out to fix the bunch meant for the car onto the Mercedes Benz. It did not take long before she walked back into the house for the next action. She reached into her bag and handed me a neatly decorated jewellery box. 'This is our gift to you for your wedding, please put it on,' she said. 'Thank you,' I replied, but as I walked to my bedroom with the box clenched in my hand, I thought to myself, 'What about all my things I've bought?' I had no time to debate all this with myself when Wilfried walked in. As he was hurrying to get ready and was busy adjusting his tie, he quickly explained that his mother would not expect anything other than me making use of the items she brought.

When I thought about it, this was probably the least I could do. My mother-in-law had taken time to construct the colourful and well-arranged hairband out of fresh flowers from her garden. She had further made two pretty bouquets. Also from her garden! Did she care for and look after the flowers for a long period of time? Just for my wedding? And had she taken extra care and transported the whole lot in ice all the way from Swakopmund? The flowers looked extraordinarily pretty. I must confess that I did not expect all of this. My mother-in-law to be, whom, half a year earlier, I did not expect to meet at all, had spent so much of her time to do this for my wedding? It was incredible. Then I opened the jewellery box. And there was the most beautiful piece of jewellery I had ever had. An orange stone, a piece of diamond and a golden chain: everything Namibian. I was not sure what to do with it at that time, but Wilfried highly recommended that I should wear it for the wedding. He was pleased when I put it on. You know why? The necklace was to be part of my father-in-law's speech at the reception later the same evening. Can you imagine the dilemma if I had not worn it? I am glad I did. Such is the beauty of cultural diversity.

We were married in the Roman Catholic Cathedral, St Mary's, in central Windhoek. Our wedding was not like any other wedding. In church, although I had my back to the audience, I could feel the heavy look at us. This was not a common wedding in the Namibia of those days. It was indeed a bold statement as late Comrade Dr Mosé Tjitendero put it the same evening. We brought two different cultures together, he underlined. I gladly sat back as Comrade Tjitendero, the first Speaker of the National Assembly of the Republic of Namibia, eloquently described our marriage. In conclusion, he stated how difficult it was for him to stop talking as he was among his people, the only family he knew. He briefly recalled the persuasive approach he used to get me to study in France. He called it a 'struggle in a classroom' advising me to take up the French Government scholarship. Since this was a speech on my wedding day, he made it sound straightforward and concluded the topic: 'I knew I was advising a young person who knew what she wanted in life.' From his speech, and the attentiveness that everyone in the room accorded to it, I felt that closeness and bonding of those of us who had just returned from exile. It was indeed a source of pride and pure belonging. In fact, looking at it closely, we brought three cultures together. For Wilfried and me, there was our common culture of our family from exile. That was the easiest. Then there was Wilfried's home culture which I was to discover only later. Then there was my home culture which Wilfried was also to discover fully later, but he already knew a bit about it. We were both, however, happy to have our common family: our leadership, comrades and friends from exile.

In his speech, my father-in-law stressed that although we had our home in Windhoek, we were welcome in Swakopmund. With my encounter with them at our wedding and this specific pronouncement of my father-in-law, I made it my business to get used to going to Swakopmund and to start the process of discovering my family-in-law. That was where Wilfried was from and that would remain his initial home.

The following day was the beginning of the discovery of my family-in-law. I cannot remember the exact address but we met Wilfried's parents and siblings at a house in Eros for lunch and for a swim. Although swimming is not my cup of tea, I went by the Oshiwambo saying, 'oto faathanitha onkalo' similar to the saying 'when in Rome, do as the Romans do'. I appeared to enjoy swimming and every moment of that afternoon. Yes, that's how you start getting to know others.

Before leaving Windhoek, my father made it clear to me that for him, my wedding would not be complete without a celebration at home. He expected Wilfried and me at home and this would be the following weekend. Cultures are what they are and my father expected no other answer than a yes. He had invited all our relatives, friends and the entire village. There was no question of postponement. Wilfried agreed to get this behind us. My father insisted that he would have a real wedding, meaning we should dress up once more. For me it was fine, but it was a bit hard for poor Wilfried. He had to wear his black suit in the heat of the month of December. We braced ourselves for the occasion. My father was proud and I was happy for him. So were my siblings and other relatives. Wilfried and I were not expected to do anything for the second wedding celebration except to be there. My father, my siblings and other relatives provided everything including four cattle, a few goats and a sheep. Food and drinks were plentiful. And when my eldest brother Noro realised on the morning of the wedding celebration that there was no bottle of whisky for the bridal table, he rushed off to get one. In the end we had a wedding the proper Oshiwambo way.

⌁

What did I really know about the coastal town of Swakopmund? Absolutely nothing! During the days of my youth, Swakopmund was a place that we occasionally heard about because someone's dad, older brother or male neighbour worked there as a contract labourer. More than that, I really did not know. But like any other town in Namibia under the then apartheid system, suburbs and locations were laid out according to skin colours. Each of them had the same face: white suburbs right in the middle of town, a suburb for coloureds at the outskirts of town and a township for blacks preferably further away. This was the standard layout of all towns in Namibia. Although towns that developed after independence do not have the same set up, it will take time to erase the ugly face of the older towns.

So I was fully aware that my stay in Swakopmund would stand out. Although there would be many other black people moving around during day time, they would have to move to where they belonged at the strike of the knocking-off hour. As much as we were an independent country and dismantling the apartheid system was our first priority, changes take time. Seeing black people staying in the neighbourhood of Wilfried's home would take some time, indeed a long time. I was therefore the only black person staying in this particular part of Swakopmund. I had married Wilfried knowing that his home was in the part of Swakopmund where people of my colour were previously not allowed to stay. And since this was where his home was, that was where I was going to stay whenever we went to Swakopmund.

Of course the beginning was going to be difficult, and I knew this. Initially, it really felt awkward and unreal for me. Nothing was comparable to what I knew. Wilfried glided back into his home environment and Paleni, being a child, just smoothed into this new set up. Before I knew it, they were both moving around, joking and enjoying themselves. Paleni was running around and speaking to anyone she came across in the house or in the garden. Would I ever manage to wrestle my way through? I was my own biggest opponent. I simply could not find the basis to convince myself that things would be alright one day. I would sit there among Wilfried's family, sometimes up to 20 people at a time, and my entire concentration was focused on taking care that I did not make a wrong move. And mind you, that is exactly when accidents happen. This constant carefulness was to strain me for a number of years.

Then there was the rigorous routine and discipline. Specific daily things must happen only at a particular time and a few minutes later was regarded much too late. Where had I experienced that before? A little bit at the Catholic mission stations but there we were a crowd and operating from a larger space. One could get away with a few things without the priest or the nun noticing. But here I was now having to act as if I had done things at precise times all my life. Boy, my background was just too different for me to easily fit in with what was expected from me.

The first thing I never managed was to arrive in Swakopmund on time. I am not sure whether the problem was compounded by my many young children. Once the parents knew that we intended to go to Swakopmund on such a date, my mother-in-law would phone to find out the exact time we would arrive. Her preferred arrival time was just before lunch and this meant that we were invited for lunch. To my horror, we hardly ever made it on time, and this was not for only a few times, but often; it was almost every time. Did this really only have to do with me? Or were Wilfried and I just disorganised and slowed down by our children? I was not sure, but in the end we decided not to promise to be there for this or the other meal. We chose to arrive in the late afternoon when there was no fixed family commitment.

Meals in Swakopmund became another nightmare for me. Having a meal is not a big deal among the people I am from. We eat at midday and in the evening but eating can happen any time over the span of the approximate time. If the cooking takes slightly longer because the wood happened to be a bit wet or because we had to quickly finish sowing before the imminent rain, then the eating happened a while later. Or if someone is taking some time to arrive, then he or she can catch up with the others or eat alone whenever it suits him or her. The essential is that we eat at least twice a day.

Although in the meantime I had been elsewhere in the world and was aware of timed meals, I had some serious adjustments to make when it came to the meticulously structured and regulated Swakopmund meals. It had to happen this way, at this time and in this order and not even slightly different in any way. It was not only the punctuality and the sequences. The seating arrangement was part of it as well. No free sitting. And when things are so orderly, one cannot imagine making a false gesture. What if by accident I dropped my fork, or worse, spilt my drink? Those were my constant fears throughout the meals for a good number of years. And of course one had to plan other activities in relation to the meals. If you happened to be at the end of town for whatever business, you kept a constant eye on your watch and had to get your calculations right.

The Swakopmund routine did not only require training of oneself, but also of one's children. The evenings were more rigorous than any other time of the day. When we all had young children, the evening always started with the feeding of the children, followed by their bath. By the time adults sat down for an undisturbed dinner, all children were in bed. Although I did all that it took to train my children, as I sat at the dining table, I could not get rid of my fear of seeing one of my eventually four children appearing in the door for whatever stupid reason. Of course this would not be a big deal. One only needed to return the child to bed, calm him or her down and make sure that the child remained there. I understood all that but I absolutely did not want to be the one standing up to return a child to bed. And you know what? If you are worried about such things, they are always likely to happen to you.

But the fact of the matter is, when one comes into a completely new environment accompanied with a number of perceptions, life can be unnecessarily difficult. You feel like saying or doing something, but there is always this concern that it might be wrongly perceived. In the end I spent days and days saying the minimum, smiling awkwardly and really feeling relieved when I was out of public view. I would even feel insecure and upset if all of a sudden during a meal, or while in the sitting room, Wilfried stood up to get water from the kitchen, or anything from the bedroom. He did not see anything wrong with leaving me there by myself. He did not realise that his constant presence right next to me was vital during his family gatherings in my early days with them. I still remember how relieved I felt every time I carried my bag to the car on the day of our departure. Although it would still take a while until we could wave goodbye, it was already the beginning of getting rid of the tension. Wilfried and his family would still stand around the car, quickly go through the things they might have forgotten to say or which required another reminder, crack a few jokes and finally hug everyone bye-bye. If need be, Wilfried would still quickly say a few more things through the open window of the car before finally turning the engine on and bringing the car to a move. Only then was it certain that we were leaving, till next time.

There were times when I doubted whether I would ever manage. When I felt better with this brother or that sister-in-law, next time would be another one I had not seen for a year or so. Then I started hesitating again. This uneasy situation would drag on for some eight years. Clearly, initially, I went to Swakopmund only because Wilfried needed to go home. The rest had to fall in place with time. We were simply from very different backgrounds and we had to learn about each other's ways right from scratch.

～

My side of the family was no different. Although my daily life is far from being structured the way Wilfried's family's life was in Swakopmund, it was certainly not easy for Wilfried not to know when exactly we were going to eat or to return home when visiting a relative. The worst was the language issue as he could not understand what was being said around him. But what was most amazing for many people in the village was his skin. It was in fact not his colour as such. Missionaries and doctors were always white. And white South African soldiers went through villages looking for 'terrorists'. So people had always seen enough Whites but none of them had lived among them before the arrival of Wilfried. It was alright to see a white person passing through a village in a car, but it was a completely different matter to see him sitting and sleeping in a homestead.

At the beginning, since we had no water in the homestead and had to collect water from a communal water point, many neighbouring children took only half full water containers home. As they turned around repeatedly with their buckets on their heads to have a closer look at a white person drawing water, they lost a good amount of water. They saw Whites on a daily basis including at the mission station, but this particular one was seen to be more interesting simply because of the action of carrying a bucket and drawing water exactly the same way as them. My children initially thought that this was an excuse not to go and draw water, but they fast understood that someone's stare does not kill.

The most hilarious thing I experienced when one of my distant uncles came for a visit one day. As we sat in a hut drinking *omalovu*, he stared at Wilfried for a while before he unexpectedly stated his case, '*Omuntu nguka oshilumbu shoyeneyene.*' This person is a real white person. When my father, out of embarrassment, ignored him as Wilfried knew very well what the word *oshilumbu* meant, my uncle repeated his statement louder and this time pointing at Wilfried with his finger. Clearly, Wilfried, despite his language deficiency, understood what was being said about him. My father desperately tried to discretely discourage his cousin to discontinue his observation. In the end he reluctantly dropped the subject, but not before he added in no uncertain terms that he was only stating the truth and that he could not understand why people did not want to hear the truth.

At one point I visited my grandmother together with Wilfried to present to her our twin daughters born in 1992, Peyombili (Peya) and Penohole (Pena). At that occasion, she absolutely wanted to confirm something with me. Since this was just supposed to be between the two of us, she thought it necessary to whisper so that no one else could hear. I found her whispering amusing as she could not really judge who was close by to catch what she was telling me. She had been told that I had a white husband. I confirmed to her that what she had heard was right. Next thing she wanted to know was where the white husband was. When I said that he was right there with us, she could not believe that I would drag a white person to what she termed *omagumbo giishwalikiti*, poorly constructed homesteads. If this was at all true, could I ask him to get closer and to bend down in front of her? I conveyed the message to Wilfried and he obliged. My grandmother carefully searched for his head and after having felt his hair, she clapped her hands and exclaimed, '*Yakwetu ihamu tila aantu, shilumbu owemukutha peni?*' meaning, 'You are pretty daring, where did you find a white man?' My story was too complex for my grandmother to understand the logic of it, and I presented it to her in a simplistic way and spared her the details. Since this specific time we went to see her for *akwate aanona,* a cultural gesture to apply traditional ointment to newborns to welcome them into the clan. She performed her cultural ritual and we enjoyed the little moment we had with her. We regularly visited her until she passed away in 1995.

⤳

Our mixed marriage status became manageable within our respective families. At least one could discuss and reassure family members. We had absolutely no control over what was happening out there. By the time we married, there were no more than five other mixed couples in Windhoek, if not in the entire country. It was a novelty and we attracted attention as we moved around. It became worse when carrying a baby around. With a baby, there was no way we could pass for colleagues or unusual friends. And this turning of heads was not only from one section of society, but from across the board. I am not sure whether my observation was correct, but what I saw in the eyes of those who turned their heads to stare at us can be divided into two classic expressions. The glare of the whites portrayed complete perplexity at a fellow White being completely out of his mind. As for my people, they clearly portrayed a sense of betrayal by a fellow Black marrying an enemy.

In any case, pioneers of any adventure always have to endure the clearing of the way. There was absolutely nothing we could do about it. Wilfried took it lightly, I did not. This was yet another challenge I had to deal with. I could have chosen not to appear in public, but we had to do shopping, go to the doctor or to a restaurant. Anywhere we were seen together onlookers' body language would be loud and clear. Wilfried's view was, 'Ignore them.' To ignore such a thing could not happen from one day to the next. I took quite some time before I started to.

⌐⊃

As I was putting all efforts into adapting to the Namibian environment with all that I had got myself into, I still had young siblings to help. This had been my dream since 1979 when I lost my mother. To console myself, I set myself this imaginary dream of, 'One day, I will be able to stand in for you.' The time had come for me to fulfil that dream. My father and my sister had struggled for the last 12 years while I was gone. It was now my turn to relieve them. And I had better do that while I still had young children, I thought to myself.

I was however not working yet. I first had to find a job. At least Wilfried was working. As soon as we started our first year in Windhoek, he applied for a teaching job at several schools in Windhoek. But just a day before he went to sign the contract for his teaching post, he received a phone call from the Permanent Secretary of the Ministry of Transport and Communication. The Ministry was looking for a cadre to head the Government Garage. The exile discipline and spirit was still at its peak and Wilfried's response was obvious, 'Yes Comrade.' Shortly thereafter, Wilfried was on his way to report for duties at the Government Garage.

My obvious job would be to teach French. Were Namibians interested in that? I was not sure. As I was tormenting myself with the question as to where I could possibly teach French in Namibia, I was summoned to the newly established French Mission which would later be turned into the French Embassy in Namibia. There I met the late Mr Buddy Wentworth, the Deputy Minister of Education and Culture. We met in the office of a certain Mr Jean Marie Langlais, a Cultural Attaché of the newly established French representation. At this stage, everything was new including Ministries and Ministers. We were still to get used to all these establishments and those who led and worked in them.

The reason for my being summoned was to discuss the introduction of the teaching of French in Namibia and the possible establishment of some sort of institution that would lead the way. The French were not eager to create yet another Alliance Française. For Namibia, they wanted something creative and innovative. In the end, they settled for the Franco-Namibian Cultural Centre (FNCC). The traditional Alliances Françaises were French institutions. This one would be Namibian as well.

Mr Wentworth would be the Namibian Government's representative in this new undertaking. It was explained that the Director of the Centre would come from France. At that time, it seemed I was to be the technical person to start the process. A few things sounded familiar. At least the teaching of French was part of it. I had done that before, but to my knowledge, I had never organised cultural events, nor had I ever participated in the establishment of an institution. And since I did not really know who these two serious looking and certainly high ranking officials were, I did not know how or what to ask for the clarity which I badly needed. After signing some papers, I left without really knowing what I had to do next. But at least I was about to get a job.

A few days later, it transpired that my first assignment was to find a suitable building for the Centre. With the assistance of an estate agent, I went around for a few days looking at some spacious buildings. As soon as I had identified a few of them that suited the description I had got from Mr Langlais, I went back to him and he came along to check them out. After several ups and downs, we settled for a church building in the middle of Windhoek. We needed to have the Centre centrally located so that it could be accessible to all residents of Windhoek. The building only needed some basic adjustments and in no time, the FNCC was fully operational. The French team (French nationals who came from France to establish and work at the FNCC), including the Director, had been in the country for a long time and I had looked up many of my former colleagues who studied with me in France. The workforce was in place and I doubled as Deputy Director and French teacher. Two to three years after the establishment of the FNCC, we expanded the teaching of French to a few secondary schools in Windhoek and to the former Academy which formed the basis for the establishment of the University of Namibia and the Polytechnic of Namibia.

As soon as I had a job, it became high time to get back to my commitment to my brothers. By the time I returned to Namibia, I practically had only my brother Roma, who was in exile like me, under my care. There were still four brothers younger than him and two of them were still in primary school. In total, I literally had five brothers who needed a bit of a push. My first brother was working and the second one was a student in South Africa. At least something positive and encouraging was happening. It was, however, clear to me that as things stood, only a master plan would do the trick. Besides the five brothers, I had two children of my own and, little did I know, there were two more on the way. The plan therefore had to take into account not only the finances, but most importantly, the time at our disposal.

∽

But to understand what I was about to embark upon, it is important to paint the picture. We are nine siblings of whom I am the eldest. By the time I came back home, my sister and two older brothers were somehow sorted out. The case of my two brothers next in line looked easy. They would require English and skills for work. It was too late for them to enroll into formal education. If everything went according to plan, they would be working in two years' time. Then I was left with the three youngest ones who would need proper secondary school and preferably tertiary education. When I sat down and went carefully through the timeframe of the master plan, I reckoned that all my brothers would be qualified by the time my first daughter got to secondary school. In the meantime, she was still in pre-school. I concluded that this was manageable. But it had to be a rigorous and time bound plan. I knew that for my poor brothers, there was hardly any time to repeat a class or change a course. Again, there was not much discussion. It is not that I did not want to hear their views. I just knew that if I gave leeway and choices, my plan would not work out. There wasn't much time. There was so much to be done, and there were so many other people lined up for the plan. The idea was to keep everyone moving on. Otherwise the chain would get stuck down the line.

I had all the necessary ingredients for the mindset of a master planner. I was the oldest sibling and a sister for that matter. In the absence of my mother, I was the mother figure. I was away for too long and I needed to catch up as fast as possible. I was dealing with much younger brothers who did not really know me and therefore would not easily contradict me. I had 12 years of a regulated life behind me, I had managed under difficult circumstances, and that was exactly what I expected from my brothers.

It was in that mindset that I set the ball rolling. At the beginning, things went pretty well. Learning English and attending some technical courses can be easy. The tough part would come with the end of primary school and the enrolment in the secondary school, especially for the two youngest, Martin and Ruben. The first challenge was to get them away from home and to bring them all the way to Döbra, in the Windhoek district. The thing is if I had to closely monitor their progress, I had to bring them closer to me in Windhoek. The two were coming to Windhoek for the first time. And their next of kin would be me, the sister they hardly knew. How nice! Martin did not have such an emotional attachment to home, but coming to Windhoek was a huge thing for him. Unlike me, he had never stayed in a hostel before. Everything would be new for him.

Catholic schools had not lost their rigour, like all other boarding schools in the country for that matter. To get admitted at Döbra, besides a good Grade 7 certificate, all new learners had to sit for an admission test. And the test was in English. I knew what the difference of this admission test was in comparison to the multiple choice test I wrote in Cassinga back in 1977. A Döbra admission test in English for kids coming from rural schools in those days was quite difficult. My brothers were already traumatised by a number of things including getting to know me. Subjecting them to an admission test was a guarantee of non-acceptance. Not to upset my master plan, I had to find a way around this admission test. And what would that be? Appearing at the school with the panicking child in front of the office of the school principal on the first day of school! There would be so many beaming school children in school uniforms in this foreign environment except this only one, my brother. After pleading with the principal and the rest of the school administration from a not too unfamiliar face, an exception was made. 'This will be the last time,' I promised and expressed my deepest gratitude. After attending to the administrative matters, I rushed off to buy school uniforms and re-appeared to deliver the child to the school.

Two years later I was back. This time I was in a red maternity dress expecting twins. I was visible from a distance. And why was I there on the very first day of school? This time for the very last time, I was there to enroll my youngest brother Ruben! Two years was certainly not long ago, but I knew that this time really would be the very last time I would un-ceremonially be standing there. The shy boy next to me was really terrified by what I was about to do to him. Firstly, a few days earlier, he made it clear to me that he was unable to live anywhere other than home. As we stood there, we were 770 km away from home. He had never been away from my father and he would not be able to sleep anywhere else. I decided to ignore that. There was no way that I could bring my father to school just for the sake of my baby brother. I was fully convinced that he would be in a position to manage. We all had been in hostels, away from home, sometimes really far away, and we had managed. Not managing was an unheard of concept. When the school administration had taken my word, and this for the very last time, I looked on as my youngest brother was led away. Martin had been here for two years and he was fine, Ruben would also be fine.

By now I had my five brothers in Windhoek. The three younger ones were at secondary schools while the two older ones were doing a language course or hanging around at technical education institutions. Over weekends I would have them at home. By then we were living in Ludwigsdorf where we moved at the end of 1992. The move was prompted by the birth of the twins as the three bedroomed house in Hochlandpark could not accommodate a family of six. There was no shortage of work. I have worked all my life and I did not know life differently. My brothers also had to work when they were with me during weekends: washing the car, working in the garden and looking after children were among the duties. They hardly said much to me but they would do exactly what I asked them to. I just assumed they were in agreement to carry out those duties. I did the same when I went home for holidays and my views were never solicited. Why should it be different for them?

I could see the closeness among my five brothers. I thought I understood it. They were close age wise, but besides being directly related to me, they did not really know me. I did not know what hardship I was inflicting on them, especially on Ruben. At the end of the first year at Döbra, he had failed Grade 8. And what was the agreement? No one was allowed to fail. The child did not react when I scolded him. In fact I could not make any sense of the look on his face. Did he regret anything? Could I just ignore him? No, I could not. I would take him back to Döbra for a second chance. As I re-registered him for the same grade, Father Faustus, my former teacher and the very same one who wrote us a letter to Lusaka and almost brought us into trouble, made a sensible offer. He was one of the Grade 8 teachers and would put my brother in his class and keep an eye on him. He was convinced that the problem was English and he was certain that with a bit of support, the boy would manage. And he was right. After that Ruben never failed any other grade or university academic year.

By the time my three youngest brothers had completed their secondary school, I could not claim to know them any better. I was solely concentrating on their academic qualifications. The rest, I did not really know how to deal with. Neither did I give serious thought about it. Once any of the three had finished Grade 12, the discussion revolved around the importance of selecting a course that would provide immediate employment. It would not be worth obtaining a university qualification and spending a year at home looking for a job. Again, my little brothers silently listened to me. Right, they understood, I thought to myself. I went through a number of options with them and we agreed. Or so I thought. After all I had to apply for their bursaries or loans from the Ministry of Education. I was also the one to follow up. I had all the documents ready: enough copies of my father's ID as a pensioner and the death certificate of my mother. Besides that, the application form stated the course which was the right priority. More than that was not necessary.

At the end of a rigorous student life, my three youngest brothers had their qualifications. One obtained a Bachelor of Science degree from the University of Namibia and became an IT professional. The second one qualified as a Health Inspector from the Peninsula Technikon in Cape Town and my baby brother as a Civil Engineer, also from the Peninsula Technikon. True to the plan, by the time Paleni got to Grade 8, all my brothers were out of school, out of my house and working. Did they really want to get into the fields they studied for? They were too polite to give me their honest opinion. But they appeared to be happy with their accomplishments. One thing is certain, they were cooperative and did not resist that much. In the end we all managed.

Today, when we sit down as equals, I get to know what exactly went through their little minds as I progressively went ahead with my master plan. While I thought I had them under control, they later on shared a few things with me. They were utterly unhappy with a number of choices. Ruben never wanted to be at Döbra. Martin never wanted to study Health Administration. Linus never wanted to be obliged to complete a science degree in the prescribed four years without any option to repeat a year. Well, I understood, but I did not have the luxury of time, emotion or money to endlessly support my little brothers. The earlier and the faster we'd got it done, the better. My own life also had to go on.

Do you know what my dear brothers nicknamed me over the years during which I thought I was carrying out my sisterly duties? They nicknamed me nothing else, but Native Commissioner. This is the harshest thing you could call a person in Namibia in those days. A Native Commissioner in the Apartheid System was a white person, normally a male, whose function was to take care of the Affairs of the Natives, meaning black people. Each so-called homeland corresponding to a tribe had a Native Commissioner and Native Commissioners were known for their oppression and brutality. At one point, the Native Commissioner in my area was nicknamed 'Shongola' referring to someone who is consistently carrying a whip around. These were some of the qualities that my brothers perceived in me those days. They could not find anything less harsh. Today, it does not really matter what they called me. We have spent time speaking and laughing about a number of things since then. After all, we have come a long way and have been through a lot together. It is now time to simply be a good bunch of siblings.

⤷

By the time I walked into the home of Wilfried's parents as a daughter-in-law, the apartheid system in both Namibia and South Africa was unabated. Apartheid is a phenomenon which is hard to explain to people who have not experienced it. To get a feel of the extent to which apartheid impacted on people's lives and perceptions of others, one needs to have experienced it. And again it all depended on which side apartheid placed you as a community. But in short, apartheid considered non-Whites as sub-humans and black people found themselves at the bottom of it all. Things were then worsened by the reaction of the oppressed to the apartheid system. Many black people supported SWAPO, an organisation which apartheid South Africa portrayed as a terrorist organisation, a perception which was held by many white people in both Namibia and South Africa. Then this same organisation brought about the downfall of the occupation of apartheid South Africa in Namibia, an event which many Whites in Namibia witnessed with scepticism. All this further deepened the division between Whites and Blacks. It was at this moment, filled with uncertainty and anxiety, that I became this unusual daughter-in-law.

My family-in-law was White and I was Black. Those were the first and overriding characteristics we perceived of each other. And, of course, each of these two characteristics had a specific string of aspects attached to them. We knew all too well about all of these attachments but of course discussing them was out of the question. But here we were and we had to start our journey together.

Looking back today, I realise that under the circumstances, my parents-in-law had a number of understandable concerns. Until my appearance in their lives, they had no black person within their yard except for the gardener and the cleaning lady. They never had a black person taking part in their life and sharing the same facilities. None of their family members, friends or acquaintances had known this either. All this was a new and abrupt phenomenon. On the other hand, I too had my concerns. I knew about the views held by white people towards black people. I knew too that they would not make an exception simply because I happened to be a daughter-in-law. And I absolutely did not want to be treated as an exception either. The reality was that the situation obliged us to co-exist. We had to learn how to be around each other. We were completely ignorant of each others' ways. The only person who appeared not to be a partaker in this rather unusual situation was Wilfried. His parents had accepted his marriage to me and I had accepted to go with him to Swakopmund. As such, his issues were settled and life went on. But for the rest of us, only time would tell how things would be in the future.

My parents-in-law and in particular my mother-in-law and I made an amazing effort. But clearly, tact was part of it. When it came to any discussion, it was initially safer for me to stay out of it. The same applied to certain activities that I was not sure about. Gradually I started feeling understood. No one insisted when I decided that going to the beach and sitting around in the sun was absolutely not my cup of tea. Or it was understandable when I did not appear for tea just two hours after lunch. Bit by bit, I started enjoying spending time on my own or simply going for walks. I occasionally bumped into colleagues or friends who also happened to be in Swakopmund. These inbetween occurrences started to make my life in Swakopmund liveable.

As time went by, I found myself occasionally participating in some of the conversations although initially at a minimal level. It is simple to engage someone on a banal happening, but it can be challenging to do so when it comes to certain specific issues. Meaningful discussions in most cases can only happen when the interlocutors share the same background and experience, otherwise the discussion will remain superficial. Sure, one can have a sensible discussion about children, work, daily routine and similar things, but that is where it ends. When it comes to serious matters, one applies caution or else remains silent.

Despite all these barriers, there was a clear determination to get along as members of the same family. In 1993, my parents-in-law decided to take the next step. They wanted to see my home in the north. Why not? We travelled up together and they discovered the traditional and rural life of the community where I am from. This first time they booked accommodation at a nearby settlement, Ongwediva. For the subsequent visits, there was no need to stay elsewhere. They stayed with us at the homestead. They were part of the wedding celebrations of two of my brothers. Oshiwambo weddings are overwhelming, both in terms of the numbers of guests and the drawn-out festivities. But the experience of the first wedding did not deter my parents-in-law from attending the second one. Of course the language was a barrier. My father would murmur his greetings in Oshiwambo and they would say something to him in German or English. They did not really need to say much to each other. For my father, the fact that my parents-in-law had come to his home and continued to do so was a sufficiently cordial gesture. For my parents-in-law, they were pleased to discover the life of the people among whom their son sometimes spent time. Their facial expressions did not seem to suggest that the environment and life in this rural set up was not liveable.

Mingling with each other became a natural state of affairs for our two families. We expanded the mingling to the extended families and friends and the circle became ever bigger. Valuable time was spent during family occasions, braais in the Swakop River and in the gardens of various houses in Windhoek, as well as during evenings under bright stars in Omayanga. All these and many others were unforgettable moments. In the process we got to know each other better and to appreciate each other's ways.

The two of us finally found our rightful places in each other's family. Wilfried would not hesitate one bit to stop by at my family home when he was up in the north for work. He would even bring along colleagues and they would sit in a hut waiting for the *omahangu* porridge and chicken being prepared for them. That is always a treat among my community. In the early days, Wilfried also spent days there together with the children, but without me. I too had no difficulty to bring family members and friends along to Wilfried's family home. I also recall turning part of my parents-in-law's house into a meeting room when some colleagues and I could not find a meeting venue to complete a work assignment. My mother-in-law wanted to get a glimpse of our discussion and offered to serve us tea.

Today, I have nothing but appreciation and admiration for my parents-in-law. Despite my evident caution during the initial years, they made every effort to reach out to me. My slow pace to reciprocate did not discourage them in any way. In no time, I became one of their daughters-in-law and one of the mothers of their grandchildren. My mother-in-law, in particular, became a strong pillar for me especially when it came to children. She saved us from buying many children's clothes, beds, bedding and curtains. She just made them. All we had to promise was that we would put them to good use. The other thing which I highly appreciate, is my mother-in-law's availability to look after her grandchildren. When I had to travel for work, sometimes for weeks, I did not need to worry about the kids. She would either come to look after them in Windhoek or she simply picked them up and took them to Swakopmund. This was quite a relief. *Danke Mutti!*

There is certainly a conclusion to be drawn from this unexpected turn of events. Cordial relationships and appreciation are after all possible among diverse human beings. Wilfried's family and I started off as two distinct communities, convinced that we had absolutely nothing in common. Even our belonging to the same human race did not enter our mind as a unifying factor. We initially could not see much beyond our skin colour. The only thing that we certainly had in common was that we mistrusted each other. Black people lumped white people together as oppressors, and white people lumped black people together as Kaffirs. There was no room for individual consideration, and not even the slightest effort was made to establish facts. Perceptions spread like wildfire and became anchored in people's minds and as soon as the other race appeared, one saw nothing else but flashing red lights.

Evolutions normally do not need force, they just happen. Valuable time spent together and constant communication made both sides realise that we are after all not as bad as we initially perceived each other. In fact we came to a point where we clearly demonstrated to each other that we were not bad at all. There was no need to speak about it, we just knew it. And that is really the beauty of a human heart. We are all endowed with good hearts filled with the abilities of compassion, love and care. We only need to allow our hearts to do so. And that is exactly what happened between me and my family-in-law, particularly my dear parents-in-law. They initially saw trouble in the idea of an unusual daughter-in-law. I too could not see how I possibly would fit into their environment. But these were immediate conclusions even before we met each other.

As soon as we were confronted with this unusual reality in our particular society, we unleashed our real human characteristics. Yes, they were the first in their closed society to have a black daughter-in-law but they set themselves to welcome me in their family. I know what all this meant for them. I know the anguish they went through. And this happened when they were not so young which certainly didn't make things easy. Yet, they managed to turn around and to gradually embrace me. As soon as I had rid myself of mistrust, I too started my move towards them. Somewhere along the long road, the genuineness just emerged. This was beautiful especially between my mother-in-law and me. It's not that I don't appreciate the genuineness of my father-in-law, but fathers-in-law are not as complicated.

Today, all this is in the past. Going to Swakopmund has become part of the rituals. Sitting around and chatting with the large Brock family has become part of my life. In short, I am a proud, tested member of the Brock clan.

⌐

I am sure you are wondering what other surprises I have left out of this book. Of course there are others. Life is always full of surprises. But after having lived and overcome some of the surprises I have recounted, nothing else will ever surprise me. It is perhaps an overstatement, but after having emerged intact from several challenging situations, I guess I've become immune to my perceived dramatic events. With age things do change!

But I must also say that I was very lucky to have run into so many incredible people. And every time my elephant started charging, there were so many helping hands stretched out to me. With every charge, these readily available helping hands reassured me and every single time I was able to calm and pacify my poor ever charging elephant. And finally it was tamed!

When last did my tamed elephant show up? Surprisingly, it turned up as recently as 1 May 2014. I was serving at UNESCO in Paris, and as I sat in my apartment that evening, my phone rang. There was absolutely nothing unusual about a phone ringing. So, I casually picked it up. Guess who was on the phone all the way from Windhoek! None other than Hon. Netumbo Nandi-Ndaitwah, the then Minister of Foreign Affairs and the current Deputy Prime Minister and Minister of International Relations and Cooperation of Namibia. Why was she phoning? To inform me that the then President of Namibia, His Excellency Hifikepunye Pohamba, wanted to appoint me Ambassador to the Republic of Senegal. As usual, my mind went blank and Hon. Nandi-Ndaitwah sensed that. She right away suggested giving me a few days to allow the information to filter through.

I shared with Wilfried what I thought had just been communicated to me over the phone. I wasn't sure though whether I had heard correctly. We gazed at each other. You know why? I was about to complete my assignment and we both looked so much forward to returning home after five years in Paris. Wilfried was in particular happy to return to his job after over four years of being a house husband. He had even been offered a promotional position as an Executive Officer, an offer which does not come by every day. Here we were now, and we had to take a decision. Hon. Nandi-Ndaitwah would call again very soon.

And she did. On 6 May 2014, I was at our Embassy in Paris. In the absence of Ambassador H.E. Frieda Ithete, I stood in for her to chair a meeting of the SADC Ambassadors to UNESCO which the Embassy hosted. To date, I vividly recall the moment my phone rang. I had just given the floor to the Ambassador of Zimbabwe. When I saw my phone flashing and saw the name of the caller displayed on the screen, I quickly cut the intervention of the Ambassador of Zimbabwe short and requested him instead to take over the chair for a while. On that note I stepped out of the meeting room. I had no office at the Embassy, my office was at UNESCO. I however knew that I needed a quiet place where I could close the door behind me and listen attentively to the Minister. This time around I couldn't afford not to get the message right. I opted for the bathroom. Under the circumstances, I couldn't figure out another, quieter place.

As I randomly gazed at the garden of the Embassy through the bathroom window, I made every effort to follow what the Minister was telling me. Again I wasn't quite sure, not about what was being said to me, but this time about what was expected of me. Am I being expected to go and open an Embassy of Namibia in Senegal while the Government is identifying an Ambassador? The answer was short and clear, 'No, you will be the Ambassador.' Me, the Ambassador? I had no time to respond to my own question. The Minister continued her clarification and part of it still echoes in my mind, 'Namibia's population is 2.2 million and the choice for this specific mission fell on you. It is not me, it is the Head of State and I need to go back to him and inform him on your position in relation to his request.'

I was again humbled by my leadership. I might have been making my humble contribution from a distance but I was moved by the fact that this was noticed and that the highest office of my country wanted to put this trust in me. In this humbling moment, I gave my word to the Minister. If my Head of State and my government were of the opinion that I was the person that they could entrust with the responsibility of establishing a Namibian Embassy in Senegal and of renewing and strengthening relations between our two nations, then I was ready to commit myself to the mission. But I must confess that at that moment and during a few months that followed, I had no idea what the establishment of an embassy entailed. Yes, I was part of the team that established the Franco-Namibian Cultural Centre in Windhoek in 1991 and four years later, I had established the Secretariat of the Namibia National Commission for UNESCO. Would this experience be helpful in this new mission in Dakar, so far away from home?

Although I had no specific answer to any of my many questions, I quickly wound up my assignment in Paris. I undertook to complete some of the pending UNESCO activities from Dakar, my new duty station. These were activities to which Namibia had committed itself prior to my re-assignment and which I simply couldn't drop. One of these was the candidature of Namibia to the Presidency of the 38th UNESCO General Conference in November 2015 for the period 2015-2017. Hon. Stanley Simataa, the Deputy Minister of the Ministry of Information and Communication Technology, who represented Namibia on the UNESCO Executive Board for the period 2011 to 2015, became that admired President of the UNESCO General Conference on behalf of Africa.

Back in early 2014, we had also committed Namibia to the hosting and chairing of the 10th session of the Intergovernmental Committee of the UNESCO Intangible Cultural Heritage Convention. The idea emanated from the 8th session of the same Committee held in December 2013, but in a venue to which many Namibians cannot relate: Baku in Azerbaijan. That was our first time there, yet we took the chance of committing Namibia to hosting the 10th session two years later. It also so happened that I had been identified as the chairperson of the session. The challenge was that, due to UNESCO's standard practice of geographical representation among Member States, my four vice-chairpersons could only be from other regions. Should I all of a sudden as an individual, for whatever reason, not be available, only one of the four vice-chairpersons would have chaired a meeting hosted by Namibia. An exception was therefore made and in December 2015, Namibia successfully hosted and chaired this international event attended by delegates from 110 countries. With this, my chapter with UNESCO came to a close.

It was amidst all these commitments that I learned I was to be appointed Namibian Ambassador, not only to Senegal but to a couple of countries in the sub-region. I readied myself for any eventuality. On 12 November 2014 I stood at State House and was commissioned by former President Pohamba as Ambassador-designate to The Gambia, Guinea-Bissau, Guinea-Conakry, Mali, Mauritania, Niger and Senegal. Our first mission was of course to establish our operational base in the Senegalese capital, Dakar, where I arrived on 31 January 2015. It took us a bit of time to identify buildings for offices, Residence and houses, and in May 2016, as I conclude the manuscript of this book, the Namibian Embassy in Senegal has just celebrated its first year of existence in the Senegalese capital. Life goes on and I do not see any more chance for this daring elephant to show up.

Many thanks

I owe many thanks to so many institutions and individuals. I firstly would like to thank those who participated in my upbringing: my parents, the Roman Catholic Church and SWAPO. My wonderful parents, without being educated themselves, had thought that a girl growing up in the rural set up in the 1960s was worth sending to school. The Roman Catholic Church in Namibia fortified the efforts of my parents and turned me into a trainable person. The South West Africa People's Organisation, SWAPO, turned me into a Namibian, a participant in the heroic liberation struggle of the people of Namibia and a well moulded adult. Without your interventions, my life would have definitely turned out differently, but certainly not for the better.

Secondly, I would like to thank my many national leaders both in exile and in independent Namibia, many of whom I have mentioned in the book. Without knowing who I was, you have shown indisputable interest in my well-being, in my education and in my future. The same goes for my families in exile. You were prepared to take this strange girl into your households and treated me as one of you. I will remain indebted to you for your support and care.

Thirdly, I would like to thank my many comrades and friends who shared many moments of anguish with me and whose togetherness had mutual benefit for all of us. This comradeship and solidarity over many years away from home have bound us together with cords which will never break as long as we live. Thank you so much for this unique lifelong experience.

Fourthly, I would like to express my gratitude to the gallant Namibian sons and daughters who served in the People's Liberation Army of Namibia (PLAN). I am not only thanking you for bringing me in contact with our liberation movement, but I am in particular paying tribute to your courage and prime sacrifice. Your constant pressure on the South African military machinery in Namibia enabled some of us to study. We are what we are today because you were prepared to endure hardships including shedding your precious blood for the sake of all of us. I salute you, dear comrades.

Lastly but not least, I sincerely wish to thank my family: my parents-in-law for your unreserved welcome into your family; my dear husband for your love, patience and companionship; my four daughters for turning me into a happy mother; and my sister and seven brothers for being there for one another. I thank you all for a sound family life.

The liberation struggle and life in exile 1958-1990

In 1958 in Cape Town, South Africa, a group of contract labourers from South West Africa formed a political party known as Owamboland People's Organisation (OPO). Very soon the contract labourers realised that this oppressive contract labour system did not only affect people from the so called Owambo homeland in northern Namibia but the entire black population of South West Africa. In 1960, OPO was therefore renamed the South West Africa People's Organisation (SWAPO).

Having understood that the Western powers under whose mandate the former German colonies were placed had an obligation to administer those territories and prepare the inhabitants for independence, the pioneers of the Namibian liberation struggle initially believed in the United Nations. By the mid-1950s, all indications pointed to the independence of African countries including the former German colonies (South West Africa, Tanzania, Cameroon, Rwanda and Togo). Having realised that South Africa had no interest to move in that direction, Namibians started sneaking out petitions to New York. As complex as this process was, a few petitions reached the United Nations. South Africa responded that the inhabitants of South West Africa were not yet ready for independence.

The unwillingness of South Africa and the non-responsiveness of the United Nations made Namibians realise that petitioning from within would not bring much change. They decided to sneak out of South West Africa to campaign for support and to put pressure on the United

Nations. Sam Nujoma was the first to leave in early 1960 and by 1965 a group of Namibian freedom fighters under SWAPO had established themselves in Tanzania. They had long presented the Namibian case to the United Nations, and Liberia and Ethiopia had also taken it to the International Court.

Having spent five years doing nothing else but pleading with the world to end the occupation of Namibia by South Africa by peaceful means, SWAPO understood that words alone would take them nowhere. They too understood that no one else but themselves would liberate Namibia. To strengthen the ongoing diplomatic efforts, SWAPO established the People's Liberation Army of Namibia (PLAN) and launched an armed liberation struggle against South Africa on 26 August 1966.

With the mobilisation of the Namibian masses, many Namibians streamed out of Namibia to neighbouring countries to join SWAPO in exile. The biggest groups started leaving the country in 1974 and this exodus continued unabated until 1988. Many young people joined PLAN while others were sent for studies all over the world.

SWAPO established settlements in neighbouring countries to receive and accommodate Namibians in exile. The first settlements were established in Tanzania and these were relocated to Zambia. After Angolan independence in 1975, SWAPO could establish more settlements in Angola, a neighbouring country with whom Namibia shares a large stretch of border through which the majority of Namibians crossed into exile.

These settlements were different from military camps. There were in fact two types of settlements, namely the transit camps and the Health and Education Centres. Transit camps were really for transiting on the way to somewhere else. The two transit camps were Cassinga and the transit camp on the outskirts of Luanda, both in Angola. Cassinga received new people arriving in exile. It was here where people were identified for various programmes, destinations and study opportunities. The transit camp on the outskirts of Luanda provided temporary residence for those departing from or returning to Angola. Transit camps were interesting places as people were constantly on the move and new faces appeared each morning. There were however always familiar faces as some people moved on faster than others.

Health and Education Centres were meant for the elderly, women, the sick and children. These centres had permanent communities because the majority lived there for longer periods.

These settlements had similar features. Since they were meant to accommodate thousands of people at a time, they were sizeable establishments. They each had an amazing administration, a big structure where food and other provisions were kept, one or several common kitchens, an agricultural field, sometimes cattle, and a hospital. In addition to these, the Health and Education Centres had a kindergarden, a primary school and a large maternity section. Only a few patients were referred to the hospitals of host countries. They were indeed self-reliant settlements for Namibians. It was from the primary schools of these centres that many young Namibians were sent to secondary schools mainly in Africa (Nigeria, Cameroon, Kenya, Ghana, The Gambia and Sierra Leone). SWAPO also had its own secondary schools in Cuba and in Congo Brazzaville. In Europe, a number of Namibian youngsters did their secondary schooling in the former German Democratic Republic and former Czechoslovakia. When it came to tertiary education, SWAPO had no choice but to have its students scattered all over the world.

While Namibian civilians were living in the settlements and studying abroad, PLAN fighters were intensifying the war of liberation. Only then did the United Nations and the international community start to pay attention and subsequently assum its responsibility towards the Namibian people. A UN Council for Namibia and the UN Institute for Namibia were established. A UN Commissioner for Namibia was appointed and the Namibian question became prominent on the agenda of the UN Security Council. In 1978, the five Western powers (West Germany, France, Canada, Great Britain and the United States of America) volunteered to mediate between South Africa and SWAPO. The negotiations took an eternity. To complicate matters and to delay Namibian independence, the Reagan Administration fabricated a linkage between the presence of the Cuban forces in Angola and the independence of Namibia. If the Cubans remained in Angola, there would be no independence of Namibia. With such a condition, it became clear that the negotiations with South Africa would lead nowhere. The war continued for another ten years until 1988 when South Africa showed serious interest in negotiating for a peaceful settlement. A ceasefire was signed and free and fair elections could be held under the supervision of the United Nations.

With the accession to independence in March 1990, Namibia firmly turned the page. Up till today, Namibians have taken the destiny of their country as their collective responsibility.

Acronyms

ALITALIA	(*Società Aerea Italiana*) National airline of Italy
CAVILAM	(*Centre Audio-visuel des Langues Modernes*) Audio-visual Centre of Modern Languages
CDM	Consolidated Diamond Mines
FF	French Francs
FNCC	Franco-Namibian Cultural Centre
GDR	German Democratic Republic
IT	Information Technology
OPO	Owamboland People's Organisation
PAN AM	Pan American Airways
PLAN	People's Liberation Army of Namibia
SADF	South African Defence Force
SNCF	(*Société nationale des chemins de fer français*) French National Railway Company
SWABOU	South West Africa Building Society (*Bouvereniging*)
SWATF	South West African Territorial Force
SWAPO	South West Africa People's Organisation
UN	United Nations
UNCN	United Nations Council for Namibia
UNESCO	United Nations Educational, Scientific and Cultural Organisation
UNIN	United Nations Institute for Namibia
UNITA	(*União Nacional para a Independência Total de Angola*) National Union for the Total Independence of Angola
UNTAG	United Nations Transitional Group
UTA	*Union de Transports Aériens* (A former French airline which was absorbed into Air France in 1990)

Glossary of Oshiwambo terms

The people living in northern Namibia referred to as Aawambo speak the Oshiwambo language, but there are seven variations that are sometimes considered as dialects. However, all Oshiwambo-speaking people are conversant with the vocabularies belonging to all seven variations. The other remarkable feature of the Oshiwambo language is the peculiarity of the letters *l* and *r*. The two letters are considered to be one and the same because a variation or dialect cannot have both. For this reason, the following words are considered as one and the same word: omukwaniilwa/omukwaniirwa; ombala/ombara; olufuko/orufuko.

Eehamba	kings of Uukwanyama (singular: ohamba)
Egumbo	homestead
Eholo	a milking can made of wood
Ekwambashu	totem name for the locust clan
Elenga	senior headmen, in charge of a district of a kingdom, appointed by the Ohamba
Elimba	food storeroom
Ezimo	clan
Iigonda	valuable presents given to a young woman by her Omuushiki
Iimpungu	heaps of soil on which millet and sorghum are planted to avoid flooding during heavy rainy seasons

Iishana	plains, flat areas that are flooded during heavy rainy seasons (singular: oshana)
Odhikwa	baby carriers that Aawambo women use to carry their babies on their backs
Ohamba	king in the Oshikwanyama dialect (plural: eehamba)
Okagumbo	a small homestead headed by a woman, but if mentioned in relation to a man, it refers to a homestead of a woman having a relationship with a married man. A diminutive of egumbo (homestead).
Okushwa	process of separating omahangu grains
Olufuko	a rite of passage for young girls to enter womanhood; once the young girls have gone through olufuko, they are ready to be married.
Omagongo	a seasonal alcoholic drink made from marula fruit
Omahangu	pearl millet, staple food for the Aawambo
Omahola	boiled omahangu served as a light meal or snack
Omalovu	alcoholic drink made from sorghum or omahangu
Omashisha	grain bins for omahangu
Omashwarari	people who sleep in the bush
Ombara	palace, the residence of Omukwaniirwa
Omukwanekamba	person who belongs to the hyena clan
Omukwaniirwa	king in the other dialects (other than Oshikwanyama)
Omuushiki	a man who has promised marriage to a young woman
Ondjugo	sleeping hut of a woman with young children
Ontanda	campsite or a temporary shelter (plural: eentanda)

Oshana	plain, flat area that gets flooded during heavy rainy seasons (plural: iishana)
Oshikayiwa	a head-tie made of cloth worn by women and normally not touched by men
Oshilongo	the word oshilongo has three meanings. In general, it means a country. But in the context of the book, it has two meanings: 1.) an inhabited area in contrast to a forest and 2.) one of the seven districts where Oshiwambo speaking people lived: Ondonga is oshilongo, Uukwanyama is another oshilongo, so are Uukwambi, Ombalantu, Ongandjera, Uukolonkadhi, Uukwaluudhi and Ombadja.
Oshilumbu	White person
Oshipale	large clay area where mahangu is cleaned and prepared for storage
Oshithima	millet porridge
Uuhamba	palace, the residence of Ohamba, the Uukwanyama king

Afrikaans term: *Boer*

The general meaning of the term *Boer* in English is a farmer. However, this term is also widely used to refer to the Dutch descendants in Namibia and South Africa. In other words, the word *Boer* has the same meaning as white Afrikaans speakers. Since the majority of soldiers in the SADF were Afrikaans speakers, we referred to all white soldiers as *Boers*.